THE PRĀKṚITA GRAMMARIANS

THE PRĀKṚITA GRAMMARIANS

BY

LATE LUIGIA NITTI-DOLCI

TRANSLATED FROM THE FRENCH

By

PRABHĀKARA JHĀ

M.A., LL. B., Docteur-es-Lettres (3rd Cycle)

Lecturer in French, Banaras Hindu University.

MOTILAL BANARSIDASS

DELHI :: VARANASI :: PATNA

MOTILAL BANARSIDASS
Indological Publishers and Booksellers
Head Office : BUNGALOW ROAD, JAWAHARNAGAR, DELHI-7
Branches : 1. CHOWK, VARANASI (U. P.)
2. ASHOK RAJPATH (OPP. PATNA COLLEGE), PATNA (BIHAR)

First Edition
1972

Printed in India

BY SHANTI LAL JAIN, AT SHRI JAINENDRA PRESS, BUNGALOW ROAD, JAWAHARNAGAR, DELHI-7 AND PUBLISHED BY SUNDARLAL JAIN, FOR MOTILAL BANARSIDASS, BUNGALOW ROAD, JAWAHARNAGAR, DELHI-7.

TABLE OF CONTENTS

AUTHOR'S PREFACE

This book could not have come into being without the constant help and collaboration of my teacher, Mr. Jules Bloch. I read with him elements of Sanskrit and principles of scientific research. In addition I believe to owe to him in a great measure my representation of historical facts and linguistic data about India. I can simply acknowledge this debt of which I do not have even the capacity to measure the extent.

Messrs Alfred Foucher, Louis Renou, Helmer Smith of the University of Upsala and my friend Madame Stchoupak have helped me most ungrudgingly in my study of the subject and they have spared no pains in doing this. I alone am aware of amount of the facility that my researches have obtained from them.

Although Mr. Sylvain Lévi had all through been very kind and cordial towards me, I could not dare often disturb him whose disciples had been my teachers. But chance has deprived me of the anxiously long-awaited happiness to carry the first printed copy of my book to him and to request him to go through it—alas the work of publication was interrupted by his death ! The results of any serious research never left him indifferent; on so many occasions it so occurred to him that he would, even in books of mediocre merit, find an unexpected confirmation of a circumstance anticipated by him, and thus he would supply the last necessary link to complete the chain of facts coming closer together about the earth, so that the course of an idea could traverse in the world in the span of time and space.

In case he were still amongst us, I would have been less doubtful about the utility of my work and about the fruitfulness of these researches that at times appear so far remote from our daily occupations.

1. INTRODUCTION

11. In case any value can be attributed to the dates whatsoever, I should just rejoice at the fact that the present study has come to appear exactly one century after the publication of *Institutiones Linguae Prakriticae* of Christian Lassen. If I would have been born a century earlier, I think, I would have written to the author the words that Eugéne Jacquet had addressed to him, "Your book is a masterpiece: not only all your observations are precious, but in Germany you alone still share with M. de Schlegel the credit of knowing method of handling the entire stock of materials with clarity and in a perfect order in writing a book.[1]"

12. In these old pages, in these Latin sentences, that even today evoke certain amount of elegance, I began assiduously the study of Prākrit Philology: in 1837 a rapid survey of available literature was made; till then scholars were not confronted with so large a mass of books and critical studies : in between these narrow limits one enjoys a bit of rest and he is able to cast his glance without fear from time to time on the Indian sub-continent.

13. When later I took up to the study of more complex and mature work of Richard Pischel, it was astonishing to discover that most of the opinions expressed in it had already been discussed, either in dissertations *de grammaticis Prācriticis* or in later works, going back to Lassen.

14. Lassen was the first scholar who, for example enunciated the rule by which later grammarians have described more dialects than the ancient ones. It was he who explained the superior status accorded to Māhārāṣṭrī on the basis of its stronger resemblance with Sanskrit. It was he who identified Paiśācī with the dialects of North-West India etc.

15. These hypotheses have been partly refuted with the growth of our knowledge, but all of them find justification in

---

1. Letter cited by F. Nève *Mémoire sur la vie d'Eugène Jacquet de Bruxelles*, Bruxelles, M. Hayez, 1866.

the age when L a s s e n postulated them. Sometimes it would have been necessary to discard them rather, and I do not know the force of the inertia by which they often obstruct the passage of P i s c h e l's thought.

16. If we examine for example, the second paragraph of his Grammatik der Prākrit Sprachen and then compare it with the exposition of L a s s e n, we are obliged to recognise that still L a s s e n is most analytical and most precise.

17. But since it is P i s c h e l alone who is being studied these days, we shall try, before we come to our subject proper, to clear away the ground of some preconceived ideas that are still found in P i s c h e l.

18. When we refer to D a ṇ ḍ i n's verse (*Kāvyādarśa* 1, 34) about Māhārāṣṭrī, we should not stop at the first half, because the second one offers the explanation :—

mahārāṣṭrāśrayāṁ bhāṣāṁ prakṛṣṭāṁ prākṛtaṁ viduḥ I
sāgaraḥ sūktiratnānāṁ setubandhādi yanmayam II

"Above all they consider the language spoken in the Mahārāṣṭra country to be the best Prākṛta (prācritica praecipua-says Lassen): ocean of beautiful expressions—these pearls! with which Setubandha and other poems have been composed."

19. D a ṇ ḍ i ṇ does not think of giving a linguistic classification: Māhārāṣṭrī is the best Prākrit, because it has the richest literature.

110. As for the explanation that Māhār āṣṭrī was considered to be the best Prākrīt because it was probably closer to Sanskrit, it cannot be accepted without reservation, and none of the Indian grammarians has ever expressed such a heresay. Śaurasenī, on the contrary, was for them, as for us, nearer to the source : cf. for example the formula of Mārkaṇḍeya. (*Prākṛtasarvasva*, IX, 1).

śaurasenī mahārāṣṭryāḥ saṁskṛtānugamāt kvacit

"(In some places Śaurasenī, on account of Māhārāṣṭrī being closer to Sanskrit)."

111. It is no longer considered correct to make the large or small number of dialects criteria for a chronological classification of grammarians. The date of a grammar is independent of the number of the dialects that are treated by it.

112. We shall find many cases attesting to what I have put forward in course of my exposition; for the present it

suffices merely to refer to the fact that the *Nāṭyaśāstra*, in the recension of Abhinavagupta, consequently earlier than all the Prākrit grammarians, excepting Vararuci, names many more dialects than a most recent grammarian does.

113. In general, the grammarians who had written for the theatre admit existence of a large number of dialects, thus for example, Puruṣottama, who wrote certainly before the 13th century A. D.

114. On the contrary, Māhārāṣṭrī-gramamarians studied only this dialect and that upto a very recent date. The books on the oth er dialects of the *Prākṛtaprakāśa* are interpolations made by Bhāmaha or of other commentators, but the *Prākṛta-sañjīvanī* and *Prākṛtamañjarī* for example treat only Māhārāṣṭrī.

115. On the contrary, one is often confronted with the phenomenon that is in verse to what had been supposed by Lassen and Pischel : a more recent a grammarian, the less the number of the dialects. It is the case with the Jainas who considered Prākrit mainly as the language of their preaching, and for them, therefore, the dialects of the theatre were not of interest. One often finds among their works some treatises that contain exclusively rules on the principal Prākrit reproduced from a treatise which on the contrary, had taken into consideration also the other dialects. The *Vālmikisūtras*, preserved in the library of Madras, furnish a good example of this (cf. § 735).

116. It can no more be argued with Pischel (Grammar § 2) that Vararuci devotes only a few sūtras to the dialects other than Māhārāṣṭrī, and that in this regard he provides few cases in comparison with the value that he attaches to them. Leaving aside the question of authenticity of the last books of Vararuci, it may be advantageous to refer to methods of Indian grammars : all sorts of repetition is carefully avoided. Now, when the author of *Prākṛtaprakāśa* begins to treat for example Paiśācī, he assumes all that has been said before about the principal Prākrit holds good, excepting those referred to in particular, for the new dialect. Therefore, it is not the 14 sūtras, that he devotes to Paiśācī, but the 424 sūtras concerning the principal Prākrit in addition to these 14 sūtras that serve to restrict the scope of the first ones and to add certain treatments that were holding good for Paiśācī. And so on.

117. It is also unjust to accuse Indians for considering Sanskrit to be the source of Prākrit, although the latter contains some Vedic peculiarities (cf. Pischel, Gramm. § 6). A Paṇḍit would be greatly astonished if he is told that the Vedic language did not belong to Sanskrit. Pāṇini himself has never considered Vedic as an independent language : there it is always referred to by the word *Chandas*.

118. Even if the Indian grammarians had noted the affinities existing between the language of Veda and Prākrit, they would have continued to consider Sanskrit (=Vedic Sanskrit +Classical Sanskrit) as the source of Prākrit.

119. In addition to the illustrious names of Lassen and Pischel and the criticisms that I have taken liberty to raise up against some of their statements, perhaps one will be disappointed not to find in this book anything excepting a study and a solution of a few problems in matters of detail.

120 I have talked only about the Prākrit grammarians whose works could be accessible to me : readers will notice that I have given quotations only from the treatises that I myself have consulted. If in some rare cases I have chosen to be content with notices thereof given in a catalogue of manuscripts or with extracts published by some other person it has been done only when the notices and extracts left no doubt about the nature of the work in question.

121. This is equivalent to admitting that my book does not exhaust the question: Virtually I believe so; but I am in a position to assure that it is neither due to idleness nor due to fear of difficulties.

122. Possibly, one will feel that some of my conclusions, on account of their being of a more general character, should have been suitably grouped and classified. I am, however, convinced that the book would thus have acquired a more harmonious appearance; nevertheless to me it seemed preferable to leave these conclusions by the side of logical development that have resulted in them. Thus it would be easier to check them : if there is an error in reasoning, it will become vivid to the eye.

123. With this very motive, I have attempted throughout my discussions not to concentrate my view to any particular system;

I have grouped together only the works that were of demonstrable origin; and perhaps this limitation has made my researches less interesting, although it has made them more accurate and definite.

124. Consequently it will be indispensible-when this entirely exterior primary classification of the grammatical schools would have been well established—to superpose another for it, on the basis of the functions of the Prākrit-dialects. There are three important ways of their use : the Prākrits of the dramas, the Prākrits of the regional lyrics (Māhārāṣṭrī of the *gāthā*, Apabhraṁśa of the *dohās*, etc.) the Prākrits of religious propaganda (canonical texts and non-canonical texts of the Jainas). The use in the first way is certainly very ancient, but it has not given birth to real grammatical treatises, except the fragment preserved in the *Nāṭyaśāstra,* which would lead us to believe that the rules of these scenic dialects had in the beginning been drawn up in Prākrit.

125. Actually at present, the only treatises on the scenic dialects written in (or retranslated into) Sanskrit are found in the grammars of the Eastern School (Puruṣottama, Mārkaṇḍeya and Rāmaśarman). On the whole these grammars depend on the *Nāṭyaśāstra*: there we find again the division of languages into *bhāṣā* and *vibhāṣā*, the attribution of languages to the diverse personages according to a social classification rather than to some geographical one.

126. An attempt has been made in the chapter on Bharata to interpret the data provided by the *Nāṭyaśāstra* : the result has not been very clear. We can see that in the beginning possibly there was some connection between the language spoken by an actor and his birth, but this rule appears to have force in a remote past, and when treatises on dramatic art were written and classical dramas were composed, this lien was to be felt no more.

127. The scene of action of the Mṛcchakaṭika, for example, is laid in Ujjayinī, although the conventions regarding the dialects of different actors is not in the least affected on this account.

128. The grammarians of the Eastern School are all posterior to the classical dramas and to the treatises on dramatic art: consequently they only codify the same condition of things

and cannot be of any help for historical study of theatrical conventions. This is only after the success of a literary character of the Māhārāṣṭrī *gāthās* and after their entry into drama not without difficulty that we know that certain authors, like Bhavabhūti and Bhaṭṭa-nārāyaṇa, are not associated in this regard and that the grammarians of the scenic dialects, it appears, had developed the habit of writing their treatises in Sanskrit in imitation of the treatises of classical Māhārāṣṭrī.

129. The grammar of this lastly mentioned dialect is, on the contrary, always modelled on Sanskrit : it had been, from the very outset, conceived according to a more methodical plan. Without entering into the question of the spontaneity more or less grand of this language, it is to be recognised that it had been fixed and codified almost like classical Sanskrit : with the help of the grammar of Vararuci and of the lexicons like the *Pāiyalacchī Nāmamālā* of Dhanapāla, one can even today learn, I believe, to compose *gāthās* of the type of those of Hāla. This is so particularly about classical Māhārāṣṭrī that people had made the famous subdivision into three groups: *tatsama*, *tadbhava*, *deśī*, which so often intrudes upon all later-day classifications. Then the task had been to write in a connected and stylish language on the basis of knowledge of Sanskrit, and that starting from Sanskrit. It was normal to divide the vocabulary into three big groups: Sanskrit words that one was authorised to use whatsoever, that needed not be learnt; words derived from Sanskrit according to the rules propounded for Māhārāṣṭrī grammars; words, independent of Sanskrit, probably borrowed partly from dialects spoken in the regions where Māhārāṣṭrī had originated, and of which the list is found in Prākrit dictionaries. Western scholars have a tendency to attribute a shade of contempt with regard to the word *deśī*. I believe they are wrong. At the moment when one begins to write in Māhārāṣṭrī probably he is sick of Sanskrit, *deśī* being savoury for these tired palates.

130. Jayavallabha, who compiled an anthology of *gāthās* that is analogous to that of Hāla, states that the first quality of a Prākrit stanza is to contain *deśī* words :

desiyasaddapaloṭṭaṁ mahurakkharachandasaṁṭhiyaṁ laliyaṁ ।
phuḍaviyaḍapāyaḍatthaṁ pāiyakavvaṁ paḍheyavvaṁ ॥

"Replete with local words, constituted of stanzas composed with sweet phonemes, graceful, clear, extensive and explicit in respect of meaning—Prākrit poetry that is such, is worth reading.[1]"

131. On this very account I believe the identification of *deśī* and of *dhātvādeśa*, for example made by Jacobi and Grierson, as correct[2]. Among the verbs of Prākrit there are many that cannot be derived directly from Sanskrit; it is a thing that is beyond the scope of our present discussion. But on this account we need not assume that the grammarians did not have the idea of including in their lists "substitutes" roots excepting what Jacobi calls "fremdes sprachgut" (foreign linguistic commodity).

132. Vararuci is certainly the most ancient of the grammarians who have given lists of *dhātvādeśas*. We can only say that the *dhātvādeśas* of Vararuci never had correspondences in Sanskrit or that they could not be derived from Sanskrit verbs without disregard to phonetical laws.

133. The change of the root *tvar*-into *tuvar*-(Vr. VIII, 4), for example, could be taken to be the general case of insertion of an *u* in a group with -*v*-as the second element (cf. Vr. III, 65, Pkr. *taṇu*(*v*)*ī* from Skt. *tanvī*); the rule *ṛto-'raḥ* for the roots in -*ṛ*- (Vr VIII, 12) puts for the verbs an entirely normal phonetic equivalence; the case of *bhoktum* becoming *bhottum* (Vr. VIII, 55) is an example of regular assimilation of consonants in a group. And, since the Prākrit conjugation has a tendency to become thematic (cf. Vr. VIII, 71), it is not amazing to find one speaking *ṭhāī* and *thāaī*, *jhāi* and *jhāaī*, *gāi* and *gāaī* (√*thā*-, √*dhyā*- and √*gā*-).

134. It may be remarked further that in all the chapters that precede the conjugation, Vararuci never cites a single verbal form in support of a phonetic law. His commentators do the same. The equivalences are postulated for nouns exclusively. It is only in the book on conjugation that Vara-

1. *Über das Vajjālggaṁ des Jayavallabha*; inaugural-dissertation by Julius Laber, Leipzig, 1915, p. 7. Here is the Chāyā :—
deśyaśabdaparyastaṁ madhurākṣarachandaḥsaṁsthitaṁ lalitam ।
sphuṭavikaṭaprakaṭārthaṁ prākṛtakāvyaṁ paṭhanīyam ॥

2. Introduction to the edition of the *Bhavisattakaha*, pp. 63 and the *Prākrit-Dhātvādeśas*, p. 77.

r u c i has brought in some rare irregular or difficult verbal forms : thus the present of the verb *as*-"to be" (Vr. VII, 6-7), the future of the root *śru*- (*socchaṁ*, Vr. VII, 16), etc.

135. There is, perhaps one explanation to this fact : Māhārāṣṭrī-grammarians and the rest of other Prākrit grammarians wrote in Sanskrit; among them there were some (Hemcandra, Kramadīśvara) who conceived Prākrit grammar as an appendix to Sanskrit grammar. There existed in Sanskrit for every system of grammar a *dhātupāṭha*; there the verbs were collected together in a section. The Prākrit grammarians were of the opinion that students would refer to the *dhātupāṭha*—so much the more that Paṇini admitted *dhātvādeśa* (cf. 11, 4, 52 ff.)—and be able to construct different types of Prākrit verbal forms, in analogy with nouns.

136. In fact Māhārāṣṭrī grammarians had taken into consideration the difficulty of adopting their system of correspondences, that is often so artificial and is created for a particular word, to the variable unity such as the verbal themes. From a single Sanskrit root are derived different themes, that, in their turn are combined with varied affixes : every case falls under the stroke of a different phonetic rule.

137. This difficulty was experienced in the indexes prepared by Europeans for the Prākrit text; G o l d s c h m i d t, in the index to R ā v a ṇ a v a h o, W e b e r in that of the S a t t a s a ī of Hāla, P i s c h e l in his edition of the grammar of H e m a c a n d r a group all the verbal forms under the Sanskrit roots.

138. Concluding, the Prākrit grammarians did not take into account the verbs, at the time of framing of the rules on the phonetic correspondences. Consequently they have expounded the alterations that the affixes have undergone without troubling their mind about the form of the verbal themes. Lastly they thought of filling up the lacunae by inserting as examples certain verbal themes of Prākrit, either in the section on conjugation or in the small supplementary list of *dhātvādeśas*, that is rather a collection of samples, than an exposition of the whole.

139. The sūtras of Vararuci represent perhaps the first and in any case the most systematic effort made towards codification of Māhārāṣṭrī of the gāthās. So far as we are concerned

with this dialect, truly speaking nothing new has been done as yet. Later-day grammarians are satisfied merely with adding certain remarks about the details. In places where they seem to have brought in some sort of innovation, in fact they have merely introduced, some force into the rules, trying with some other conditions of the language. After Vararuci, the first man, who has attempted to examine afresh the texts in Māhārāṣṭrī with a view to draw grammatical rules on the basis thereof is W e b e r in the introduction to his first edition of the *Sattasaī* of Hāla.

140. We must take into account the fact that the task of Vararuci was less difficult than that of the grammarians of other Prākrits : the language that he wanted to describe was not current among the common people, nor was it taken to far away regions of India by troops of actors, it did not spread among the flocks for attracting the sectarian scholars; it remained quite prudently among the men of letters by whom it had been brought into existence, and he who liked to describe it could always turn his face towards it and see if the portrait still bore the resemblance of the original.

141. We can hardly say anything about grammars of the Jaina-dialects. If we exclude the stray sūtras that are found in the works of commentators, the only treatise that deals with them is the *Prākṛtalakṣaṇa* of C a ṇ ḍ a. But the actual condition of this work does not permit of arriving at any firm hypothesis. Without a grammar, probably these dialects had been employed the most and had spread far and wide in India.

142. Even if there had been treatises written about the Jaina dialects, they have disappeared, almost without leaving a trace, and have been perhaps relegated to the background through the splendour of the grammar of Classical Māhārāṣṭrī. The Jaina scholars seem to have felt that their grammars could not have the merit of the sūtras of the school of Vararuci, and since the Prākrits of their canonical and non-canonical texts offered strong similarities with Māhārāṣṭri, they preferred to use the grammars of Māhārāṣṭrī by adapting it more or less according to their needs.

143. It is why we do not have a veritable Jaina grammatical school, and since we do not possess independent grammars of the scenic dialects, the three currents got inseparably mixed up together. We shall see later that the Jaina monk H e m a-c a n d r a, who probably wanted to teach the diverse dialects of his religion, dresses his materials about the frame-work of the sūtras of Vararuci on classical Māhārāṣṭrī, while L a k ṣ m ī d h a r a, who was a Brāhmaṇa, perhaps wanted to frame rules for the Prākrits of some Rāma-drama, and when he did not find in his locality even these traces of the grammar of *bhāṣā* and *vibhāṣā* utilized by the Eastern grammarians commented upon the adaptation of the Māhārāṣṭrī lyrics made by H e m a c a n d r a to serve the needs of the Jainas. But his intention is further revealed in the prologue to his work.

144. In these few examples, it is seen that in the wholly exterior classification based on the form of the sūtras, only the classification of the grammatical schools applies to the data that can be checked. It just examines what has really been done by every grammarian, leaving aside what they wanted to do, what they could have done, in case he did not have the intention of just copying out a preceding work, of which the objective had some times been quite different from his own.

145. However, it so happens that a grammarian, while copying out merely inserts in his exposition certain facts taken from the languages of the texts that are of particular interest to him : the remarks on Ārṣa or Ardhamāgadhī that Hemacandra has made in his commentary is the result of this attitude. The study of these external influences, separating the sūtras of the classical Māhārāṣṭrī from later interpolations will constitute the second phase of the study of the Prākrit grammar.

146. I think I have prepared the ground for research of this type and have assisted in utilization of the testimony—so much discussed, but so badly known—furnished by Prākrit grammarians.

CHAPTER I

2. VARARUCI

21. *The author of Prākṛtaprakāśa.*

211. Prākrit grammar claims very nearly the same aristocratic heritage as Sanskrit grammar, and in case a god did not come down from the heaven to teach the technical terms, there are sages, almost legendary, who are considered to have contributed to its formation : Pāṇini, the great Bharata, Vararuci etc.

212. Only book of the Vararuci, according to Indian tradition, has come down to us, is the Prākṛtaprakāśa, the basis for the study of Prākrit grammar from the most ancient times upto our days.

213. Vararuci has been identified with Kātyāyana, the author of the Vārttikas on Pāṇini. This very Vararuci-Kātyāyana passes for the author of the fourth book of the Kātantra. He is such an illustrious and ancient personality that it seems difficult to include him among the mortals. Harirāma, while commenting upon this stanza, found in the introduction to the fourth book of the Kātantra :

kātyāyanena te sṛṣṭā vibuddhipratibuddhaye[1]

"Kātyāyana wrote this chapter for the instruction of the ignorant, says : *kātyāyano munir vararuciśarīraṁ parigṛhya śāstramidaṁ kṛtavāniti śrutiḥ* : "the sage Kātyāyana took the body of Vararuci and composed this treatise; so goes the tradition"[1]. From this sentence it is sufficiently clear that little value was attached to this identification in the opinion of the Indians themselves. Evidently here we have a legend transmitted from generation to generation, enriched and complicated in the course of its passage, but always received with an amount of scepticism. Consequently it appears simply useless to try to prove some sort of relationship between

1. B. Liebich, Das Kātatnra, Sitzungsberichte der Heidelberger Akademie der Wissenschaften, Philos.-histor. Klasse, 1919; 4te Abhandlung, p. 10.

Prākṛtaprakāśa, on one hand, as we know it and Vararuci—Kātyāyana on the other.

214. But yet it appears further vain and more arbitrary to deny the ascription of the Prākṛtaprakāśa to Vararuci—Kātyāyana on linguistic grounds, as was done for example by Th. Bloch in his bitterly critical dissertation on Vararuci and Hemacandra[1]. It is true, as he says, that Kātyāyana could not have lived after the third century B.C. and that the inscriptions of Aśoka of this age manifest more archaisms in respect of linguistic usage than do the Prākrits of the grammarians and of the dramas; but this leads us simply to conclude that they had not come into existence at all till then. By the side of this language of the chancellory of Aśoka, that is almost identical throughout the length and breadth of the peninsula, the different regions could use Prākrits of every kind, more or less "corrupt". The coexistence of diverse stages in course of evolution of languages is a very much current and undisputable fact : in case, some day, all the proofs disappear, then it will be possible for one to suspect the antiquity of even Dante, under the pretext, that the language used by him in the 13th century represented a much more developed stage of Indo-European than does Lithuanian of our days. The discovery of the fragments of the dramas of Aśvaghoṣa already has allowed to take further back the period generally assigned to the use of literary Prākrits and the circumstances in which this discovery has taken place ought to make us wiser in the matter of advancing of arguments *a silentio*.

215. The ancient data on the identity of Vararuci and Kātyāyana were put together by Pischel[2]; we should now add to them the important article of Sylvain Lévi on Aśvaghoṣa and the introduction of Liebich to his edition of *Kātantra*[2]. As regards myself I admit that I have not, a century after, been able to set aside the opinion of Lassen.

"De vita Vararuchis nil nobis traditur, nec de aetate

1. Th. Bloch, *Vararuci und Hemacandra*, Gutersloh, 1893 =KZ XXXIII, p. 328.

2. R. Pischel, *Grammatik der Prākrit Sprachen* (henceforward Pischel, *Gramm.*) 32; S. Lèvi, Le *Sūtrālamkāra et ses sources* (JA, 1908, pp. 57-184), B. Liebich, *Das Kātantra,* p. 11 ss.

certi quid elici potest; nam fabulas, quas de eo circumferuntur, repetere supersedeo" : (about the life of Vararuci nothing new has been delivered to us, his age is not certain; it will not serve any purpose to reproduce the legends that circulate about him[1].)

22. *The Prākṛtaprakāśa—the title.*

221. While leaving aside the question of the identity of this author, we have still to establish that the *Prākṛtaprakāśa* has during all the times been considered to be the most authoritative treatise concerning the Prākrit languages. Even though there are scholars, in whose opinion the *Prākṛtalakṣaṇa* of Caṇḍa is the most ancient, yet the hopeless condition in which it has come down to us and the rarity of citations that have been taken from it, prove that its authority had never been great.

222. As regards Vararuci, it is just the contrary: there is perhaps not a single catalogue of manuscripts that does not contain an entry for a copy of the *Prākṛta-prakāśa* and there is no commentator on the drama or on the treatises on dramatic art who has not referred to it.

223. However, the name of *Prākṛtaprakāśa* is not generally mentioned and adopted except when European scholars take delight in believing it. Lassen, who was capable of taking a clear judgment and who had no predecessor to influence his ideas, and therefore, was free from most of our wrong ideas said in a dubitative fashion: "Incipiam a *Vararuche* Cuius liber *Prākritaprakāśa* sive *Chandrikā*, illustratio sive lumen lunare dialectorum Prākriticarum inscriptus omnes qui in eodem argumento versantur, auctoritate et antiquitate facile antecedit." ("I shall start from Vararuci with his book Prākṛta Prakāśa, or the Candrikā, illustration or lunar brilliance of the writings in the Prākrit dialects that is authoritative, ancient and unquestionably excellent.[2])

224. In reality the *Prākṛta-Prakāśa* has the appearance

1. Christianus Lassen, *Institutiones linguae pracriticae*, Bonn, 1837, p. 4.
2. Lassen, *inst.*, p. 3.

of being the title of rather of a commentary than of an original work. The variations in manuscripts are sufficiently characteristic of this subject. In a catalogue of manuscripts of the Deccan College[1] we find the same called by the following names :—

1. VIII, 293 (p. 89) :—*Prākṛtaprakāśaṭikā-Manoramā* attributed to *Bhāmaha* alone;

2. XIII, 92 (p. 201) *Manoramāvṛtti* or *Prākṛtaprakāśa*, author : Vararuci.

3. XV, 182 (p. 256) *Prākṛtaprakāśa*, author of the text : Vararuci : author of the commentary : Bhāmaha.

225. The new catalogue of the Sanskrit and Prākrit MSS of the India Office mentions a copy of the text provided with another commentary (No. 5122, p. 296). The work is named as *Prākṛtavyākaraṇa*, and the name of the author is Kātyāyana[2].

226. Besides we find the title of *Prākṛtamanoramā* for the entire work—text of Vararuci and the commentary of Bhāmaha in a MS deposited at the college at Benares[3].

227. There have appeared two indigeneous editions, one twenty-one years after the other, under two analogous titles that show that the editors consider *Prākṛtaprakāśa* to be title of the commentary alone[4].

228. Moreover, the introductory stanza of Bhāmaha neither gives the name *Prākṛtaprakāśa*, nor the *Manoramā* :

vararuciracitaprākṛtalakṣaṇasūtrāṇi lakṣyamārgeṇa l
buddhvā cakāra vṛttiṁ saṁkṣiptāṁ bhāmahaḥ spaṣṭam ll

"Vararuci composed the sūtras dealing with rules con-

1. A catalogue of the collections of Manuscripts deposited in the Deccan college, with an index, compiled by S. R. Bhandarkar, Bombay, 1888.

2. Catalogue of the Sanskrit and Prākrit Manuscripts in the Library of the India Office, Vol. II, Brahmanical and Jaina Manuscripts by A. B. Keith, with a supplement Buddhist Manuscripts by F. W. Thomas, Oxford, Clarendon Press 1935. "The usual name *Prākṛtaprakāśa* is not found here.

3. List of Sanskrit, Jaina and Hindi Manuscripts purchased by order of Government and deposited in the Sanskrit College, Benares, during the year 1905, Allahabad, 1906.

4. *Prākrita Prakāśa* by Pandita Bhamaha with the sūtras of Vararuchy revised by Pandit Rama Shastri Tailanga, Benares, 1899; *Prākrita Prakāśa* by Bhāmaha A commentary on Bararuchis Prakrit Sūtras by Jaykrishna Dass Gupta, Benares, 1920.

cerning Prākrits, by means of examples; Bhāmaha entered into its meaning and prepared a short and neat commentary."

2209. According to D o l c i, the Indians habitually call the grammar of Vararuci "The Sūtras of Prākṛta" or "The Sūtras of Vararuci" It is thus that the commentators of the ancient works call it. It is in that manner that for example Gaṅgādhara, the commentator of *Saptaśataka* of Hāla[1], has referred to it.

2210. *The Text*—The present discussion about the title may possibly appear useless; still D o l c i considers it necessary simply to warn the readers against considering the work attributed to V a r a r u c i, commented upon by B h ā m a h a, and published by C o w e l l as one indivisible whole. The printed letter possesses a sort of imaginary prestige, against which it is desirable to guard ourselves, and as such a manuscript that may appear to be very much spurious on account of its being presented before our eyes with its errors and inconsistencies acquires an indisputable authority the day some other person has read it and some printer has reproduced it by presenting the same in the form of a book. The beautiful edition of C o w e l l that is so convenient to handle and the authority of Bhāmaha are mostly responsible for the wrong notions that still are prevalent about Vararuci and his work. Nobody has even paid any attention to the other commentaries, such as the *Prākṛtasañjīvanī* and the *Prākṛtamañjarī* or to Vararuci's disciple M ā r k a ṇ ḍ e y a, who in any case faithfully preserves even the inconsistencies of his master. It is in this respect that Th. B l o c h deserves particular condemnation : he preferred to rejoice in pointing out minutely the apparent faults of Vararuci and Hemacandra and he did not exert his critical acumen in respect of the text as a whole.

1. *Das Saptaśatakaṁ des Hāla*, published by Albrecht W e b e r, Leipzig, 1881, Ex. p. 137 (366) *jño jāṇamunau Prākrtasūtram* (=Vr. VIII 23); p. 168 (414) *khider visūra iti prākṛtasūtram* (—Vr. VIII, 63) etc; cf. also U j j v a l a d a t t a on the *Uṇādisūtra*, I, 108, (A u f r e c h t, p. 26, 1, 1); *śaṣoḥ saḥ* (Vr. II, 43) *iti prākṛtasūtrād antyasaḥ*.

2. *The Prākṛita-Prakāśa*: or *the Prakrit Grammar of Vararuchi with the commentary* (*Manoramā*) *of Bhāmaha*, The first complete edition, by E. B. Cowell, London, 1868, Second Issue. (Reprint. Calcutta 1962.)

2211. In course of her repeated perusal of the *Prākṛta-prakāśa*, in the edition Cowell, Dolci says she often wonders as to why Th. Bloch did not take notice of certain contradictions of the text which seem to pass within the range of our vision every time. She thinks his blindness and her clairvoyance have had the same causes: he had in his mind a theory that he wanted to defend and he tried to find in the texts only the weapons that were suitable for his use; but as far as she is concerned her task has been to edit a grammatical text and she claims to have tried only to understand the methods of the grammarians and even their manias. The study of the *Prākṛtaprakāśa* in the ed. Cowell inspired her to make the following preliminary remarks :

1. None of the manuscripts utilized by Cowell had in it the text of the commentary on chapter XII, that deals with Śaurasenī. Cowell (p. 183) has reported about the "loss of the commentary of Bhāmaha". This explanation has been generally accepted;

2. This is the book XII that alone gives the name of Māhārāṣṭrī for Prākrit and that also in its last sūtra : (XII, 32) : *śeṣaṁ māhārāṣṭrīvat*. Nowhere, either in the beginning or at any other place in the book Vararuci has defined Prākrit as being Māhārāṣṭrī.

—3. The base of Paiśācī and of Māgadhī (cf. X 2; XI, 2) would have been Śaurasenī, a dialect, that had not yet been treated. This is against not only the constant practice of the grammarians and the principle of *adhikāra*, but against even common sense.

4. The commentary on the sūtra X, 11, that describes the devocalisation of *-jja-* as *-cca-* in Paiśācī refers to a rule relating to Śaurasenī : *jja cca.*

jjaśabdasya śaurasenīsādhitasya cca ityayamādeśo bhavati ll *kaccaṁ-kāryam* ll

"In place of *-jja-* enters (in Paiśācī) *-cca-*". Commentary: "This is *-cca-* that is substituted for the sound *-jja-* taught for Śaurasenī.

Ex. *kaccaṁ* (*kāryam*)". We do not find in chapter XII any rule that deals with the group *-jja-*. On the contrary this rule expressly concerns the principal Prākrit (III, 17).

5. The technical terms used in the sūtras of the last three

chapters, (leaving aside the commentary for the purpose of rendering the proof free from doubt), do not always correspond with those of the first nine books dealing with the principal Prākrit. We shall be able to appreciate the position by simply keeping our eyes open with regard to the grammatical literature of India and then we shall arrive at this very decision. It will not amount to exaggeration in case we say that the schools of grammarians are classified according to the technical terms employed by them[1]. Now :

The pronouns are called *sarvādi* in the first part (VI, 1), *sarvanāman* in the second (XII, 26).

The vocative is called *āmantraṇa* in the first part (V, 27, 37), but *sambuddhi* in the second (XI, 13).

The neuter is called *napuṁsaka* in the first part (V, 25, 30; VI, 18, 22), but *klība* in the second (XII, 11).

"Dropping" is *lopa* in the first part (I, 4; II, 2: III, 1; IV, 2: V, 2, 13, 42; VI, 21); but it is replaced by *luk* in the second (XI, 20).

Yuj—which means in the first part "pair", hence the "aspirate consonants" (since they constitute the second and fourth letters in the groups of mute consonants [varga]) has the signification of "combined in group" in the second part. Cf. *ayuj*-"single consonant" X, 3; XII, 3. For "combined" and "single" the first part uses *yukta*-(I, 31; III, 9) and *ayukta*-(I, 30; II, 1).

The list is capable of being made longer by addition of more examples, but some of them will require a long and dull discussion.

Sometimes even demonstration would become impossible, in case we base our studies particularly on the dialect of Vararuci; that may have its own value, but that may not be communicable. It is surprising to note that Vararuci has employed the word and the meaning of *prakṛti*-"base, origin" in chapters on the dialects (X, 2: Śaurasenī is the base of Paiśācī; XI, 2 of Māgadhī; XII, 2: Sanskrit that of Śaurasenī), while in the beginning of the work he did not consider Sanskrit to be the *Prakṛti* of the principal Prākrit.

1. It is true that Pāṇini employs two different terms for expressing the same fact, but there is always some distinction in meaning.

2212. The terms *adīrghya*—"lengthening of the vowel *a*" (XI, 13), *svaradīrgha-* "lengthening of the vowel" (XII, 11, 21) are used in the last three chapters only and appear stranger not only to the grammatical vocabulary of Vararuci, but also to that of the grammatical terminology in general. The instrumental form *prakṛtyā-* (XII, 31), that is used to indicate that a form undergoes no modification, occurs only once in chapter XII :—

16. The title in chapters V and VI,as found in the colophones, are typically different from those found in other chapters :—

(i) *ajvidhi*—"rules of vowels";
(ii) *ayuktavarṇavidhi*—"rules on single consonants";
(iii) *yuktavarṇavidhi*—"rules on conjunct consonants";
(iv) *saṁkīrṇavidhi*—"miscellaneous rules";
(v) *liṅgavibhaktyādeśa*—"substitutes for nominal affixes";
(vi) *sarvanāman*—"pronouns";
(vii) *tiṅvidhi*—"rules on the conjugation";
(viii) *dhātvādeśa*—"substitutes for verbal roots";
(ix) *nipātasaṁjñāvidhi*—"rules on the indeclinable particles.'

2213. These very subdivisions occur in the other commentary on Vararuci, namely in the *Prākrtasaṁjīvanī*; but here the fifth and the sixth chapters have been combined into one under a single title *subvidhi.* This list may be traditional, since Vasantarāja has reproduced it in a metrical form in the beginning of his work :

ajvidhir-ayuktajavidhiḥ[1] *saṁyuktavidhistatastu saṁkīrṇaḥ* I
suptiṅdhātu-nipātajavidhayo 'ṣṭāviha paricchedāḥ II

2214. We do not understand the reason of this differentiation between nouns and pronouns, a thing that does not occur in any other Sanskrit grammarian, and what is still further astonishing in Prākrit, in which frequently we come across cases of confusion between nominal and pronominal declensions. If we examine these two chapters more closely we shall be convinced that this division was brought in neither by the author of the text nor possibly by its commentator. Indeed it would be difficult to explain the position that the sūtras 60-62 of the sixth book again take up the matter of declension of *-i* and *-u* stems after the pronoun; besides this exten-

1. Ed. : *ayuktavidhiḥ* that makes the metre (*āryā*) wrong.

sion of the *adhikāra idutoḥ* (V. 14) which had lost its force long before is absurd. The two sūtras (VI. 63) *dvivacanasya bahuvacanam* and (VI 64) *caturthyāḥ ṣaṣṭhī,* that bring the sixth chapter to its end, have their jurisdiction over the whole of the nominal and pronominal declensions. We are not in a position to comprehend as to why they have found place under the section on the pronoun, i.e. in the *sarvanāmapariccheda.* These five sūtras, on the contrary, form the logical conclusion of the declension as a whole, that is of the *subvidhi.*

2215. It has been said above that to us it appears that this division into two of the fifth chapter is of a later date than that of even Bhāmaha. We have arrived at this conclusion since the commentary on the sūtra VI, 60 *śeṣodantavat-śeṣaḥ subvidhiradantavad bhavati,* "all that has not been specifically spoken of among the rules on the declension, is formed on the model of the theme ending in *-a.*" Hence Bhāmaha had probably before him a single chapter that comprised of the fifth and sixth chapters of the edition of Cowell and what was designated as *subvidhi* exactly as in other commentators on Vararuci.

231. The edition Bhāmaha—Cowell, from what has been said above, suffices to bring to light a very important fact: the sūtras of Vararuci have within their purview a single Prākrit i.e. the "Prākritica praecipua" in the beautiful nomenclature given by L a s s e n. The last three chapters on Śaurasenī, Māgadhī and Paiśācī were added later by some commentator (Bhāmaha ?). Lastly the twelfth chapter, that relates to Śaurasenī, is certainly not the work of Bhāmaha, since it is not found with his commentary in any of the manuscripts. All these facts that have been stated here combine together and confirm this hypothesis. Even the division of the *subvidhipariccheda* into two incomplete chapters, on the noun on one part, and on the pronoun on the other, is the consequence of this intrusion of the dialects that were not in the work in its original form. The works on Indian grammars in general and the Prākrit grammars in particular are divided either into four or into multiples of four. The sūtras of Pāṇini are grouped under eight *adhyāyas,* each of which has four *pādas.* The Indians generally call the whole of the work *Aṣṭādhyāyī.* Originally the K ā t a n t r a too consisted of four *prakaraṇas,* each

having four pādas[1]. Ś ā k a ṭ ā y a n a has four *adhyāyas* of four *pādas* each, etc.

232. The grammar of H e m a c a n d r a consists of eight adhyāyas, each of which is divided into four *pādas* : the eighth one deals with the Prākrit languages. Even the grammar of K r a m a d ī ś v a r a was written in eight *pādas*, of which the last one is devoted to Prākrits. This practice was adhered to even later : P u r u ṣ o t t a m a d e v a and Mārkaṇḍeya should have divided in twenty sections the abundant materials that they had to study[2].

233. We do not find any exception to this general rule. In order to escape this practice R a m a ś a r m a n was obliged to imagine a miraculous tree of Prākrit (*Prākṛtakalpataru*), with three branches (ś ā k h ā), divided into a large number of bunches (*stabakas*) of flowers (*kusuma*) corresponding to the four feet of the cow or cows that haunted the minds of other grammarians. L a k ṣ m ī d h a r a does not come at all into question, since he is writer of a commentary on the Prākrit grammar of T r i v i k r a m a (which, moreover, contains twelve pādas, grouped under three adhyāyas). It is a sort of *Sidhānta-Kaumudī*, in which he has faithfully preserved the sūtras of his principal. There remains Caṇḍa only, who, in the edition H o e r n l e, consists of only three *vidhānas*. His work does not contain any rule about verbs, and as such we consider this but a fragmentary work on Prākrit grammar.

234. Hence it comes that Vararuci studied a single dialect,

1. Cf. B. L i e b i c h, Das Kātantra, p. 9.

2. Mārkaṇḍeya, without distinguishing between them, calls all these divisions as *pādas*, that relate to a section of the principal Prākrit (e. g. *mahārāṣṭryām ajvidhiḥ prathamaḥ pādaḥ*) or of a different dialect (e. g. *śaurasenyanuśāsanaṁ navamaḥ pādaḥ*). Puruṣottama does not have the courage to take the same freedom: the chief Prākrit is divided into eight *adhyāyas*, but to each dialect or group of dialects he devotes one sūtra (e. g. colophon to the chapter on Śaurasenī: *śaurasenī-bhāṣāsūtraṁ samāptam*). The detail has certain importance for a knowledge about these two writers. Mārakaṇḍeya was more a man of letters than a grammarian; his use of the word *pīda* is not orthodox. On the contrary Puruṣottamadeva, who was a commentator of Pāṇini, accentuates the analogy of the famous eight adhyāyas of Sanskrit grammar with the eight *adhyāyas*, that Vararuci should have devoted to the principal Prākrit. Furthermore he attributes a chapter, sūtra, to each language or each group of languages. On the value of the *sūtra* in the singular, cf. Th. G o l d s t u c k e r, *Pāṇini*, London 1861, p. 22.

the principal Prākrit. This conclusion, that has been attempted to be drawn merely on the basis of the only text of Bhāmaha-Cowell, gets corroboration from diverse sides.

None of the other commentaries on Vararuci has dealt with the dialects : all of them are limited to the study of the principal Prākrit.

236. *The eastern grammarians, the followers of Vararuci (Puruṣottama, Mārkaṇḍeya, Rāmaśarman), who faithfully reproduce the sūtras of Vararuci in respect of the main Prākrit, place the dialects in an order quite different from that in Bhāmaha-Cowell.* They begin with Śaurasenī, to which they devote a number of sufficiently important sūtras and study Māgadhī only thereafter. Further they throw Paiśācī to the end of the work, after Apabhraṁśa.

237. *Kramadīśvara, who had amply utilised the sūtras of Vararuci on the principal Prākrit, completely keeps himself aloof from Prākṛtaprakāśa in respect of the dialects.* The chapter on the dialects is called *apabhraṁśārambhaḥ* and he cites Ardhamāgadhī that is omitted in Bhāmaha-Cowell.

238. *Hemacandra often cites (twenty-six times) the opinion of other grammarians, whom he does not mention by name* (cf. §. 611ff.) *in the portion dealing with principal Prākrit.* These quotations are not found in the section on the dialects[1].

239. Thus it follows from what has been said above that the treatment of the principal Prākrit was fixed and traditional in difference to that of the dialects. Hemacandra considered it necessary to discuss the opinion of his predecessor or predecessors in respect of the principal Prākrit, but he did not recognise their same authority in respect of the dialects.

2310. With the exception of Caṇḍa, all the Prākrit grammarians, notwithstanding differences that they maintain in respect of the details, knew the sūtras of Vararuci on the principal Prākrit. And they knew them alone. Therefore, when we speak about Vararuci, we should always remember that reference is only to the first nine chapters of the edition Bhāmaha-Cowell and keep this in mind that its fifth and sixth chapters constitute a single whole.

1. Hc. does not cite the opinion of other grammarians, except in the case of Cūlikāpaiśācī. But even this case may be considered simply as an isolated exception to the rule that has been set down above. The twenty-six other citations are all found in the commentary, whilst this one is in the sūtra (IV, 327). Cf. besides §. 612ff.

2311. Hence it ensues further that the criticisms of Th. Bloch are mostly unjust[1].

2312. But the problem remains whether or not, the sūtras of the edition Bhāmaha-Cowell are wholly reliable even for the principal Prākrit? It is hoped that we shall be able to find its solution by comparing them with the other commentators and followers of Vararuci and such a comparison will help us in rectifying a number of current erroneous ideas. We presume that the reader has read the *Prākṛtaprakāśa* in the edition of Cowell and hence we proceed to study the other commentaries in this regard[1].

2313. Since this edition Bhāmaha-Cowell will be used as the basis of the present study, there will be no objection to eliminate a small number of inaccuracies of the English translation: this translation had rendered us a great service in the beginning and our present criticisms simply aim at making them still better.

(i) III, 9, p. 124. The interpretation of the commentary is wrong and reference to Pāṇini is out of place. Bhāmaha wants to say in a simple manner that henceforward substitution should be made for the groups of consonants inside the body of a word. Thus in the word *asthin*—we should put *ṭha* in place of *stha*—and not in place of the final *n* according to the sūtra 11. And let us add that in the word *sphoṭaka* of the sūtra 16 *kha-* replaces the group *spha* and, not for example the single consonant *ṭa-*.

(ii) VIII, 40, p. 169. The explanation of *yogavibhāga uttarārthaḥ* is not exact. The two sūtras are separated

1. Cf. particularly KZ XXXIII, 346-348, 358, 360.

2. This edition is generally available in libraries, and sometimes also in bookshops. In any case it has been reproduced several times in India by unscrupulous publishers. The only exception is Mr. P. L. Vaidya, who has acknowledged his indebtedness to Cowell. Vaidya is alone to have done partly an original work as well. It is true that he has reproduced the edition of Cowell, but he has also added an introduction on the Prākrit grammarians in the beginning and a table of variants from the *Prākṛtasaṁjīvanī* and *Prākṛtabodhinī* at the end. Its moderate price will make this edition accessible to all workers: *Prākṛta-prakāśa* of Vararuci with Bhāmaha's commentary Manoramā, edited with Translation, Introduction, Glossary etc. by Dr. P. L. Vaidya, Poona, The Oriental Book Agency 1931, 3 Rs. (Also included in the edition with Kumārapālacarita. A recent reprint of Cowell's edition has been brought by Punthi Pustak, Calcutta, 1962. But it contains a very large number of printing errors.)

"on account of what follows", on account of the following sūtra. It is the root *veṣṭ* alone that undergoes special treatment after a preposition. Unless we separate the sūtras 39 and 40 we shall have a form like *-kvallaï*, a thing that is to be checked.

241. The exclusion of the dialects, other than the principal Prākrit, and the unification of the fifth and sixth chapters of the edition Bhāmaha-Cowell have been based partly on the examination of the commentaries of Vararuci and chiefly on the *Prākṛtasañjivanī* of V a s a n t a r ā j a.

242. While we shall now proceed to the work of a critical study into the text of the sūtras of Vararuci, we shall have occasions to refer to these frequently. These two things, therefore, deserve to be constantly kept in view.

243. In addition to the commentary of Bhāmaha, which was published by C o w e l l , we actually know four other commentaries, all of which have been published.

244. The *Prākṛtasañjīvanī* of V a s a n t a r ā j a has been known since long. Vāsudeva, a commentator of the Karpūramañjarī, has referred to it. Mārkaṇḍeya mentions it as a source of his information. It was consulted by Cowell and Aufrecht. According to Pischel it is not a commentary on Vararuci, but an original work. This is an error of point of view that has surrounded the edition Bhāmaha-Cowell. Besides the final colophon reads as follows : *iti vasantarājaviracitāyāṁ prākṛtasañjīvanīvṛttau nipātavidhiraṣṭamaḥ paricchedaḥ samāptaḥ.* The author did not dare call his work by a name other than a *vṛtti*, commentary.

245. The same P i s c h e l (*Gram.* § 40) has discussed the question of its author, and if his line of argument be accepted, the age of the *Prākṛtasañjīvanī* would fall towards the end of the 14th and beginning of the 15th century. The work has been published by Batuk Nath Sharma and Baladeva Upadhyaya[1].

1. The P r ā k ṛ t a p r a k ā ś a of Vararuchi with the "Sañjīvanī" of Vasantarāja and the "Subodhinī" of Sadānanda, edited with Introduction etc. by Baṭuk Nath Sharma and Baladeva Upādhyāya, Benares, 1927. The editors promised an introduction that has not been provided with the text. This is a nice publication, no doubt, but it is regrettable that we have even by now not been able to know about the results of the study of these two scholars. (Unfortunately Sharma is already dead and Upādhyāya is working at a new edition.)

246. This commentary is the best corrective of the edition Bhāmaha-Cowell. A few examples will suffice to show the advantage that can be derived from it. It is interesting in its ownself. The examples have been given copiously and they appear quite old. A great number of kārikās have been quoted here, and several of them are found also in the text of Bhāmaha; in any case it is a testimony to the vitality of the tradition about Vararuci : we have tried to fill the lacuna in the text with its help. On the contrary it is remarkable that Vasantarāja has not cited passages from authors in support of the sūtras of Vararuci : only isolated words and, very rarely a short and common sentence. He never refers to a Prākrit grammarian by his name; but at the end (VIII, 19) he makes the general declaration that all cases, that do not constitute the subject-matter for a special rule should in Prākrit be taught as in Sanskrit as in the treatises of the grammarians like Śākaṭāyaṇa, Pāṇini and Śarvavarman.

247. The *Prākṛtasubodhinī* of Sadānanda has been published with the *Prākṛtasañjīvanī*. It does not offer any interest, since it is absolutely an imitation of the former, of which it is an abridgement : it did not deserve at all the honour of passing into print. It simply serves to provide some of the sūtras that are missing in the manuscript of the Prākritasañjīvanī. Nothing is known about its author or his age.

248. The third commentary, the *Prākṛtamañjarī*, has the peculiarity of being written wholly in ślokas. Pischel knew of its one incomplete manuscript written in Malayalam characters and preserved in the Library of the Royal Asiatic Society of London[1].

249. About the author, Pischel says that probably he belongs to South India, whose name and date are not known. He is sometimes called Kātyāyana, but it is simply an error: we find in the introductory stanza the name of Kātyāyana merely as a substitute for Vararuci, the author of the sūtras, that have been commented upon by the author of the *Prākṛtamañjarī*[2].

1. Pischel, *Gramm.* § 33; *de gramm.—Prācr*; 10-16.
2. Cf. Pischel, *de gramm. Prācr.*, p. 10-11.

2410. The edition of the Nirṇaya Sāgar Press[1] has been utilized in this work. In the appendix (see below § 277) will be found the list of the variants of the sūtras of Vararuci in these three main commentaries. I do not think that anybody will fully be inclined to agree with Pischel, when he says that *Prākṛtamañjarī* was certainly known to Bhāmaha[2].

2411. The examples quoted in the section devoted to indeclinables, the only ones that sometimes happen to have the length of a small sentence, are never identical with those of the *Prākṛtaprakāśa* and the *Prākṛtamañjarī*. Moreover, the *Prākṛtamañjarī* does not have the section on the declension of nouns and pronouns bifurcated, and it comes to an end with the indeclinables, without dealing with the dialects.

2412. The *Prākṛtapāda* of Nārāyaṇa Vidyāvinoda (see below § 511). As regards the principal Prākrit the *Prākṛtaprakaśa*, the *Prākṛtasañjīvanī* and the *Prākṛtamañjarī* are remarkably in accord with others. The tradition about Vararuci has been sufficiently strong, for being honoured, but still neither the *Prākṛtasañjīvanī* nor the *Prākṛtamañjarī* has accepted the innovations of the *Prākṛtaprakōśa*[3].

2413. So the two other commentaries *were not acquainted with Bhāmaha*, and we do not subscribe to the opinion that Bhāmaha himself was not responsible for these innovations and that the chapters dealing with the dialects for example had been interpolated at a later date. In all eventuality it seems important that we insist on the point that Bhāmaha-Cowell recension of the *Prākṛtaprakāśa* was neither known to nor imitated by any of the commentators of Vararuci. But it is also possible to assume that either the *Prākṛtaprakāśa* or all these other commentaries explain almost the same sūtras concerning the principal Prākrit.

1. Bombay, 1903, Mukundaśarman, editor. The Introduction in Sanskrit (pp. 1-8) contains some beautiful theories about Sanskrit and Prakrit, but nothing has been said there with regard to the source of the manuscripts that have been utilized by the editor, nor do we find there any note regarding the personality of the author or on the date of the work. According to P. L. Vaidya (Introduction to the edition of the *Prākṛtaprakāśa*, p. VIII), the *Prākṛtamañjarī* had been published by Basanta Kumar Chattopadhyaya after the *Prākṛtaprakāśa* (Calcutta, S. K. Lahiri and Co.).

2. Pischel, *Gramm.* § 33: Der Verfasser hat offerbar Bhāmaha gekannt—The author certainly knew Bhāmaha."

3. All that has been said about these two commentaries is valid also for the *Prākṛtapāda* of Nārāyaṇa Vidyāvinoda.

2414. In the following pages, for the purpose of comparison with the *Prākṛta-prakāśa*, we have purposely selected only the *Prākṛtasañjīvanī*. The commentary of Vasantarāja is much bigger than the *Prākṛtasañjīvanī*. The kārikās cited by him lead us to think about the existence of a more active grammatical school. However, the appendix, as already mentioned, gives all the variants from the *Prākṛtamañjarī*.

2415. [After publication of the work of Dolci there has come to light the *Prākṛtasaprakāśa* of Vararuci with the commentary of Rāmapāṇivāda[1] based on two MSS in the Malayalam script. To Rāmapāṇivāda Prākrit is not a language. It is only a metamorphosis of Sanskrit. This work is divided into eight chapters. Here also the chapters V-VI of Bhāmaha-Cowell are contained in a single chapter V. At the end it is said "*aparam apabhraṁśāderlakṣaṇamanyantra vijñeyam*, the characteristics of Apabhraṁśa and others should be known from other works". This commentary is more detailed than that of Bhāmaha and it is clear that its author knew Bhāmaha. There are more examples and there are citations from well-known texts. It is interesting to note that sometimes the citations given here differ in reading from the published editions. The work has the importance that it is based on the Prākrit as known in Malabar[1].]

251. A single example will suffice to prove the point at which Vasantarāja and Bhāmaha are in agreement. The affix of the instrumental singular is everywhere -*ṭā*-, but the sūtras VI, 32 and 45 (=Vas. V. 61 and 79 give -*āṅ*. In fact he has made use of the term *āṅ* already employed for indicating in certain cases the affix -*ā* of the instrumental singular by Pāṇini : Vararuci uses this -*āñ* for indicating the affix of the instrumental of the personal pronouns *mayā* and *tvayā*. The later day grammarians have normalised, cf. for example MK (V. 92 and 103), who uses -*ṭā*.

252. From what has been seen above, it appears quite legitimate to try to correct the text given by Bhāmaha (or by those who have made use of the commentary of Bhāmaha) according to the version of Vasantarāja and vice-versa. Moreover, it

(1. Edited by C. Kunhan Raja and K. Ramachandra Sarma, Adyar Library Series No. 154, Adyar, 1946.).

may here be noted that Bhāmaha has not always understood the text upon which he has written a commentary. As already pointed to by Cowell, p. 137 and Th. Bloch, p. 346, the most striking example is that of the sūtra IV, 14. This error does not occur in the version of Vasantarāja.

The two readings are :—

Prākṛtaprakāśa IV

mo binduḥ[1] // 12// *antyasya halo*
makārasya bindurbhavati // *accham̐ caccham̐*
aci maśca //13// *aci parato mo bhavati vā*[2] //
phalam avaharaï / *phalam̐ avaharaï*
nañorhali // 14 // *nakārañakārayor hali parato*
bindurbhavati makāraśca //
nasya am̐so amso (sic ?) / *kam̐so kamso* /
ñasya / *vam̐caṇīam̐ vamcaṇīam̐*, *vim̐jho vimjho* //

Prākṛtasañjīvanī, IV

mo bindur aci valopaśca // 13 //
atraiva sūtre trīṇi sūtrāṇi—
mo bindurityekam /....../ *aci veti*
dvitīyam sūtram /....../ *alopaśceti*
tṛtīyam̐ sūtram......
nañor hali // 14 // *bindurityanuvartate* /
yayi tadvargāntam̐ yāvat /
hali vyañjane pare nakārañakārayoḥ
bindurādiśyate / *sam̐jhā bam̐jhā*
sandhyāvandhyayoḥ // *pam̐tī paṅktiḥ* //

254. Thus it is seen that the sūtras 12-13 of the edition Bhāmaha-Cowell form a single whole in the version of Vasantarāja. The reading of the latter evidently appears closer to the original. Moreover, the manuscripts used by Cowell leaves us in some doubt as regards the actual reading. The MS A adds *vā* in the margin, and *mas'ca* may possibly be a wrong reading for *paśca*: *aci vā* [*lo*] *paśca*

This sūtra 13 of Bhāmaha, as it is, does not merit acceptance :

12 "In place of a final *m* we have the *anusvāra*"

1. *vinduḥ*—Dolci.
2. *bhacati*—Dolci.

13 "But before a vowel (in place of *ṁ*) we have also *m*. A grammarian can never give expression to his ideas in this manner.

The last sūtra should rather have been *aci vā* as we find in MK. : "But before a vowel this change is optional".

Perhaps the error committed by Bhāmaha is due to analysis of the sūtra 14 : *binduḥ* does not occur in the immediately preceding sūtra; he does not have it as implied as *adhikāra*, and he has to try for some extraordinary graphic for an impossible rule that would permit replacement of *n* or of *ñ* before a consonant by *m* : **vaṁcaṇīaṁ* 1

255. Let us leave him aside and see if others beginning from Vasantarāja down upto Th. B l o c h have understood this sūtra well. There is a difficulty that should not be ignored in silence. In case this sūtra 14 ordains the change of *n* and *ṅ* (or *ñ* according to Bhāmaha) into *anusvāra* before a consonant, it stands in contradiction to the sūtra 17 that teaches that a nasal may stand optionally before a homogeneous consonant or be changed into *anusvāra* (*Prākṛ. Pr.* IV 17 : *yayi tadvargāṁtaḥ*, *Prākṛ. Sañj.* : *kapi tadvargyāntaḥ*). Vararuci should have prescribed a compulsory change of *n*, *ṅ* (or *ñ*) into *anusvāra* under the sūtra 14 for stating in the three succeeding sūtras that this change is optional for all the nasals.

256. However, the explanation seems to be quite clear. Vasantarāja gives as examples *saṁjhā*<*sandhyā*, *baṁjhā*<*bandhyā*, *paṁtī*<*paṅkti-* : MK IV, 23 has this very sūtra and he gives the examples *viṁjho*<*vindhya-*, *paṁtī*<*paṅkti-*. Kī II, 12 has the examples *paṁttī*<(for *paṁtī*) *paṅkti-* and *bhaṁttī*<**bhaṁkti*< *bhakti*.

257. In these examples the rule is limited to the cases in which a nasal precedes a group of consonants. When on account of assimilation of the group the nasal is no more homogeneous to the consonant following it, it should be compulsorily changed into *anusvāra*.

Ex. *paṅkti*, **paṅtti*, *paṁti-*. The examples go to suggest that the reading of Vasantarāja is the better one : we should read *ṅ* and not *ñ* here.—Vr. IV, 14 *nañorhali*, in that case, is to be translated as *na* and *ña* are replaced by *anusvāra* when it happens to occur (on account of assimilation of a group) before a (non-homogeneous) consonant[1].

258. I, 17. It is evident that the value attributed to *ca* (that in addition is not found in the corresponding sūtra of Vasantarāja or of Mārkaṇḍeya) is excessive : *cakāronuktasamuccayārthaḥ*. And this rule is meant to cover the cases of lengthening of the type *visattha-<viśvasta-*, that is not restricted exclusively to the vowel *i*, but possibly takes place in the case of the vowels in general undergoing compensatory lengthening for which Vararuci does not have any special sūtra.

259. II, 42. It is generally admitted that in Māhārāṣṭrī the (dental) *n* is replaced in all positions by the (cerebral) *ṇ*. It has been affirmed as an indisputable fact by Pischel in his grammar and he has cited Vararuci, Hemacandra, Kramadīśvara and Mārkaṇḍeya in support of it[2]. Now these grammarians have in fact put certain limitations and made certain reservations. Hemacandra (I, 228-229) teaches that cerebralisation is optional in the initial syllable and never takes place if *n* stands in the beginning of a group (ex. Skt. *nyāyaḥ*, Pkt. *nāo*) Kramadīśvara admits the (dental) *n* in the initial syllable and appears to require duplication of the *n*.

2510. II, 106. *noyugnasya*

Comm. *viṇṇajaṇo* (more correctly *vinnajaṇo<vijñajana-*?).

2511. 107 : *ādau vā<ṇaī naī vā.*

Mārkaṇḍeya knows about certain cases of duplicated dentals (II, 42) and considers the treatment *n>ṇ* as optional in the initial syllable (II. 43).

2512. Consequently the affirmation of Pischel is based only on Vararuci (II, 42) of the edition Bhāmaha-Cowell. We expressly leave aside Caṇḍa, whose silence was interpreted very eloquently in support of our thesis by Hoernle (pp. XXIV-XXV and LX-LXII).

But Vararuci, is he so explicit ? *no ṇaḥ sarvatra* appears to leave no doubt about it. But it is significant to note that the MS W in particular does not have *sarvatra* and, over and

1. Cf. also the note of Pischel on Hc. I, 25.

2. Gramm., § 224 : "*Na* geht im Anlaut, wie Inlaut stets in *ṇa* über. (=*na* in the anlaut as in the inlaut becomes *ṇ*). Mr. Jules Bloch (L'Indo-Aryen, Paris, 1934, p. 78) shows that this phenomenon may simply be a provisional thing concerning orthography.

above, Prākṛtasañjīvanī and Prākṛtasubodhinī, both comment upon the sūtra *no ṇaḥ*. Consequently the word *sarvatra* appears probably as a gloss[1]. Moreover, the commentary of the Prākṛtasañjīvanī is very instructive.. It cites a *kārikā* ; *ādau kvāpi nakārasya ṇatvabhāvopi drs'yate*>*ṇūṇaṁ* ("however) in the initial position as well, sometimes the (dental) *n* becomes the (cerebral) ṇ. Ex. *ṇūṇaṁ*." We ought here in this context make a note of the fact that the force of the *adhikāra ādeḥ* might still have its force and that Bhāmaha has interrupted its influence. The *kārikā* appears to solve the difficulty.

The single example of an accessory word having two nasals *ṇūṇaṁ*<Skt. *nūnam* is very much suggestive.

2513. It would be possible to assume that in the beginning the treatment *n*<*ṇ* was exclusively restricted to the intervocalic syllable by Vararuci and that when he permitted this treatment for the initial syllable in a few cases of the initial *n* he had before him the only form, the enclitic *ṇūṇaṁ*<*nūnam*. This followed by the example *ṇūṇam* in Vasantarāja would be the unique residue of this doctrine of Vararuci badly understood by grammarians and editors of the texts. It seems that there existed a sūtra *vādau* or *nādau* and the graphic unification of *ṇ* for *n* caused it to disappear from the Prākṛtaprakāśa[2]. It would be preferable to assume *nādau* that finds its correspondence in Vasantarāja and has been accepted by other grammarians, all of whom have introduced the option : *vādau*.

2514. Vr. III, 53 This difficult sūtra", as remarked by Cowell, p. 131, is perhaps reduced to a little artifice of the grammarian.

The problem remains as to how to explain this treatment :

Skt. *āṁra* — Pkt. *ambaṁ*
Skt. *tāmra* — Pkt. *tambaṁ*

1. It occurs generally over the head of the sūtra and more especially in the grammatical usage.

2. This opposition to *n*, initial or duplicated, *ṇ* intervocalic (and initial of enclitics)is attested in a great number of modern Indian languages. Cf. Jules Bloch, L'Indo Aryen, p. 79. This has its origin in the Vedic language. For cerebralisation of the initial of the enclitic, cf. Wackernagel, Altindische Grammatik I, p. 191, § 171a.

In this connection Vararuci talks about "reduplication". This is a point that is certain. The sūtra has the same place in the Prākṛtasañjīvanī and in Mārkaṇḍeya. The *adhikāra dvitvam* "reduplication" should play the special role necessary for the following sūtras.

The difficulty was quickly felt.

Kramadīs' vara (II, 64) and Hemacandra (II, 56) resolved it by including these words in the general treatment of the groups and by simply giving the equivalence : *-mra-*= *-mba-*.

Mārkaṇḍeya dares not speak about reduplication, but with his habitual honesty he does not make any alteration in the sūtra and while so doing he gives a very embarassed explanation. It seems desirable that we should accept the sūtra of Vararuci as such. Let us take the word *āmra-*. The *r* drops on account of III, 3. Consequently the *m* should have been doubled (III, 50) ; but in this particular case the reduplication of the *m* is effected through *b* : *āmra-*>**āmba-*> *amba*.

Most of the manuscripts utilized by Cowell have *avva-*, one of them has *aṁvva-*. It seems that we should not attribute any importance to these graphics. The forms *amba-*, *tamba-* are well attested (cf. Pischel, Gramm. § 295), the others are unhappy creation of the commentators who did not understand the sūtra.

2514. III, 56 is certainly interpolated : it is wanting in Prākṛtamañjarī, Prākṛtasañjīvanī and Mārkaṇḍeya. This reminds of Hc. II, 92 (*na dīrghānusvārāt*) that forbids reduplication after a long vowel and *anusvāra* : ex. *ājñā*>*āṇā*, *saṁjhā* <*sandhyā*. In reality neither Vararuci nor his followers could release the law of the long vowel in an open syllable and short vowel in a closed syllable.

2515. V—13. The first sūtras of the declension present difficulties in the edition Bhāmaha—Cowell. It is worthwhile to study them closely, although some of the problems remain unsolved. We have the impression that Vararuci was not firmly decided as in the case of the forms of the type acc. plur. *vacche*, abl. sg. *vacchā*, etc., the *e* and the *ā* ought to be considered as affixes added to the theme or as modification of the thematic vowel.

2516. The following table will enable us to appreciate this hesitation:—

Declension of the masculine in *-a*

Sg. Nom. *vacche* (V, 1)
Acc. *vacchaṁ* (V, 2)
Inst. **vacchaṇa* (V, 4), *vaccheṇa* (V, 12)
Abl. *vacchā* (V, 6 or V, 13, 11)
**vacchao*, **vacchaü*, **vacchahi* (V, 6)
vacchāo, *vacchāu*, *vacchāhi* (V, 11)
Gen. *vacchassa* (V, 8)
Loc. *vacchammi* (V, 9)
vacche (V, 9 or V, 13, 12)
Pl. Nom. **vaccha* (V. 2), *vacchā* (V, 11)
Acc. **vaccha* (V, 2), *vacche* (V, 12)
**vacchā* (V, 11)
Ins. **vacchahiṁ* (V, 5), *vacchehiṁ* (V, 12)
Abl. **vacchahiṁto*, **vacchesunto* (V, 12)
**vacchehinto*, **vacchasunto* (V, 7)
Gen. **vacchaṇa* (*ṁ*) (V, 4), *vacchāṇa* (ṁ) (V, 11)
Loc. **vacchasu* (V, 10), *vacchesu* (V, 12)

2517. Even the text of the sūtras is not authoritative. The sūtras 1-5 are identical in Bhāmaha, Vasantarāja, Mārkaṇḍeya and Hemacandra. Kramadīśvara shows innovations that render his work unsuitable for its utilization for restitution of the text of Vararuci. Every time he has spoken about the thematic changes he has also taught the affix in a manner that offers no correspondence to the sūtras 11-13. Ex. (for the genitive singular) *āmo ṇaḥ prāg dīrghas'ca.*

2518. V, 6 is a little different in Hc (III, 8):
ṅases ttododuhiṁtolukaḥ

2519. V, 9 *ṅer emmī*, but the MS W
has *ṅeremmi* and Kramadīśvara (III, 15) *ṅer mmiḥ.*

2520. V, 11 *jaśśasṅasyāṁsu dīrghaḥ*, cited also under the same form under the sūtras 2 and 4; but MS B.
jasṅasyāṁsu[1] *dīrghaḥ*;
MS D *jasbhyasṅasyāṁsu*; but under the sūtra 4
jaśśasbhyasṅasyāṁsu dīrghaḥ; E *jasṅasyāṁsu*

1. Cf. Variants to the sūtra V, 2.

Vasant. V, 11—*jasṅasyāṁsu dīrghaḥ*
Mk. V, 12 *dīrgho jasṅasyāṁsu*
Hc. III, 12 *jasśasṅasittododvāmi dīrghaḥ*

2521. V, 12 *e ca supyaṅasoḥ*
Vas. V, 12 *e supyaṅiṅasoḥ*
Mk V, 14 *ṅiṅasau vinā supyet*
Hc III, 13 *ṭāṇa s'asyet*

2522. V, 13 *kvacidṅasiṅyorlopaḥ* :
Vas. V, 13 *kvacadapilopaḥ*
Mk. V, 16 *asya kvacillopaḥ*

2523. A single correction appears certain; it is *jasbhyas°* and not *jass'as°* that should be read in the sūtra V, 11. The other manuscripts of the edition Cowell that have been seen authorise this. With the help of this simple correction we are able to suppress the accusative plural from *vacchā*, that is not normal in Māhārāṣṭrī, and to bring in *vacche* which, in fact, is not taught in the text of Vararuci, since the sūtra 12, cannot check the force of the sūtra 11.

2524. The *ca* of this very sūtra 12, that occurs only in the edition Bhāmaha-Cowell, proves the embarrassment of the commentator in the face of this problem[1]. The same correction will enable us to postulate the forms *vacchāhiṁto*, *vacchāsuṁto* that Bhāmaha is obliged to accept on account of this helpful *ca* (comm. upon V, 7). These are the only forms attested in the classical texts of Māhārāṣṭrī, although they mostly occur as the ablative singular[2].

2525. This too is certain that the sūtras V, 6 and 13 cannot coexist : either the *ā* of the irregular ablative is considered as an affix or it represents a sort of compensatory lengthening after dropping of the affix. The same question holds good also for the locative singular in -e (V, 9 and 13). In the last case the sūtra is not attested by Vaṣ. and Mk.

1. Cf. the commentary on the sūtra V, 2.

2. Cf. Hāla *cheppāhiṁto* (240) explained as *lāṁgūlebhyaḥ*, which, however, can be better translated by an ablative singular; *hiaāhiṁto* (451) explained as *hṛdayāt* and *hṛdayebhyaḥ*, that can be taken either as singular or plural; lastly *raiharāhiṁto* explained as *ratigṛhāt* and *ratigṛhebhyaḥ*, but what necessarily appears to be in the singular. Cf. also Pischel, *Gramm.* §§ 365 and 360.

2526. It would be possible for us to assume that originally Vararuci admitted dropping of the affix in the forms like the acc. plur. *vacche*, abl. sing. *vacchā*, etc. He begins with enumeration of the affixes; then he gives the affix zero ("dropping") and then he describes the cases of modifications of the theme before the same affixes. In order to arrive at this coherent result we have to read V. 6 *ṅaserdoduhayaḥ*; V, 9 *ṅermmiḥ*; V, 11 *jasbhyasṅasyāṁsu dīrghaḥ* and V, 2 *e supyaṅiṅasoḥ*; V, 13 would add, moreover, the locative in *-e* and the ablative in *-ā*, that interchanging with the forms having affixes *-mmi*, *-do*, *-du*, *-hi* would create a number of confusions : *ṅi* and *ṅasi* of the *sūtra* 12 would correspond to the locative and ablative forms already explained above, and, therefore, exclusively to the forms of the type *vacchammi* (due to the sūtra V, 9 emended) and to *vacchāo vacchāu vacchāhi* (according to corrected V, 6 and 11).

Evidently these corrections are arbitrary, but the actual condition of the text of Vararuci is not acceptable.

2527. V. 16. *jasaśca o yūtvam* ll *idudaṁtayor jasa okārādeśo bhavati* l *idutos'ca īūtvaṁ vā* l *cakārād ṇo ca* l *aggīo vāūo* l *aggiṇo vāuṇo* ll

The three best manuscripts utilized by Cowell add one *vā* after *jasaśca*. We at once see that the sūtra as it stands is devoid of any meaning. Bhāmaha explains the *ca* as meant to introduce some other forms of the types taught for the accusative. Normally the *ca* should in this case follow *o* : "in the nominative plural we have also the affix *o* ". Placed after *jasas* the *ca* has also a different value : "in the nominative plural too we have the affix *o*". Moreover, the technical term *yūtvam*, singular abstract for indicating the two elements, is at least astonishing. The forms *aggīo* and *vāūo* taught by this *sūtra* are not found in Māhārāṣṭrī, while the forms *agga*(*v*)*o* and *vāa*(*v*)*o* are well confirmed[1].

Having taken cognition of the difficulty created by the edition Bhāmaha, we may examine the other grammarians[2]. Probably through an accident of the scribe the sūtra is wanting in Vasantarāja, but it is given by the Prākṛtasubodinī of Sadānanda :

1. Cf. Pischel, Gramm., §§ 380-381.
2. Cf. also the variants of the MS W in the edition Cowell.

jasa o vo vātvaṁ ca
Examples : *rāsao rāsivo rāsiṇo rāsī*<
rāśayaḥ, veṇao, veṇuvo, veṇuṇo, veṇū<*veṇavaḥ*
Mk. V, 20 *jasa o vo acca prāk*
Examples : *aggao aggavo aggiṇo, vāao vāavo, vāuṇo.*
Kramadīśvara has two sūtras (III, 19 and 20)
jasa o roriṇas'cāt (corr. *vor*)
Ex. *aggao, aggaro* (corr. *aggavo*), *sāhao*
sāharo (corr. *sāhavo*).

Hemacandra (III, 20-22), while adding certain details, has expressed almost the same thing.

The forms *aggio-* and *vāūo* taught by Bhāmaha are not authorised by any of the grammarians.

The *vā* added in the margin in the MSS A B D of Cowell, the badly placed *ca* and the strange word *yūtvam*, without being able to effect any paleographic certitude make us feel that the sūtra preserved by the Prākṛtasubodhinī should be substituted for the one given by Bhāmaha. So we should read *jaso o vo vātvaṁ ca.*

2528. V, 25 and 30.

The sūtra V, 25 of the edition Cowell is not intelligible. It is not accurate to say, as implied by Bhāmaha, that the adhikāra *dīrgha* (sūtra 18) "a long one" has its force in this place. The sūtra reads *napuṁsake sorbīnduḥ* in Vasantarāja and *sornapuṁsake binduḥ* in Mārkaṇḍeya : in both of them its place is between the sūtra on the feminine suffixes *-ā* and *-ī* and that on the neuter plural suffix. The sūtra *sorbindurnapuṁsake* is found also in Bhāmaha, but under the number 30. On the testimony of other grammarians we may presume that this sūtra 30 should take the place of 25 of the edition Bhāmaha-Cowell. On account of copyist's error the sūtra 25 has been this presented in mutilated form; the commentator tries to make use of it, but on the other he is astonished to note the absence of a more explicit sūtra on the neuter nominative singular, he reconstructs it in its primitive form and allotting to it another place, to speak truly rather a badly selected place.

A confirmation of this hypothesis is furnished by the

sūtra 27. With regard to the vocative Vararuci says :

nāmantraṇe sāvotvodīrghabindavaḥ

Ex. inter alia : *he vaṇa, he dahi, he mahu.*

"When the nominative performs the function of the vocative, the suffix *-o* (of the masculine theme in *-a*) should not be used, there should not take place either the lengthening (of the theme in *-i* or in *-u*) or the addition of *anusvāra* as the affix (after neuter themes)". This presupposes that the affix of the neuter singular had already been indicated : The sūtra 25 in its actual form does not do it.

2529. Vr. VI, 62 has to be corrected certainly. This sūtra is governed by the adhikāra *adantavat* of the sūtra 60, of which, like the preceding one, it should limit the force.

e bhyasi "(all the themes not ending in *-a* are declined like the theme in *-a*, apart from the cases examined above and reminding also that they) do not have *-e* in the ablative plural".

This sūtra has the same form in Vasantarāja (V, 108); however, the manuscripts B and W of the edition Cowell give *ā bhyasi*. It is not found in Mārkaṇḍeya, Puruṣottama and Rāmaśarman and not in Kramadīśvara or Hemacandra. [Rāmapāṇivāda too reads it as *ā bhyasi.*]

Vasantarāja felt the difficulty that did not appear to Bhāmaha : in his commentary he gives it an altogether a different interpretation; to him the sūtra should cover the numerals ending in *-n* and would go to teach **pañcāhinto, pañcāsunto,* etc. rejecting **pañcehinto, *pañcesunto,* etc. It is evident that this interpretation is not admissible and Vasantarāja, in order to be consistent with his ownself, should have at least changed the place of this sūtra. Now there is no question of the names of the number that have been explained already above.

Cowell has accepted the commentary of Bhāmaha as it is[1]. In case we interpret it in its real value, it would, authorise formation of **aggehiṁ, *ṇaehiṁ* etc.! Since in case it would prohibit the thematic *-e* only in the ablative plural, it would follow that this *-e* enters into all the other

1. Cf. also the note to the English translation, p. 157.

cases according to the sūtra V, 12. Evidently the only way out remains to correct the text, and the reading *e supi*, "the thematic vowel may be *e* before all the nominal affixes", is what first comes to the mind, It is not very audacious from the point of view of paleography. The fault must be a very old one, in case the two commentators Vasantarāja and Bhāmaha, geographically and traditionally widely separated from each other, found it in their respective texts. Bhāmaha did not take notice of it, but Vasantarāja attempted to give it a reasonable explanation. It is curious to find that the sūtras V, 124-128 of Mārkaṇḍeya appear to be an extension of the commentary of Vasantarāja; they have been interfered with the sequence of the sūtras 122-123, 129-134, since their logical place would be after 121. On this fidelity of Mārkaṇḍeya with regard to the order of the sūtras of Vararuci, cf. § 475.

2530. VI, 9-10.

We think Vararuci was not aware of the form *to* that the later day grammarians consider as an ablative singular of the theme of the demonstrative pronoun *ta*-[1].

VI, 9 *tto do ṅaseḥ* l *kiṁyattadbhyo ṅaseḥ tto do ityetāvādeśau bhavataḥ* ll *katto kado* l *jatto jado* l *tatto tado* ll

VI, 10 *tada os'ca* l *tada uttarasya ṅaser okarādes'o bhavati vā* ll *to tatto tado* ll

Bhāmaha is wrong. This last sūtra does not authorize to form *to*, but *tao*.

In fact this is the opinion of Vasantarāja, who substitutes a single more general sūtra for the two sūtras of the edition Bhāmaha.

V, 56. *otto do ṅaser anidamaḥ*

Examples : *savvao savvatto savvado* l
aṇṇao aṇṇatto aṇṇado l *tao tatto tado.*

At the end of the commentary he reproduces a kārikā : "*to ityapi tadaḥ prāhurādeśaṁ ṅasinā saha* ll *to tasmāt.*

This makes us feel that this sūtra has been interpolated by somebody who had wanted to attribute to Vararuci the form *to.* The kārikās served to supply the lacunae of the text and later came to pass for the text itself. But it is not

1. Cf. Pischel, Gramm. § § 142 and 425.

understandable as to how something that was provided for already in the sūtra could be rejected in a kārikā.

2531. VII, 20, poses a problem :

vartamānabhaviṣyadanadyatanayor jja jjā vā :

This sūtra occurs in this very form in Bhāmaha and in Vasantarāja. But in any case in order to justify the use of the affix of the dual, we ought to separate *vartamāna-* and *bhaviṣyadanadyatana*. The second word, in which the substantive precedes the adjective, would serve to indicate a periphrastic future. It is so understood, for example, by Mārkaṇḍeya (VI, 36).

But the question arises whether or not it is correct to say that the potential, about which there is the talk here, should be exclusively used as a substitute for the periphrastic future. It is further doubtful if the term *bhavīṣyadanadyatana* is admissible. It has been translated by Cowell as definite future". On the contrary we ought to read *anadyatana-bhaviṣyat*.

An example of the *anadyatana-* for "periphrastic future" is not known in Sanskrit grammar, but this use is capable of being deduced from the definition of the periphrastic future given by Pāṇini (3, 3, 15) : *anadyatane luṭ*[1]. [Rāmapāṇivāda adds *ca* to the sūtra to extend it to cover also vidhyādi.]

2532. VII, 25 : Bhāmaha as well as Rāmapāṇivāda limits the use of the imperfect *āsi* (<*āsīt*) to the singular. The sūtra of Vararuci does not authorize this limit, nor does the usage of the text goes to support this[2]. This limitation is unknown to Vasantarāja.

2533. VIII, 61 is not acceptable :

graherdīrgho vā ll *gāhijjaī gahijjaī*

The MS W has *graher vā vetthaḥ...*

vetthaī geṇhijjaī gṛhyate.

The Prākṛtasañjīvanī has the sūtra as expected (VII, 66).

1. Mr. Renou had proposed to interpret the word *vartamānabhaviṣyadanadyatanayoḥ* as consisting of two members, of which the second one should be considered as a dvandva. He also points out that Kāśikā explains this sūtra of Paṇini as *bhaviṣyadanadyatanerthe*, may be in the sense of the periphrastic future.

2. Cf. Pischel, Gramm. § 515.

graher gheppaḥ...gheppaī gṛhyate,
pakṣe geṇhiaī geṇhijjai

Possibly we may quietly correct the text of ed. Bhāmaha according to Vasantarāja : perhaps *vā* too is added : in the MS W it is found at another place and there it is exclusively used with the intention of adding a form that is possible, though it is not attested : *gahijjaī*, by the side of *gāhijjaī*, that is deduced from the sūtra and is candidly inadmissible. It is, however, true that option may be allowed also in favour of a form *geṇhijjaī*, that is not attested by the text, but is admitted by some other grammarians[1].

261. We have here examined the text of Vararuci only at the places where a correction has appeared as strongly justified or even necessary and has modified the basis of the doctrine.

262. There would still remain the work of examining the sūtras of Vararuci : this will have to be done rather by some other editor of Vararuci. A new edition of the sūtras would render great service to our knowledge of Prākrit. And such an edition should be based not only on Bhāmaha or on Vasantarāja[2], but also on all the commentators of Vararuci and on the grammarians who depend upon him. One would be astonished to find that Kramadīśvara at several points presents himself as an innovator and that Mārkaṇḍeya would furnish an example of intelligent fidelity to a text. In case he had not taken into his head the bad idea to versify his

1. For details compare P i s c h e l, Gramm. § 548.

2. Cowell, for example, has attached too little importance to the variants found in the MS W that he has designated as a modern recension. It is evident that the other manuscripts guarantee a text as a whole; but what value can we attach to this text? In case we assume that the MSS A B C D and E are the five copies of one and the same MS and that the manuscript that served as their source was just one of the editions of the sūtras of Vararuci, we would not be very far from truth; even in the face of certain sūtras concerning some dialects other than Māhārāṣṭrī or in the face of a number of absurdities like the division of the section on declension into two books, without taking into consideration the import of the concluding sūtra, we wonder whether this manuscript represents the original *Prākṛtaprakāśa* on which Bhāmaha had written his commentary, or if it is not a posterior resetting, a great success, in case we are to judge by the large number of its copies that are preserved in India.

grammar, he would have perhaps represented for the time being the actual and best edition of Vararuci, a revised and supplemented edition and still a fine edition.

263. In case it is accepted that the sūtras of Vararuci form a work independent of the commentary of Bhāmaha and if it be admitted that there were also some other commentators and some other imitators, who would not have necessarily known Bhāmaha, it would follow that the text of Vararuci has to be reconstituted after utilization of all the accessible sources. The few examples of textual criticism of Bhāmaha cited above show, it is hoped, that this method is sufficiently fruitful. It is why that in anticipation of a critical edition of Vararuci based on all the known commentators and the grammarians who derive their materials from him, it may be believed that the present writer has not executed a useless work even by pointing to the sūtras that occur exclusively in the edition of Bhāmaha or in that of Vasantarāja. There have been added references to the sūtras corresponding to Mārkaṇḍeya, Hemacandra and Kramadīśvara. The fact that a particular sūtra does not occur in the one or in the other or in none of these grammarians or that one occurs there in a different form too has its importance.

264. List of sūtras commented upon by Bhāmaha alone :—

I, 7 *lavaṇanavamallikayor vena*

Vas. I, 6 devotes to the first of the these two words a kārika : "*otvaṁ saha vakāreṇa lavaṇepyasa ceṣyate*". The second word has been pointed too by Hc alone. It is wanting in the Prākṛtamañjarī.

Mk. I, 9; Kī. I, 8; Hc. I, 170-171.

II, 5 *śīkare bhaḥ*

is contained in Vas. II, 4 (cf. Pischel Gram. § 266). It is wanting in the Prākṛtamañjarī.

Mk. II, 5; Kī. II, 26; Hc. I, 184.

II, 19 *kabaṁdhe bo maḥ.*

Mk II, 17; Hc. I, 239

II, 26 *pho bhaḥ*

cf. Vas. II, 24 (*khaghathadhaphabhāṁ haḥ*).

cf. Mk. II, 24; cf. Kī. II, 16; cf. He. I, 236

II, 37 *panasepi*

Vas. devotes a *kārikā* to this word in his commentary :
"*panasepi pakārasya phakāradeśa īṣyate*"

It is wanting in the Prākṛtamañjarī; cf. Mk. II, 36 : Hc. I, 232.

III, 37 *si ca*

It is wanting in the Prākṛtamañjarī; cf. Kī. II, 101; cf. Hc. II, 174.

III, 56 *na bimdupare*

It is wanting in the Prākṛtamañjarī; cf. Hc. II, 92.

V, 30 *sorbindurnapumsake*; cf. § 2528.

VIII, 5 *kte turaḥ*

Mk VII, 7, Hc. IV, 172.

VIII, 8 *dūno dūmaḥ*

Mk. VII, 10; Hc. IV, 23

VIII, 10 *padeḥ pālaḥ*

added in the margin in the MS A.

VIII, 20 *jighrateḥ pāpāaü*

It is wanting in the MSS A and C also.

IX, 7 *ṇavaraḥ kevale*

Vas. says in the commentary on the sūtra VIII, 9, *ānantarye ṇavari*=Bhāmaha IX, 8 : *kecit tu ṇavari kevalānantaryayor ityekam sūtram paṭhanti* l *tanmate nipātadvayamapi ubhayanivṛttau paryavasyati*" Mk. VIII, 11-12; Hc. II, 187.

IX, 13 *ṇavi vaiparītye*

Mk. VIII, 21; Hc. II, 178.

IX, 17 *ajja āmantraṇe*

It is wanting in the MS A and is added in the margin of D, and is wanting in the Prākṛtamañjarī.

The sūtras I, 30; V, 16-17; V, 38-42 are wanting even in the edition of the Prākṛtasañjīvanī, but they are found in the Prākṛtasubodhinī; so it is by an accident that we have lost the corresponding commentary of Vasantarāja.

List of sūtras commented upon by Vasantarāja alone :

I, 17 *ūduta upasarge visarjanīyena*
(continued in Bhām. I, 17). It is wanting in the Prākṛtamañjarī.

I, 18 *īd itaḥ*;
cf. Hc. I, 93.
It is wanting in the Prākṛtamañjarī.

III, 47 *ādes'ca* (follows Bhāmaha III, 47)
cf. Mk. III, 63 comm. Hc. II, 58.
It is wanting in the Prākṛtamañjarī.

IV, 10 *kṣudho haḥ* (follows Bhām. IV, 8)
Mk. IV. 16; Hc. I, 17
It is wanting in the Prākṛtamañjarī.

IV, 26 *svārthe ko vā* (follows Bhām. IV. 25);
cf. also the comm. in the MSS A and C;
cf. Mk. IV, 51; Hc II, 164.

IV, 31 *mahārāṣṭre haroḥ* (follows Bhām. IV, 29)
Mk. IV, 56; Hc II, 119.
It is wanting in the Prākṛtamañjarī

V, 111 *kvacinna tādyarthe* (follows Bh. VI, 64)
Mk. V, 131; Hc. III, 132;

VIII, 20-26 (follow Bh. VIII, 23; it is wanting in the Prākṛtamañjarī)
ghaṭer gaḍhaḥ
Hc. IV, 112
samo galaḥ

Hc. IV, 113
sraṁso lhasaḥ

Hc. IV, 197
neḥ sadaḥ sajjaḥ
āṅo rabher ḍhavaḥ

Hc IV, 155
udi śaleḥ thallo vā.

Hc. IV, 174
pibater ghoṭaḥ[1]

Mk. VII, 115 (*ghoṭṭaḥ*); Hc IV, 10(*ghoṭṭaḥ*).
It is wanting in the Prākṛtamañjarī.

VII, 40 *padervalaḥ* (follows Bh. VIII, 36)
cf. Bh. VIII, 10 in the preceding list.
It is wanting in the Prākṛtamañjarī.

VII, 68 *takṣe raṁpavacchau* (follows Bh. VIII, 62)

VII, 77 *evam anyepi* (follows Bhām. VIII, 70)

VII, 79-80 *anadantānām ad vā* (follows Bh. VIII, 71)
It is wanting in the Prākṛtamañjarī
aḍādes'ā bahulam

VIII, 2 *kīsa kimarthe* (follows Bh. IX, 1)
cf. Mk. VIII, 16; cf. Hc. III, 68.
It is wanting in the Prākṛtamañjarī

VIII, 8 *ijerāḥ pādapūraṇe* (follows Bh. IX, 6)
cf. Mk. VIII, 31; Hc. II, 217

VIII, 10 *u kṣepavismayasūcanāsu* (follows Bh. IX, 8)
Mk. VIII, 6 (*uṁ*); cf. Hc. II, 199 (*ū*)

VIII, 15 *vecca āmantraṇe* (follows Bh. IX, 12)
(to be corrected as *ve ca*? cf. Mk. VIII, 26).

1. Dolci—pivaterghoṭaḥ.

265. In case we remember that the total number of sūtras of Vararuci exceeds 400 in the two commentaries[1], the number of the sūtras uniquely attested in one or the other is not very large. The difference in the radaction of the sūtras is neither big (cf. Appendix I, § 277).

266. The quotations from the commentaries of dramas or of other works in Māhārāṣṭrī are generally traced out without difficulty[2].

267. Even a later day grammarian like Rāmaśarman, or his commentory shows in the citations that he had before him a text that on the whole was similar to what was commented upon by Bhāmaha and Vasantarāja[3].

268. The sūtras of Vararuci are old and have come down to us withuot much of mischances; but can they be called to

1. Vas. 431 sūtras, Bhām. 424 sūtras, are divided thus :

	Vas.	Bhām.
(i)	44	44
(ii)	43	47
(iii)	65	66
(iv)	35	33
(v) (=Bh. V-VI)	111	47+64
(vi) (=Bh. VII)	34	34
(vii) (=Bh. VIII)	80	71
(viii) (=Bh. IX)	19	18

2. Weber, (p. XXXIV of the introduction to the edition of Hāla, 1881) is astonished not to find a reference to Vararuci and to Hemacandra. Hemacandra needs not merit to have any authority in the eyes of knowers of Māhārāṣṭrī. As regards Vararuci it is not astonishing that he is not named—it is the practice with the commentators,—but the citations followed by *iti prākṛtavyākaraṇe* or *iti prākṛtasūtram* are totally borrowed from him. Cf. for example H. 354 where the commentator refers to the *prākṛtavyākaraṇa* at the place where he justifies the use of the genitive with the value of the dative and where he dares say *iti prākṛtavyākaraṇe*, probably because he wrote *caturthyarthe ṣaṣṭhī* in place of *caturthyāḥ ṣaṣṭhī* of Vr. (VI, 64); 366 *jño jāṇamuṇau prākṛtasūtram* (Vr. VIII, 28), etc. Vararuci is mentioned by name only once and that for ascribing to him a sūtra that he did not write; but certainly it is a fault of the author of the commentary (546 *prākṛte pūrvanipātāniyamāt iti vararuciḥ*). The other commentators do not name Vararuci and this very sūtra is again quoted at 153, 407 and 533 without ever having been followed by the indication *iti prākṛtasūtram* or *iti prākṛtavyākaraṇe*.

3. A single example will suffice to show that sometimes the interpretation of the sūtra may be different : Vr. I, 21 *ulūkhale lvā vā* (s. understood *ot*) would serve for Bhāmaha to form *okkhalaṁ* and *ulūhalaṁ ohalaṁ* and *ulūhalaṁ* for Vasantarāja, *okkhalaṁ* and *udukkhalaṁ* for Ramaśarman (commentary to RT I, 1, 13—*vararucistu okkhalaṁ udukkhalaṁ, nīḍāditvāt*. But the sūtra admits of these diverse interpretations.

constitute a complete grammar of Prākrit ? Let us first of all take note of a fact that perhaps has not as yet been noticed : the work of Vararuci does not begin either with an introductory stanza nor with any general sūtra on Prākrit. In the very beginning, without telling us that the technical terms of Sanskrit grammar will be used, without restricting the scope of the study of the subject, without uttering a word of *maṅgala*, the work begins with the phonology of vowels : *āderataḥ*. Neither Hemacandra, who, nevertheless wrote an appendix to his Sanskrit grammar, nor Caṇḍa, who is older than Vararuci according to Hoernle, nor Mārkaṇḍeya dares just rush forth thus *in medias res*; Kramadīśvara alone follows his master Vararuci even in abruptly beginning his work, but firstly he writes the 8th chapter of the Saṁkṣiptasāra and so he had before him a reader who already was in course of grammatical methods; and in addition he was armed with the force of tradition and of habit. But even Kramadīśvara adds in his commentary *lokānusārāt prākṛte* and comes along the right path by extracting a word of *maṅgala* from the first sūtra : *samṛddhyāder ādir ad ād vā*.

There are only two ways of justifying this situation : it may be that Vararuci too wrote an appendix to his Sanskrit grammar, or that he was content with framing a number of rules for Prākrit without claiming to have written a complete Prākrit grammar. They were possibly grouped, arranged, and provided with headlines (by introducing changes and that by making them badly sure, cf. § 224) by somebody, and the commentators began working on them. And so in case I call Vararuci the author of these primitive sūtras, that is for the sake of simplification !

269. In case these sūtras are read one after another, like a class-manual of our days, one is struck with their general character : starting from a Sanskrit model, they struggle to justify such and such forms, but they do not describe Prākrit : They make the clear impression that they refer to a text or to an aggregate of definite text. This impression is confirmed by the commentators.

Let us take for example Bhāmaha : The dropping of intervocalic consonants is governed by euphonic considerations : *prāyograhaṇād yatra s'rutisukham astī tatra na bhavatyeva* (on Vr. II, 2) ;

the *anusvāra* may be dropped or introduced for metrical reasons; *yatra kvacid vṛttabhaṅgabhayāt tyajyamānaḥ kriyamāṇaśca bīndurbhavati sa māṁsādiṣu draṣṭavyaḥ* (on Vr. IV, 16); the use of the particle *o* should be marked in the verses : *gāthāsu draṣṭavyāh*. Evidently it is the books in verses that the commentory has in view, the works to which the sūtras would correspond.

2610. I am naturally tempted to identify these works. Unfortunately little can be derived from the examples that Bhāmaha has added to the sūtras of Vararuci. There are hardly sentences having a complete sense except in the 9th book on the subject of invariable particles. Everywhere we find only isolated words. These sentences of the book on *nipātas* have passed through several lacunae : the penetration of Th. Bloch and the erudition of Pischel have disclosed the identity of three only[1], but they are extremely common :—

Vr. IX, 2 *huṁ sāhusu sabbhāvaṁ*
Hāla 453 *sahi ! sāhusu sabbhāvaṁ*
Vr. IX, 9 *kiṇo dhuvvasi*
Hāla 369 *kiṇo dhuasi*
Vr. IX, 10 *avvo ṇam iva attuṁ*,
an error for
Hāla 204 *avvo ṇa jāmi chittaṁ*.

2611. But there are about twenty cases that are not found in the Saptaśataka of Hāla; those that are the longest have a better determined meaning. Their identity would have been decisive, since several authors had the occasion to say "why do you wash yourself ? "tell me the truth"[2].

2612. The quotations from the commentary offer us little that may be of any use. So naturally attempt is here made to analyse the vocabulary of the sūtras of Vararuci; all the words that have been studied in the sūtras and exclusively in the sūtras have been examined; all the forms that they assume in Prākrit, either in the edition of Bhāmaha[3] or

1. Th. Bloch, KZ, XXXIII, p. 329.

2. These three quotations occur in Hemacandra (II, 197; 204; 216). Another sentence of the commentary of Bhāmaha occurs in Hc., although it is not found in Hāla : Vr. IX, 2 *huṁ geṇha appaṇo jīaṁ*=Hc. II, 197 *huṁ geṇhe appaṇo ccia*.

3. The words attested in the sūtras and found in Bhāmaha or in Vasantarāja have been omitted.

in that of Vāsantarāja have been carefully noted. There was altogether a collection of 406 words (sometimes there being two or three Prākrit forms in this list corresponding to a single Sanskrit word); 233 of these words are included in *Weber's* index to the second edition of Hāla. Their number may be increased still further; it is true that there are certain mistakes of reading in the rest of the words that have nothing corresponding in Hāla. Thus **apelo* (Bhāmaha I, 19); while *āmelo* is taught by Bhāmaha II, 16 **isi<īṣat*; (Bhām. I, 3) that should certainly be read as *īsi*; **gauravaṃ* (Bhām. I, 43) that is impossible in Prākrit and owes its existence merely on a wrong understanding of the adhikāras; **ṇiakka-* (Bhām. VIII, 69), which too is an error committed by Bhāmaha (cf. Cowell, p. 173); **via* and **vea* (Bhām. IX, 3) that should be read as (*c*)*cia* and (*c*)*cea*, etc. Excepting these six examples we find nothing in the ratio 239/166. So at least 59% of the words studied by Vararuci are found in Hāla. It is already a considerable result, particularly so when we notice certain striking correspondences like the derivative *bhisiṇī>visinī* (II. 38), that actually occurs in the Saptaśataka (4 and 8)[1]. Mk. (II, 37) formulates the rule for *visa>bhisam*, although he gives only one example of *bhisiṇī* (—Hāla 8).

For the purpose of rendering this impression more precise all the doublets authorised by Vararuci have been picked up, almost all of them are found in the Saptaśataka. Their list, followed by a list of the invariable particles and of the affixes taught by Vararuci is given below. The coincidences are striking.

2614. A number of doublets occur in the Setubandha and in the Gaüḍavaho: perhaps we have not taken account of these texts here. I have the impression that literary Māhārāṣṭrī was formed in the gāthās and that the epic poems have borrowed from it the language without modification. In fact the doublings and fluctuations of spelling are attested very well in the anthologies of the gāthās that are compositions of different authors who perhaps spoke different dialects. These doublets—these variations—are notice-

1. Cf., however, *visa* in the recension Teliṇga 952.

able in a smaller measure in works composed leisurely by a single same author. But the Indian have taste for thoughtless imitation. Māhārāṣṭrī, that had seen the great success of the gāthās, was fast becoming almost intangible. The later-day epic poets were imitating it with delight.

Doublets of Vararuci

Sanskrit	Reference	Prakrit		
samṛddhi-	I, 2	*samiddhī*		H
		sāmiddhī		
mayūra-	I, 8	*moro*		H
		maūro		
mayūkha-		*moho*		H
		maūho		
yathā	I, 10	*jaha*		H
		jahā		H+
sadā	I, 11	*saï*		H
		saā		H+
piṇḍa-	I, 12	*peṇḍaṁ*		H+
		piṇḍaṁ		H
iti	I, 14	*ia* (in the beginning of a sentence)		H
		(*t*)*ti*		
ulūkhala-	I, 21	*okkhalaṁ*	Bh.	
		ohalaṁ	Vas.	
		ulūhalaṁ		
dukula-	I, 25	*duallaṁ*		
		duūlaṁ	——	H
vṛkṣa-	I, 32; III, 31	*rukkho*		H
		vaccho		
daiva-	I, 37	*daïvaṁ*		
		devvaṁ		H
prakoṣṭha-	I, 40	*pavaṭṭho*	Bh	
		pavuṭṭho	Vas.	
		paoṭṭho		
uttarīya-	II, 17	*uttarīaṁ*		
		uttarijjaṁ		
-anīya-	II, 17	(*rama*)*ṇīaṁ*		
		(*rama*)*ṇijjaṁ*		H

-daśa° II, 49	*daha (muho)*	
	dasa (muho)	
sthāṇu- II, 15	*khāṇū*	
	thāṇu "Hara"	H
sūrya- II, 19	*sūro*	
	sujjo	
kṣamā Bh. kṣmā Vas. III, 31	*chamā*	
	khamā	H
kṣaṇa- III, 31	*chaṇaṁ* ("feast", com.)	H
	khaṇaṁ	H
bāṣpa- III, 38	*vāho* "tear"	H
	vappho	
vihvala- III, 47	*vebbhalo* Bh.	
	vibbhalo Vas.	
	vihalo	
	vibbhalo Vas.	
sevā III, 47	*sevvā*	
	sevā	H
kṛṣṇa- III, 61	*kasaṇo* ("black," com.)	H
	kaṇho ("Viṣṇu", com.)	H
sneha- III, 64	*saṇeho*	H
	ṇeho	H
kālāyasa- IV, 3	*kālāsaṁ*	
	kālāasaṁ	
bhājana- IV, 4	*bhāṇaṁ*	
	bhāaṇaṁ	H
yāvat IV, 5	*jā*	H
	jāva	H
māṁsa IV, 16	*maṁsaṁ*	
	māsaṁ	
pṛṣṭha- IV, 20	*puṭṭhī* Bh.	
	paṭṭhī Vas.	H
	puṭṭhaṁ Bh.	
	paṭṭhaṁ Vas.	

Sanskrit	Prākrit	
akṣi IV, 20	*acchī*	H
	accharṁ Bh.	H
	acchiṁ Vas.	
praśna- IV, 20	*paṇhā-*	
	paṇho	
ava	*o-*	H
apa IV, 21	*ava-*	H
malina- IV, 31	*maïlaṁ*	
	maliṇaṁ	H
gṛha- IV, 32	*gharaṁ*	H
	gaha (vaī)	H
ātman- III, 48; V, 45	*appā*	H
	appāṇo	H
	attā Vas.	
brahman- V, 47	*vamhā*	H
	vamhāṇo	
√*bhū* VIII, 1, 3	*ho-*	H
	huva-	H
	°*bhava-*	H
√*kṛ* VIII, 13	*kuṇa-*	H
	kara-	H
√*smṛ-* VIII, 18	*bhaar-*	H
	sumara-	H
√*bhī-* VIII, 19	*bhā*	H
	vīha	
√*mlā* VIII, 21	*vā*	
	vāa	H
√*jñā-* VIII, 23	*jāṇa-*	H
	muṇa-	H

√*sthā-* VIII, 25, 26	*ṭhāa-*		H
	ṭhā-		
√*dhyā-* VIII, 25, 26	*jhāa-*		
	jhā-		H
√*gā-* VIII, 25, 26	*gāa-*		H
	gā-		H
√*rudh-* VIII, 49	*rundha-*		H
	rumbha-		H
√*sphuṭ-* VIII, 53	*phuṭṭa-*		H
	phuḍa-		H
√*cal-* VIII, 53	*calla-*		
	cala-		H
pra + √*mīl-* VIII, 54	*pamilla-*		H
	pamila-		H
√*mṛj-* VIII, 67	*lubha-*		
	supa-	Bh.	
	puṁsa-	Vas.	
√*masj-* Bh.	*vuṭṭa-*	Bh.	
	vuḍḍa-	Vas.	
√*majj-* Vas VIII, 68	*khuppa-*		
√*dṛś-* VIII. 69	*pulaa*		
	ṇiakka-	Bh.	H
	ṇiaccha-	Vas.	
	avakkha		H
	saccava-	Vas.	

śak- VIII, 70	*tara-*	H
	vaa-	
	tīra-	H

Doublets of Bh. alone

√*ghrā-* VIII, 20	*pā-*	
	pāa	

Doublets of Vaṣ alone

√*ṛṣi-*	— *isī*	
I, 30	— *risī* (?)	
airāvata- II, 10	*erāvaṇo*	
	erāvao	
udumbara- IV, 2	*umbaraṁ*	
	uumbaraṁ	
√*ghūrṇ-* VII, 5	*ghola-*	
	ghumma-	H
ud + √*śal-* VII, 25	*utthalla-*	H
	ucchala-	
nir + √*mā-* VII, 39	*ṇimmāṇa-*	
	ṇimmava-	
√*takṣ-* VII, 68	*rampa-*	
	vaccha-	

2616 Particles from Vararuci

huṁ IX, 2 *dāna-pṛcchā-nirdhāraṇeṣu* (Vas. °*nivāraṇeṣu*)

ccia, *ccea*, Vas. (Bh. *via*, *vea* wanting) IX, 3 *avadhāraṇe*
H

o IX, 4 *sūcanā-paścāttāpa-vikalpeṣu*
H

ira } IX, 5 *aniścitākhyāne* Bh. *aniścayākhyāneṣu* Vas.
kira } H
kila } H

huṁ } IX, 6 *niścaya- vitarka- saṁbhāvaneṣu*
kkhu } H

ṇavara- IX, 7 *kevale* Bh. alone, but cf. com. Vas. VIII, 9.
H

ṇavari IX, 8 *ānantarye*
H

kiṇo IX, 9 *praśne*
H

avvo Bh. *abbo* Vas. IX, 10 *duḥkha-sūcanā-saṁbhāvaneṣu*
(Vas. °*saṁbhāṣaṇeṣu*)
alāhi IX, 11 *nivāraṇe*
H
ai H
vale Bh. *raṇe* Vas. IX, 12 *saṁbhāṣaṇe*
ṇavi IX, 13 *vaiparītye* only in Bh.
H
sū Bh. *dhū* Vas. IX. 14 *kutsāyām*
re H.
are (cf. H. p. 290 IX, 15 *saṁbhāṣaṇa-ratikalaha-kṣepeṣu*
hire (Bh. *hare* Vas.
mmiva Bh. *piva* Vas.
H. H. IX, 16
miva Bh. *miva* Vas.
via Bh. *viva* Vas.
H. H. *ivārthe*
va Vas.
H
ajja IX, 17 *āmantraṇe* only in Bh.
H.
kīsa VIII, 2 *kimarthe*
H
H.
je VIII, 8 *pādapūraṇe*
ra H.
u VIII, 90 *kṣepa-vismaya-sūcanāsu*
H.
vecca VIII, 15 *āmantraṇe*

2617 Suffixes of Vararuci

-*dā* (*tal*) IV, 22
-*ttaṇa* (-*tva*) IV, 22 H.
-*ūṇa* (*ktvā*) Bh., -*tūṇa* Vas. IV, 23.
-*ira* (-*tṛn* *śīle*") IV, 24 H.
-*alu* H
-*illa* H.
-*ulla* H.
-*āla*
-*vanta*
-*inta* (*matup* IV, 25 H. (-*ala*)
-*ā* or -*ī* optional for the feminine IV, 24 H.
-*ka* *svārthe*, only in Vas. IV, 26 H.

* * *

271. The lexical coincidences are striking between the sūtras of Vararuci and the Saptaśataka of Hāla; in case these were much more numerous, it would have been proved that Vararuci had before him the same selection of the gāthās that has been edited by W e b e r. This would be demanding too much !

272. A later day anthology like the Vajjālagga of Jayavallabha is composed of 795 verses, of which 76 are found in Hāla[1]. The Saptaśataka possibly contained, in a proportion impossible to measure, a portion of the gāthās that have been provided with a grammatical commentary by Vararuci. But probably it does not contain all of them, and does not contain all those that were known to Vararuci.

273. I have already spoken above about the necessity of a critical edition of Vararuci based on all the commentators and all the grammarians who have drawn materials from his work; and now we are in a position to venture to say that such an edition should be based also on thorough utilization of the Saptaśataka of Hāla and of all the anthologies of verses found in Māhārāṣṭrī that are accessible to us. Vararuci would singularly get elucidated better by this confrontation and often the gāthās would become better intelligible thereby. An example confirms this hypothesis :—

Hāla 550

Ed. W e b e r :— *voḍasuṇao vivaṇṇo*
attā mattā paī vi aṇṇattho l
phaḍahī vi modiā mahi-
saeṇa ko kassa sāheu ll

Translation :—The nasty dog is dead. The mother-in-law is intoxicated. My husband too is elsewhere (or the mother-in-law is intoxicated with presented "*sura*"). Even the cotton plant is twisted by a buffalo (so that nobody can be pricked?) Who will speak this to whom ?"

The edition D u r g ā p r a s ā d and P a r a b (VI, 49) has *phalihaṁ va moḍiaṁ mahisaeṇa* paraphrased in Sanskrit as : *kārpasyāpi bhagnā mahiṣakeṇa.*

1. J. L a b e r, Ueber das Vajjālāggam des Jayavallabha : Leipzig 1913, pp. 35-37.

The "cotton-plant" was inconvenient for an amorous sport; it is unexpected. Hemacandra (Deśī. VI, 82) explains, it is true, *phalahī* as *karpāsa-* "cotton-plant", but he has succeeded in thrusting this word into his anthology on the affirmation of the commentators of Hāla.

274. Vr. II, 36, on the contrary teaches us that some Sanskrit words change the initial *p* into *ph* in Prākrit. These words are *paruṣa->pharuso*, *parīgha->phaliho* and *parikhā>phalihā*[1]. The stanza at once becomes clear, *phaliham phaḍahī* has to be translated in the chāyā as *parigha-* in its ordinary meaning of "iron-bar", "bolt".

"The wicked dog is dead, the mother-in-law is in intoxicated, my husband is elsewhere and (by a stroke of fortune) the bolt has been broken by a buffalo. Who will ever speak this ?"

* * *

275. To sum up, the last three books of the edition Bhāmaha-Cowell are additions made by later-day authors. As regards the book on Śaurasenī, it was not even known to Bhāmaha.
267. The sūtras of Vararuci studies only a single dialect, that is of the Māhārāṣṭrī lyric. And even for Māhārāṣṭrī these sūtras cannot aspire to be named grammar; they are written in Sanskrit for persons knowing Sanskrit with the intention of teaching them to compose Prākrit gāthās. It is possible that originally these stanzas were of relatively popular creation, but they were meant to become in a certain moment to serve as mental diversion for the learned, who knew the dialect on one hand and Sanskrit on the other and their effort terminated in writing in this artificial language the Māhārāṣṭrī lyric dotted with Sanskrit reminiscences and extraordinary dialectical words.

276. The sūtras of Vararuci were composed for this public.[2]

1. Cf. also Pischel, Grammatik. § 208.

2. So far as it relates to Māhārāṣṭrī, we ought to acknowledge that the most suggestive has been the review by Garrez of the first edition of Hāla, by Weber. Cf. JA. 6e series, t. XX (1872), pp. 197-220.

278. Variants of the sūtras of Vararuci according to the three principal commentaries[1]
PP—Prākṛtaprakāśa, ed. Bhāmaha-Cowell
PS—Prākṛtasañjīvanī of Vasantarāja
PM—Prakṛtamanjarī
RV—Commentary of Rāmapāṇivāda

RV	PP	PS	PM	
1, 1	1, 1	1, 1	1, 1	
2	2	2	2	
3	3	3	3	PS °āṅgāreṣu ca
4	4	4	4	
5	5	5	5	PS *e ca śayyādiṣu*
6	6	6	6	
—	7	—	7	
7	8	7	8	RV *mayūramayūṣayorvā yvā*
8	9	8	9	
9	10	9	10	RV, PM *yathādiṣu*
10	11	10	11	RV, PS *it sadā*; PM *it sadādau*
11	12	11	12	
12	13	12	13	
13	14	13	14	RV, PM *itestaḥ*
14	15	14	15	
15	16	15	16	RV *kṛñi*
16	17	16	17	PS, PM *ītsiṁhajihvayoḥ* RV *ī siṁhajihvayos'ca*
17	—	—	18	PM *ive lopaḥ* RV *iverlopaḥ*
	—	17	—	PS *ūda uta upasarge visarjanīyena*
	—	18	—	PS *īditaḥ*

1. Cf. § 243 ff. The text of the edition Bhāmaha—Cowell has not been reproduced. The three others have been quoted so far as they differ. Orthographical differences have been ignored. The sūtras are understood up to the end, in case the word is not followed by the sign °.

PP	PS	RV	PM	
1,18	1,19	1,18	1,19	
19	20	19	20	RV *ennīḍāpīḍedṛśakīdṛśeṣu*
20	21	20	21	PS °*sameṣu*
21	22	21	22	
22	23	22	23	
23	24	23	24	
24	25	24	25	
25	26	25	26	
26	27	26	27	
27	29	27	28	
28	30	30	31	PS °*ādiṣu vā*
29	31	31	32	
30	—	28	29	(In the Prākṛtasubodhinī)
31	32	29	30	PS *yukasyāpi riḥ*
32	33	32	33	
33	34	33	34	PS *ḷta iliḥ*
34	35	34	35	PS *idvāvedana*°
35	36	35	36	
36	37	36	37	RV *daityādiṣvaīḥ*
37	38	37	38	
58	39	38	39	
39	40	39	40	RV *ī dhairye*
40	28	40	41	PS *ota udvā*°; PM *otodvā prakoṣṭhe*
41	41	41	42	
42	42	42	43	PM *paurākṛtiṣvauḥ*; RV °*ṣvaüḥ*
43	43	—	44	
44	44	43	45	
II, 1	II, 1	II, 1	II, 1	
2	2	2	2	
3	3	3	3	
4	4	4	4	PS °*cikurasīkhareṣu ko haḥ*; PM °*cikuraśīkhareṣu haḥ*
5	—	—	—	
6	5	5	5	RV *candrikāyāṁ ko maḥ*
7	6	6	6	
8	7	7	7	PS, PM *prativetasa*°
9	8	8	8	

10	9	9	9	
11	10	—	—	PS *vā*
12	11	10	10	
13	12	11	11	
14	13	12	12	PS *saṁkhyāyās'ca*
15	14	13	13	
16	15	14	14	
17	16	15	15	
18	17	—	—	
19	—	16	16	RV, PM *kabandhe yaḥ*
20	18	17	17	
21	19	18	18	
22	20	19	19	
23	21	20	20	
24	22	21	21	
25	23	22	22	PM *aṁkoḍhe ḍhasya llaḥ*
26	—	23	23	
—	—	24	24	RV, PM *yathādiṣu haḥ*
27	24	25	25	PS *khaghathadhaphabhāṁ vā* PM *khaghathadhabhām*
28	25	26	26	
29	26	27	27	
30	27	28	28	
31	28	29	29	
32	29	30	30	
33	33	31	31	
34	31	32	32	
35	32	33	33	
36	33	34	34	
37	—	—	—	
38	34	35	35	RV *bisinyāṁ bhaḥ*
39	35	36	36	
40	36	—	—	PS *lāhala-lāṅgala-lāṅgūleṣu vā ṇaḥ*
41	37	37	37	PM *ṣaṭchātasaptaparṇeṣu*; RV *ṣaṭśātasaptaparṇeṣu haḥ*
42	38	38	38	RV, PS, PM *no ṇaḥ*
43	39	39	39	
44	40	40	40	
45	41	41	41	

46	42	42	42	
47	43	43	43	
III, 1	III, 1	III, 1	III, 1	PS °*paṣasaśām*
2	2	2	2	
3	3	3	3	RV *lavarāṇām*
4	4	4	4	
5	5	5	5	PM °*sadṛśeṣu jaḥ*; RV °*sadṛśeṣu ñaḥ*
6	6	6	6	
7	7	7	7	
8	8	8	8	RV °*nalamānāṁ*°
9	9	9	9	
10	10	10	10	
11	11	11	11	
12	12	12	12	
13	13	13	13	
14	14	14	14	
15	15	15	15	
16	16	16	16	PS *kṣetake ca*; RV, PM *ṣphoṭake ca*
17	17	17	17	
18	18	18	12	
19	19	19	19	
20	20	20	20	RV, PS *riaḥ*; PM *riyaḥ*
21	21	21	21	
22	22	22	22	
23	23	23	23	PS *mṛttikāpattanayośca*; RV, PM *pattane ca*
24	24	24	24	
25	25	25	25	PS *garte ca ḍaḥ*
26	26	26	26	PM °*vicchardeṣu*; RV °*vicchardiṣu*
27	27	27	27	RV *tyathyadyānāṁ-*
28	28	28	28	RV *dhyahyayorjhaḥ*
29	29	29	29	RV *skaṣkakṣāṇāṁ-*
30	30	30	30	
31	31	31	31	RV *kṣmā-*
32	32	32	32	PM *grīṣmapakṣma*°
33	33	33	33	
34	34	34	34	

35	35	35	35	
36	36	36	36	PS *spasya*; RV, PM *spasya ca*
37	—	—	—	
38	37	37	37	
39	38	39	38	RV *kārṣāpaṇe ca*
40	39	39	39	
41	40	40	40	PM *vṛścike jjuḥ*
42	41	41	41	
43	42	42	42	
44	43	43	43	PS °*daśasu ṇaḥ*
45	44	44	44	RV, PM *ṇḍaḥ*
46	45	45	45	RV, PM *bhindipāle ca*
47	46	46	46	RV, PS, PM *vihvale bho vā*
—	47	—	—	PS *ādes'ca*
48	48	47	47	
49	49	47	48	RV, PM *kmasya ca*
50	50	49	49	
51	51	50	50	PS, RV *varge yujaḥ pūrvaḥ*; PM *varge yujaḥ pūrvam*
52	52	51	51	PM *nīlādiṣu*
53	53	52	52	PM °*mbaḥ*
54	54	53	53	
55	55	54	54	PS *jñādeśasya*
56	—	—	—	
57	56	55	55	
58	57	56	56	RV *sevādiṣu vā*
69	58	57	57	RV, PS, PM *vikarṣaḥ*
60	59	58	58	RV, PM °*śliṣṭakriyāratnaśārṅgeṣu tatsvaraḥ pūrvasya*
61	60	59	59	
—	—	60	60	PM *asaṁjñāyāṁ vā*; RV *asaṁjñāyām*
62	61	61	61	PS °*hrīklānta*° ; °*sparśādarśaharṣārheṣu*; RV, PM *iccrīhrīklāntakleśamlānasvapnasparśaharṣeṣu*
63	62	62	62	RV *atkṣmāślāghayoḥ*
64	63	63	63	
65	64	64	64	RV *ut padma*°

66	65	55	65	
IV, 1	IV, 1	IV, 1	IV, 1	RV °*maglopa*°
2	2	2	2	PS *dorvā lopaḥ*
3	3	3	3	PS *kālāyase yasya*
4	4	4	4	
5	5	5	5	
6	6	6	6	RV *antyahalaḥ*
7	7	7	7	
8	9	—	—	
9	8	8	8	
—	10	—	—	PS *kṣudho haḥ*
10	11	9	9	
11	12	10	10	RV, PM *prāvṛṣaḥ saḥ*
12	13	11	11	PS *mo bindur aci vā lopas'ca*
13	—	12	12	
14	14	13	13	RV *naṅorhali*
15	15	14	14	
16	16	15	15	
17	17	16	16	PS *kapi tadvargyāntaḥ*; PM *hali tadvargāntyaḥ*; RV *rali tadvargyāntyaḥ*
18	18	17	17	
19	19	18	58	
20	20	19	19	
21	21	20	20	
22	22	21	21	
23	23	22	22	PS *ktva tūṇaḥ*; RV, PM *ktvā tūṇaḥ*
24	24	23	23	RV *tṛna iraḥ śīle*
25	25	24	24	RV *ālviallollellavaṁteṁtā*°
—	26	25	25	RV, PS' PM *svārthe ko vā*
26	27	26	26	PS *vidyutpītayorlaḥ*; PM *ḷaḥ*
27	28	27	27	PS *do vaḥ*; PM, RV *do raḥ*
28	29	28	28	RV, PM *sthitiparivṛttiḥ*
—	—	29	29	RV, PM *kareṇvāṁ raṇoḥ*
29	30	30	30	
—	31	—	—	PS *mahārāṣṭre rahoḥ*
30	32	31	31	PS *bṛhaspatau bahor hayaḥ*: PM *bṛhaspatau vahoḥ*; RV *bṛhaspatau vahorhayau*

31	33	32	32	
32	34	33	33	RV *gṛhasya-*
33	35	34	34	
V, 1	V, 1	V, 1	V, 1	RV *ata otsau*
2	2	2	2	
3	3	3	3	
4	4	4	4	
5	5	5	5	RV *bhiso hiḥ*
6	6	6	6	
7	7	7	7	
8	8	8	8	
9	9	9	9	PM *ṅeremmi*
10	10	10	10	RV *supaḥ su*
11	11	11	11	RV, PS, PM *jasṅasyāṁsu dīrghaḥ*
12	12	12	12	PS *e supyaṅiṅasoḥ*; RV, PM *e ca supi*
13	13	13	13	PS *kvacid api lopaḥ*; RV, PM *kvacid ṅasiṅyorlopaḥ*
14	14	14	14	
15	15	15	15	
16	—	16	16	RV *jasa o vā cātvam.* (The sūtras 16 and 17, however, occur in the Prākṛtasubodhinī; probably it is a case of an occasional lacuna; the enumeration continues).
17	—	17	17	
18	18	18	18	
19	19	19	19	RV, PM *jaso vā striyām udotau*
20	20	—	—	
21	21	20	20	
22	22	21	21	PM *ṭāṅasiṅasṅīnāṁ idudadādataḥ*
23	23	22	22	RV *ṭāṅasiṅasṅīnāmidudadādetaḥ*
24	24	23	23	

25	25	24	24	RV, PS, PM *napuṁsake sor binduḥ*
26	26	25	25	PS *dīrghaḥ*
27	27	26	26	
28	28	27	27	PS, PM *ata eta* PM (*e*), RV *āta e.*
29	29	28	28	
30	—	—	—	
31	30	29	29	RV *ṛta āraḥ puṁsi*
32	31	30	30	RV, PS, PM *māturā*
33	32	31	31	PS, PM *°ṅassu*; RV *ṅassu vā*
34	33	32	32	
35	34	33	33	
36	35	34	34	RV, PS, PM *rājñaḥ*
37	36	35	35	RV *āmantraṇe binduvā*
38	37	36	36	RV, PM *°ṇo vā*
39	—	—	—	(38-41 in the Prākṛtasubodhinī)
40	—	37	37	RV. *āmo ṇaḥ*
41	—	38	38	
42	—	39	39	PM *ṅaso dvitvaṁ ṅalopaśca*, RV. *ṅasaścadvitvaṁ jalopaśca*
43	42	40	40	
44	43	41	41	RV, PM *ṇo ṇamo rād ṅasi*
45	44	42	42	RV *ātmanoppaṇo vā*
46	45	43	43	
47	46	44	44	RV, PS, PM *brahmādayopyevam*
VI, 1	V, 47	V, 45	V, 45	PS *sarvādeḥ*; RV, PM *sarvāder jasa e*
—	48	—	—	PS *jasa et*
2	49	46	46	
3	50	47	47	
4	51	48	48	
5	52	49	49	
6	53	50	50	RV *ītaḥ ssāsse*
7	54	51	51	RV *ṅerhiḥ*
8	55	52	52	RV, PM *iā ca kāle*
9	56	53	53	PS *o tto do ṅaser anidamaḥ*

10	—	54	54	RV, PM *tada o*
11	57	55	55	PS *tado ṅasā se vā striyāmapi*; RV, PM *ṅasā vā se*
12	58	56	56	
13	59	57	57	
14	60	58	58	
15	61	59	59	PS *aṁ ssiṁssayor vā*; PM *ssassimorat*
16	62	60	60	
17	63	61	61	
18	64	62	62	
19	65	63	63	
20	66	64	64	
21	67	65	65	PS °*tasya lopaḥ*
22	68	66	66	
23	69	67	67	
24	70	68	68	
25	71	69	69	
26	72		70	PM *yuṣmadaśca tuṁ tuvaṁ sau*; RV *yuṣmadastuṁ tuvaṁ sau*
27	73	71	71	RV, PM *tumam ami ca*
28	74	72	72	PS *tujjhe tujjha tumhe jasi*
29	75	73	73	
30	76	74	74	PS *taī tae tumaī tumae tume*; PM *taī tae tue tumae* RV *taī tue tume tumae*
31	78	75	75	PS °*tujjha-tuva-tumhāḥ*; PM *ṅasi tuva-tuma-tuha-tubbha-tujjha-tumhāḥ*; RV *ṅasi tuvatumatuhatumhatujjhatubbāḥ*
32	79	76	76	
33	80	77	77	
34	81	78	78	PS *tujjhehi tubbhehi tumhehi bhisi*; RV, PM *tujjhehi tumhehi bhisi*
35	82	79	79	PS °*tumāo tumāi tumāhi vā*
36	83	80	80	
37	84	81	81	PS *vote*; PM *vohau*; RV *vo ho*

38	77	82	82	PS *tumammi ca ṅau*; PM, RV *ṅau tumassi tumammi*
39	35	83	83	PS *tujjhesu tubbhesu supi*
40	86	84	84	
41	87	85	85	PS *ammirami ca*; RV, PM *mirami ca*
42	88	86	86	PS, RV *maṁ mamaṁ ca*
43	89	87	37	
44	90	—	—	PS *ṇo ca śasi*
45	91	88	88	PM *āṅi ca me mamāi*
46	92	39	89	
47	94	90	90	RV *amhehi bhisi*
48	95	91	91	PS *°mamāo mamāu mamāhi ṅasau*
49	96	92	92	
50	97	93	93	
51	98	94	94	PM *°amho āmi*; RV *ṇo amha amhāṇa amhe āmi*
52	99	95	95	PM *mamassiṁ mamammi ṅau*; RV *mamassi mamammi ṅau*
53	100	96	96	
54	101	97	97	
55	102	99	98	RV, PS *trestī*
56	103	100	99	PS *tiṇi°*
57	104	98	100	PS *doṇi vā*; PM *°doṇṇi vā*; RV *duve veṇṇi vā*
58	104	101	101	
59	105	102	102	RV *eṣāmāmo ṇhaḥ*
60	106	103	103	
61	107	104	104	RV *ṅasiṅyornādetau*
62	108	105	105	RV *ā bhyasi*
63	109	106	106	PM *dvivacane*
64	110	107	107	
—	111	—	—	*kvacinna tādarthye*
VII, 1	VI, 1	VI, 1	VI, 1	
2	2	2	2	PM, PS, RV *sipthāsoh si se*
3	3	3	3	
4	4		4	RV *ntihathamomumā bahuṣu*

5	5	5	5	
6	6	6	6	
7	7	7	7	PM °*hodhaśca*; RV *mimomumādeśānāṁ hodhaśca*
8	8	8	8	PS *yaka ia ijjau*
9	9	9	9	
10	10	10	10	
11	11	11	11	
12	12	12	12	
13	13	13	13	RV *uttame ssāhau ca*
14	14	14	14	
15	15	15	15	
16	16	16	16	PS, PM °*dṛśirūpāṇāṁ*° °*dacchaṁ*; RV "*dṛsirūpāṇāṁ* °*dacchamaḥ*
17	17	17	17	
18	18	18	18	
19	19	19	19	
20	20	20	20	RV °*tanayośca jyajjau vā*
21	21	—	—	
22	22	21	21	
23	23	22	22	
24	24	23	22	
25	25	25	24	PS *āsirasteḥ*
26	26	25	25	RV *ṇica edāderāt*
27	27	26	26	PS *āve vā*
28	28	27	27	PM, RV *āviḥ ktabhāvakarmasu vā*
29	29	28	28	
30	30	29	29	
31	31	30	30	
32	32	31	31	
33	33	32	32	
34	33	33	33	
VIII. 1	VII, 1	VII, 1	VII, 1	RV, PM *hobhuvau*
2	2		2	PM *kte tu bhū*; RV *kte bhūḥ*
3	3	3	3	
4	4	4	4	
5	—	—	—	

6	5		5	PS *ghūrṇo gholaghummau*; PM, RV *ghūrṇergholaḥ*
7	6	6	6	RV *ṇuderṇollaḥ*
8	—	7	7	RV *dūño dūmaḥ*
9	7	8	8	PS *pāṭeḥ phālaḥ*; PM, RV *pāṭeḥ phaḷaḥ*
10	[40]	—	—	[PS *padervvalaḥ*]
11	8	9	9	RV *vṛṣādīnāmṛto riḥ*
12	9	10	10	RV, PM *antyasyāraḥ*
13	10	11	11	PS °*kuṇa ca*; RV, PM °*kuṇaḥ*
14	11	12	12	PS *jṛbher jambhā*; PM, RV *jṛmbher jhaṁbhāaḥ*
15	12	13	13	
16	13	14	14	PS *ghetta*°; PM *ghe*°; RV *ghe ktvātumuṁstavyeṣu*
17	14	15	15	
18	19	16	16	
19	16	17	17	PM, RV °*bhā vībhau*
20	—	—	—	
21	17	18	18	PS *mlo vā vāa*; PM, RV *mlāyo vā vāau*
22	18	19	19	RV *tṛpasthippaḥ*
23	19	20	20	
—	20	—	—	
—	21	—	—	
—	22	—	—	
—	23	—	—	
—	24	—	—	
—	25	—	—	
—	26	—	—	
24	27	31	21	
25	28	22	22	PS, PM *sthā*°; RV *sthādhyāgāṁ*°
26	29	23	23	RV °*bhaviṣyadvartamāna-vidhyādyekavacane*
27	30	24	24	PS °*dhā*
28	31	25	25	PS *graser ghasaḥ*; RV *graserghisaḥ*
29	32	26	26	

30	33	27	27	RV *krīñaḥ°*
31	34	28	28	RV *veḥ ke ca*
32	35	29	29	PS *udhmo dhumā*; RV *°uddhumaḥ*
33	36	30	30	RV *śraddho dahaḥ*
34	37	31	31	
35	38	32	32	
36	39	33	33	PS *niro māṅo maṇa-mavau* : PM *niro mo māṇaḥ*
37	41	34	34	
38	42	35	35	
39	43	36	36	
40	44	37	37	
41	45	38	38	RV *utsamorḷḷaḥ*
42	46	39	89	PS, PM *rudo vaḥ*
43	47	40	40	RV *°vijeḥ*
44	48	41	41	PS *vṛdher ḍḍhaḥ*
45	49	42	42	
46	50	43	43	
47	51	44	44	
48	52	45	45	PS *yudhibudhigṛdhisidhikru-dhāṁ jjhaḥ* ; RV *yudhabudhayorjjhaḥ*
49	53	46	46	
50	54	47	47	PM, RV *ḷaḥ*
51	55	48	48	RV, PS, PM *śadi°*
52	56	49	49	RV, PM *dvitvaṁ vā*
53	57	—	—	PS *°calor°*
54	58	50	50	RV *°mīḷaḥ*
55	69	51	51	RV *°ktvātumunstavyeṣu°*
56	60	52	52	PS *°lū dhūnāṁ ṇonte hrasvaśca*; PM *°lūṅdhūṅāṁ ṇontyasya hrasvaḥ* RV *śrūhujilūñdhūñāṁ ṇontyasya hrasvaśca*
57	61	53	53	RV *bhāvakarmaṇorvaśca*
58	62	54	54	
59	63	55	55	PS *duhi-lihi-vahāṁ dujjha-lijjhabujjhāḥ*; PM *duhali-*

				havahāṁ dubbhalibbhavabhāḥ
60	64	56	56	PS, PM *hṛṅkrṅor°*; RV *hṛṅkṛñor hīrakīrau*
—	65	=1957	57	RV, PM *jño ṇajjaṇappau vā*
61	66	58	68	PS, RV *graher gheppaḥ*; PM *graher vā gheppaḥ*
62	67	59	59	
—	68	60	60	PS *takṣe rampavacchau* ; PM *takṣeruppaḥ* ; RV *takṣe rabbaḥ*
63	69	61	61	RV *visūraḥ*
64	70	62	62	
65	71	63	63	PS *carceścaraḥ* ; PM *carver vabbhaḥ*; RV *carvervaṁbhaḥ*
66	72	64	64	PM *traser bujjhaḥ* ; RV *bujjaḥ*
67	73	65	65	PS *°lubbhapuṁsu*; RV, PM *°luhapusau*
68	74	66	66	PS *°majjeḥ* ; RV *buḍḍakhupphau majjeḥ*
69	75	67	67	PS *°ṇiaccha avakkhasaccavāḥ*; RV, PM *dṛśeḥ pulaṇiaṇlac-chapecchāḥ*
70	76	68	68	RV *śakestaracaatīrāḥ*
—	77		69	PS *evamanyepi*; PM *anyepi*
—	—	69	—	RV *apakramerboḷaḥ*
71	78	70	70	
—	79		—	PS *anadantānām advā*
—	80	71	71	PS *anādeśā bahulam*; PM *adādeśe bahulam*; RV *aḍādeśe bahulaṁ*
IX, 1	VIII, 1	VIII, 1	VIII, 1	
—	2	—	2	PS *kīsa kimarthe*
2	3	2	2	PS. PM *°nivāraṇeṣu*; RV *huṁ... nivāraṇeṣu*
3	4	3	3	RV, PS *ccia ccea°*; PM *cia cea°*
4	3	4	4	
5	6	5	5	PS, PM *″aniścayākhyāneṣu*
6	7	6	6	RV *hu khu niścayavitarka-saṁbhāvanāsu*

7	—	8	8	RV *ṇavara°*
—	8	7	7	PS *ijerāḥ pādapūraṇe*; RV PM *ije re°*
8	9	9	9	PM, RV *ṇavaria*
—	10	10	10	PS *u kṣepavismayasūcanāsu*; PM, RV *ū°*
9	11	11	11	
10	12	12	12	PS. PM *°saṁbhāṣaṇeṣu*; PM *abbo amho duḥkha°*; RV *appo ammo duḥkhasūcanāsaṁbhāṣaṇeṣu*
11	13	13	13	RV *haḷāhi°*
12	14	15	14	PS *°raṇe°*; RV *°vaḷe°*
13	—	16	15	RV, PM *vi vaiparītye*
—	19	17	16	PS *vecca āmantraṇe*; PM *bebbe*, RV *vaḍḍhe°*
14	1ṅ	14	17	PS *dhū°*; RV, PM *ā°*
15	17	18	18	RV *are re saṁbhāṣaṇa°*
16	18		19	PS *piva-miva-viva va ivārthe*; PM *viva miva viā ivārthe*; RV *piva miva viva ivārthe*
17	—	19	—	
18	19	23	23	
—	—	20	—	RV *aggho haṁho ābhimukhyakaraṇe*
—	—	21	—	RV *haddhi nirvede*
—	—	22	—	RV *hī harṣe*

CHAPTER II

BHARATA

31. Bharata presents a number of problems that are still unsolved and these problems present themselves at every instant in respect of Indic studies. In case they could be resolved they would assist us in responding to the question that we come across, but in their actual state they stand as obstacles in our way. We feel that on their solution would depend at least partly the solution of our particular problems. But when we try thus to handle them with presentiments, we are not able to succeed in resolving them provisionally: In course of our study into the theatre, into prosody or even into the history of India, we very often find the Nāṭyaśāstra of Bharata; but the uncertainty of the text and tradition does not allow us to take advantage of this work of fundamental importance. By way of caution scholars hesitate even in borrowing quotations from this work.

32. The history of Prākrit grammar too begins with the Nāṭyaśāstra. Pischel (according to Cowell and Aufrecht)[1] have indicated that Mārkaṇḍeya in his Prākṛtasarvasva has cited a certain number of passages that he ascribes to Bharata and the name of Bharata appears in the stanzas given in the introduction to his grammar among the authors studied by him. According to Pischel the quoted passages are not found in the Nāṭyaśāstra and belong probably, if not to an altogether different work, at least to a different recension.

33, As a matter of fact, one of the passages is identical in Mārkaṇḍeya and in the *Nāṭyaśāstra* (edition Śivadatta and Parab)[2] another one presents itself in the two slightly

1. Pischel, *De Gramm.* p. I, ss; *Gramm.* § 31; Cowell, *Vararuci*, p. XI; Aufrecht, Catal-catal, No. 412, p. 181a.

2. The *Nāṭyaśāstra* of Bharata Muni, edited by Paṇḍit Śivadatta and Kāśīnātha Pāṇḍuraṅga Parab, Bombay 1894, Kāvyamālā n°. 42.

different forms. Below is given a complete list of citations by Mārkaṇḍeya :—

Mk. I, 1 *yadāha paramarṣirbharataḥ-dhātuprātipadika-kṛttad-dhitasuptiṅsamāsādīnāṁ terthās tāśca vibhaktayaḥ* l *pariṇatiriha paramanyā iti*[1] ll

Mk, X, 1 *prācyā vidūṣakādīnāmiti bharataḥ* ll

Mk. XI, 1 *yadāha bharataḥ-dāṇḍika-pāṇika-pāṇṭika-nagarādhi-padāṇḍa-pāṇikasadṛkṣeṣu madhyamapātreṣu sadā yojyāvantī tu nāṭya-vidhāviti* ll

Mk. XI, 13 *dhūrtādibhāṣā bāhlīkīti bharataḥ* ll

Mk. XII, 38 *rākṣasī-śreṣṭhi-ceṭānukarmyāder ardhamāgadhīti bharataḥ* ll

Mk. XIII, 9 *maharṣirbharataśca*[2] *āgamaliṅgavihīnaṁ viparītaṁ nyāyadeśakālāḍeḥ madamūrkhatābhimānādyaiśvaryāt syācchakāravacanamiti* ll

Mk. X, 1=*Nāṭyaśāstra* (edition Kāvyamālā) XVII, 51.—Mk. XII, 38 : cf. *Nāṭ.* (ed. KM) XVII, 50 : *ceṭānāṁ rāja-putrāṇāṁ śreṣṭhināṁ cārdhamāgadhī*—.Mk. XI, 1; XI, 13; XIII, 9 are not found in the *Nāṭyaśāstra*; the first two passages even contradict it. XVII, 52 : *yodhanāgarakā-dīnāṁ dākṣiṇātyā*; *Nāṭya.* XVII, 51; *dhūrtāṇāmapyavantijā*, but they too are in the spirit of the *Bhāratīyanāṭya-śāstra* so to say. We should not loose sight of the fact that Mārkaṇḍeya is an author of the 17th century,

1. This passage has been cited by P i s c h e l (*De Gr. pr.* p. 1)in a different form : *yadāha—°samāsādīnāṁ pariṇatiriha pravaktavyeti* II.—*terthāstāśca vibhaktayaḥ*, has in addition the appearance of a gloss.

2. Mārkaṇḍeya mentions Bharata four times, once *paramarṣirbharataḥ* and once *maharṣir-bharataḥ*. In case the last citation (XIII, 9) was not existing, it could be imagined that the appellation *paramarṣir bharataḥ* was used to refer to a different Bharata, more ancient than the presumptive author of the *Nāṭyaśāstra*. An analogous hypothesis had already been formulated by Manomohon G h o s h regarding the commentary of R ā g h a v a b h a ṭ ṭa on the Śakuntalā who attributes twentyone citations to Ā d i b h a r a t a, fourteen to B h a r a t a; now fifteen of the first group and eleven of the second group are literally found in our *Nāṭyaśāstra* Subsequently G h o s h himself renounced this explanation and refuted the identification postulated by D.R. M a n k a d of this Ā d i b h a r a t a (name of the work ? with (fol. 1-33)a part of the manuscript entitled Nāṭyasarvasvadīpikā preserved in the Bhandarkar Oriental Res. Institute. In the colophon to this work too there occurs the word Ādibharata. I think we should give up the idea of distinguishing between Bharata and Ādibharata. In this context cf. M. G h o s h, The *Ādibharata* and the *Nāṭyasarvasvadīpikā*, Annals of the Bhandarkar Oriental Research Institute, XV (1933-1934), 89-96.

when in all probability the text of Bharata may have all the divergences that are found today.

34. The single really astonishing citation is the first one : it is in prose and does not appear to be from a treatise on dramatic art, rather it looks as if from a veritable grammar. Now it is true that in the beginning of adhyāya XVII, there are certain verses that Bharata devoted to Prākrit grammar, but they are exclusively concerned with phonetics. In all events, the quotation of Mk. I, 1 does not occur there.

35. Besides Mārkaṇḍeya is the single grammarian of Prākrit who quotes Bharata. This appears to indicate that the grammatical portion of the adhyāya XVII of the Bhāratīyanāṭyaśāstra did not have a great echo in India : this fact, at least, is curious. So long we had before us only the Kāvyamālā edition, the first hypothesis that struck our mind was that these verses had lately been interpolated into the text. But since the new edition of Bharata in the Gaekwad's Oriental Series again presents this fragment of grammar, guarantied by the commentary of Abhinavagupta, we have now to reject this hypothesis.

36. So this fragment was present already in the 10th or 11th century in the text of the *Nāṭyaśāstra*, and so it is anterior to majority of Prākrit grammars that are known to us.

37. Among the other particularities we find in it certain rules written in Prākrit : a remarkable fact in face of the situation that the language of Prākrit grammar is exclusively Sanskrit.

38. This adhyāya XVII[2] of the *Nāṭyaśāstra* had never been published in Europe. During the last forty years the only available text had been that of the Kāvyamālā Series based, according to Śrī Rāmakrishna Kavi, on sufficiently recenly made transcriptions of a single manuscript preserved in the Bhandarkar Oriental Research Institute. The fragment of Prākrit grammar had been absolutely inconceivablein it. In 1934

1. Cf. p. 208.
2. Consequent to division into two sections of the adhyāya IX, it corresponds in some MSS of the Nāṭyaśāstra to the adhyāya XVIII.

appeared the second volume of the *Nāṭyaśāstra* in the Gaekwad's Oriental Series, edited by Shri Rāmakrishna Kavi[1]. This edition, based on collation of forty MSS of very different ages, roughly represents the recension of Abhinavagupta and faithfully reproduces his commentary and takes into account the reading of the ancient recension followed by Udbhaṭa and Lollaṭa[2]. It provides within brackets all the passages that are wanting in the recension of Abhinavagupta; the critical apparatus in it is sufficiently rich. With the help of this new edition we are now in a position to understand almost the whole of the adhyāya XVII.

39. It is hoped the reproduction and translation of these interesting Prākrit passages will not be devoid of interest. Following the numeration of the GOS edition the subject-matter of the adhyāya starts in the following manner :—

vv. 1-3 (śloka), 4-6 (āryā) : generalities on Prākrit.
vv. 7-24 (āryā) ; grammar of Prākrit (7-10 in Prākrit, 11-24 in Sanskrit).
vv. 25-64 (śloka) : classification of Prākrits, allocation to diverse characters, dialectical peculiarities.
vv. 65-93 (śloka) : rules regarding mode of addressing different characters.
vv. 94-102 (ślokas) : names to be given to different characters.
vv. 103-150 (ślokas) : theory of voice and of sound.

310. We quote below the stanzas 1-64. In addition to the Kāvyamālā and the GOS it has been possible to consult a copy of the manuscript of the *Nāṭyaśāstra* preserved in the library of Kathamandu. This manuscript appertains to an ancient recension, but on the other hand it presents numerous points of contact with the recension of Abhinavagupta. Its copy had been loaned to the present writer by Sylvain Lévi who had borrowed it earlier from the editor of the *Nāṭyaśāstra*

1. *Nāṭyaśāstra* of Bharata with the commentary of Abhinavagupta of Kashmir, edited by Ramakrishna Kavi, 4 vols; vol. I (I-VII), Baroda 1926; Vol. II (VIII-XVIII), 1934.

2. Cf. Introduction to the second volume, pp. XXII-XXIII.

of the GOS. It appeared that in several cases the Nepal MS was capable of presenting a text that is better than that of the GOS edition[1] and since our object has been to facilitate reading of these difficult and important passages of the *Nāṭyaśāstra* corrections have been effected here and there in the text of tke GOS, completely retaining its readings in the note.

G indicates the GOS edition (XVII, 1-64);
K the Kāvyamālā edition (XVII, 1-63);
N the Nepal MS (XVIII, f. 100a I, 1-102 b 1.5).

evaṁ tu saṁskṛtaṁ pāṭhyaṁ mayā proktaṁ samāsataḥ I
prākṛtasya tu pāṭhyasya saṁpravakṣyāmi lakṣaṇam II 1 II

etadeva viparyastaṁ saṁskāraguṇavarjitam I
vijñeyaṁ prākṛtaṁ pāṭhyaṁ nānāvasthāntarātmakam II2II

trividhaṁ tacca vijñeyaṁ nāṭyayoge samāsataḥ I
samānaśabdaṁ vibhraṣṭaṁ deśīgatamathāpi ca[2] II 3 II

kamalāmalareṇu-taraṅga-lola-salilādivākyasampannam I
prākṛtabandheṣvevaṁ saṁskṛtamapi yogamupayāti II 4 II

ye varṇā saṁyogasvaravarṇānyatvamūnatāṁ cāpi I
gacchanti padanyastāste vibhraṣṭā iti jñeyāḥ[3] II 5[4] II

yathā

eoāraparāṇi a aṁāraparaṁ a pāae[5] *ṇatthi* I
vasaāramajjhimāi a kacavaggatavaggaṇihaṇāiṁ II 6 II

vaccaṁti kagatadayavā lopaṁ[6] *atthaṁ ca se vahaṁti sarā* I
khaghathadhabhā uṇa hattaṁ uveṁti atthaṁ amuṁcaṁtā II 7 II

upparahuttaraāro heṭāhutto[7] *a pāae*[8] *ṇatthi* I
mottūṇa bhadra-vodraha-padra-hrada-candra-jāīsu II 8 II

1. Cf. *Nāṭyaśāstra*, ed. GOS, p. XXII-XXIII.
2. G : adds : *pāṭhyamekaṁtu vijñeyaṁ saṁskṛtaṁ prākṛtaṁ yathā* (K too is wanting)
3. G : *yāntyapadādau prāyo vibhraṣṭāṁstān vidurviprāḥ.*
4. G : adds : *ye varṇā varṇagatā vyañjanayuktāśca ye svarā niyatāḥ* II6II *tān aparasparavṛtte prākṛtayuktyā pravakṣyāmi* II (K too is wanting)
5. N *pāie.*
6. N. *lovaṁ.*
7. G. *heṭāhuttau* (probably a printing mistake).
8. N. *pāie.*

khaghathadhabhāṇa haāro muha-meha-kahā-vahū pahūesu l
kagatadapabāṇa ṇiccaṁ vīyammi[1] *ṭhio hoi* ll 9 ll

cha iti ṣakāro nityaṁ boddhavyaḥ ṣaṭpadādiyogeṣu l
kilaśabdāntyo repho bhavati tathā khu tti khaluśabdaḥ ll 10 ll

ḍa iti ca bhavati ṭakāro bhaṭa-kaṭaka-kuṭī-taṭādyeṣu l
satvaṁ ca bhavati śaṣayoḥ sarvatra yathā visaṁ saṁkā[2] ll 11 ll

aspaṣṭaśca dakāro bhavatyanādau takāra itarādyaḥ l
vaḍavā[3] *taḍāgatulyo bhavati ḍakāropi ca lakāraḥ*[4] ll 12 ll

vardhanagate ca bhāve dhakāravarṇopi ḍhatvamupayāti[5] l
sarvatra ca prayoge bhavati nakāropi ca ṇakāraḥ ll 13 ll

āpānaṁ āvāṇaṁ bhavati pakāreṇa vatvayuktena l
ayathātathādhikeṣu tu thakāravarṇo[6] *vrajati dhatvam* ll 14 ll

paruṣaṁ pharusaṁ vidyāt pakāravarṇopi phatvamupayāti[7] l
yastu mṛtaḥ sopi mao yaśca mṛgaḥ sopi hi tathaiva ll 15 ll

okāratvaṁ gacchedaukāraś[8] *cauṣadhādiṣu niyuktaḥ* l
pracalācirā-calādiṣu[9] *bhavati cakāropi tu yakāraḥ* ll 16 ll

aparasparaniṣpannā hyevaṁ prākṛtasamāśrayā varṇāḥ ll
saṁyuktānaṁtu punarvakṣye parivṛttisaṁyogam ll 17 ll

ścapsatsathyāḥ cha iti tathā bhyahyadhyā bhavanti tu jhakārāḥ l
ṣṭaḥ ṭṭaḥ staḥ tthaḥ ṣmo mha kṣṇo hṇaḥ ṣṇo ṇhaḥ kṣaḥ khakāra-rūpopi[10] ll 18 ll

1. The three texts : *kagatadayavāṇa*; N. *viīammi*.
2. K. *viśaśaṅkā*, N. *visasaṁkā*.
3. G. *baḍabā*.
4. G. *kakāraḥ*.
5. K. *śaṭhapāṭhapīṭhiādiṣu kāravarṇopi ḍhatvamāyāti*, N. *rakāravarṇopi ṭatvamupayāti*.
6. G, *bhakāra°*.
7. N. *paruṣaṁ harusaṁ vidyāt yakāravarṇopi hatām*.
8. N. *aukāratvam ucchantākāraś*.
9. *pracalayitācalādiṣu*.
10. N. *śca-tsa-thyāḥ cha ity ahṛvyāmvā bhavanti tu sakārāḥ* l *ṣṭa ṭṭha staḥ ttaḥ ṣmo mlaḥ kṣṇaḥ ṣṇo kṣaḥ kha iti caiva syāt* ll

āścaryaṁ acchariaṁ niścayamicchanti ṇiccayaṁ ca yathā[1] l
utsāho ucchāho paṭhyaṁ pacchaṁ ca vijñeyam ll 19 ll

tubhyaṁ tujjhaṁ mahyaṁ majjhaṁ vindhyaśca bhavati viṁjhotti l
daṣṭo daṭṭhotti tathā hastopi ca bhavati hatthotti ll 20 ll

grīṣmo gimhotti tathā ślakṣṇaṁ saṇhaṁ sadā tu vijñeyam l
uṣṇamuṇhaṁ yakṣo jakkho pallaṃku bhavati paryaṁko[2] ll 21 ll

viparītaṁ hamayoge brahmādau syād bṛhaspatau phatvam[3] l
yajño bhavati ca janno[4] *bhīṣmo bhimhotti vijñeyaḥ* ll 22 ll

uparigatodhastādvā bhavet kakāradikastu yo varnaḥ l
sa hi saṁyogavihīnaḥ śuddhaḥ kāryaḥ prayogesmin ll 23 ll

evametattu vijñeyaṁ prākṛtaṁ saṁskṛtaṁ tathā l
ata ūrdhvaṁ pravakṣyāmi deśabhāṣāvikalpanam ll 24 ll

bhāṣā caturvidhā jñeyā daśarūpe prayogataḥ[5] l
saṃskṛtaṁ prākṛtaṁ caiva yatra pāṭhyaṁ prayujyate ll 25 ll

atibhāṣāryabhāṣā ca jātibhāṣā tathaiva ca l
tathā yonyantarī[6] *caiva bhāṣā nāṭye prakīrtitāḥ* ll 26 ll

atibhāṣā[7] *tu devānāṁ āryabhāṣā tu bhūbhujām* l
saṁskārapāṭhayuktā samyaṅnyāyapratiṣṭhitā[8] ll 27 ll

dvividhā[9] *jātibhāṣā ca prayoge samuddhṛtā* l
mlecchaśabdopacārā ca bhārataṁ varṣamāśritā[10] ll 28 ll

atha yonyantarībhāṣā[11] *grāmyāraṇyapaśūddbhavā* l

1. G. adds : *vatsaṁ vacchaṁ ca yathā apsarasaṁ tadvadaccharaaṁ* l
2. K. *jakṣo jakrauryollaśca bhavati pallaṁko*; N. *yakṣo jakkho polaśca bhavati pallaṅkaḥ.*
3. N. *viparīto hamayogo...hatvaṁ.*
4. N. *jaṇṇo.*
5. N. *daśarūpa°.*
6. K. *jātyantarī.*
7. N. *satyātibhāṣā.*
8. K. *samyaggrāma°.*
9. K.N. *vividhā.*
10. N. *tathā bhāratasaṁśrayā.*
11. K. *atha yā jātyantarī bhāṣā.*

nānāvihaṅgajā caiva nāṭyadharmīpratiṣṭhitā[1] ll 29 ll

jātibhāṣāśrayaṁ pāṭhyaṁ dvividhaṁ samudāhṛtam ll
prākṛtaṁ saṁskṛtaṁ caiva cāturvarṇyasamāśrayam[2] ll 30 ll

dhīroddhate salalite dhīrodātte tathaiva ca l
dhīrapraśānte ca tathā pāṭhyaṁ yojyaṁ tu saṁskṛtam ll 31 ll

eteṣāmapi[3] *sarveṣāṁ nāyakānāṁ*[4] *prayogajam* l
kāraṇavyapadeśena[5] *prākṛtaṁ saṁprayojayet*[6] ll 32 ll

aiśvaryeṇa pramattānāṁ dāridryeṇa plutātmanām l
anadhītottamānāṁ ca saṁskṛtaṁ na prayojayet[7] ll 33 ll

vyājaliṅgapraviṣṭānāṁ śramaṇānāṁ tapasvinām l
bhikṣucakracarāṇāṁ ca prākṛtaṁ saṁprayojayet ll 34 ll

bhāgavattāpasonmattabālanīcagrahopasṛṣṭeṣu l
strīnīcajātiṣu tathā napuṁsake prākṛtaṁ yojyam ll 35 ll

parivrānmuniśākyeṣu cokṣeṣu śrotriyeṣu ca l
śiṣṭā ye caiva liṅgasthāḥ saṁskṛtaṁ teṣu yojayet[8] ll 36 ll

rājñaśca[9] *gaṇikāyāśca śilpakāryāśca tathaiva ca* l
kālāvasthāntarakṛtaṁ[10] *yojyaṁ pāṭhyaṁ tu saṁskṛtam* ll 37 ll

1. K. *°prayogajā*; N. *prayogatas*.
2. N. *°varṇyādisaṁśrayam*.
3. K. *eṣāmeva tu*; N. *eṣāmeva ca*.
4. K. *nāṭyakānām*; G. *nāyakāṇā*.
5. K. *karairavya°*
6. G. adds : *dāridryādhyanābhāvayadṛcchādibhireva ca* ll
7. K. *aiśvaryeṇa pramattasya aiśvaryeṇa plutasya ca* l
   dāridryeṇa pramattasya dāridryeṇa plutasya ca ll
   uttamasyāpi bruvataḥ prākṛtaṁ saṁprayojayet l
   N. *aiśvarye tu pramattasya dāridryeṇa plutasya ca* ll
   uttamasyāpi paṭhataḥ prākṛtaṁ saṁprayojayet ll
8. 36-36 wanting in N;
   K. *vyājaliṅgapratiṣṭhānāṁ śravaṇānāṁ tapasvinām* l
   bhikṣu-cakravaraṇānāṁ prākṛtaṁ saṁprayojayet ll
   bāle gadopaṣṛṣṭe ca strīṇām ca prakṛtau tathā ll
   nīce matte saliṅge ca prākṛtaṁ pāṭhyamiṣyate l
   paribhāṇmuniśānteṣu vākyeṣu śrotriyeṣu ca l
   dvjiā ye caiva liṅgasthāḥ samṣkṛtaṁ teṣu yojayet ll
9. N. *divyāyā*.
10. N. *taṣām kālāṁtalakṛtam*.

sandhivigrahasambandhaṁ tathā ca prāptavāggatim[1] I
grahanakṣatracaritaṁ khagānāṁ rutameva ca II 38 II

sarvametattu vijñeyaṁ kāvyamadhye śubhāśubham[2] I
nṛpapatnyā smṛtaṁ tasmāt kāle pāṭhyaṁ tu saṁskṛtam[3] II 39 II

krīḍārthaṁ sarvalokasya prayoge ca[4] *sukhāśrayam* I
kalābhyāsaśrayaṁ caiva pāṭhyaṁ veśyāsu saṁskṛtam II 40 II

kalopacārajñānārthaṁ krīḍārthaṁ pārthivasya ca[5] I
nirdiṣṭaṁ śilpakāryastu nāṭake saṁskṛtaṁ vacaḥ II 41 II

āmnāyasiddhaṁ sarvāsāṁ śubhamapsarasāṁ vacaḥ[6] I
saṁsargād devatānāṁ ca taddhi lokonuvartate[7] II 42 II

chandataḥ prākṛtaṁ pāṭhyaṁ smṛtamapsarasāṁ bhuvi[8] I
mānuṣāṇāṁ[9] *ca kartavyaṁ karaṇārthavyapekṣayā*[10] II 43 II

na barbarakirātāndhradramilādyāsu[11] *jātiṣu* I
nāṭyaprayoge kartavyaṁ pāṭhyaṁ[12] *bhāṣāsamāśrayam* II 44 II

sarvāsveva hi śuddhāsu jātiṣu dvijasattamāḥ[13] I
śaurasenīṁ samāśṛtya bhāṣāṁ kāvyeṣu yojayet[14] II 45 II

athavā chandataḥ kāryā deśabhāṣāprayoktṛbhiḥ I
nānādeśasamutthaṁ hi kāvyaṁ bhavati nāṭake II 46 II

1. K.N. *cāpyaśubhaṁ śubham.*
2. K.N. *sarvametaddhi vijñeyaṁ yasmādājñaḥ* (K *rājā*) *śubhāśubham.*
3. K. *nṛpapatnyā bhavet pāṭhyam saṁskṛtaṁ dvijasattamaḥ.*
4. K.N. *°prayogasya.*
5. K.N. *tu.*
6. K. *bhavaḥ*; N. *divyānāṁ vacanaṁ śubham.*
7. N. *hi taddhi loko nivartate.*
8. N. *ayi*
9. K. *mānuṣīṇām.*
10. *kāvyamarthavyapekṣayā.*
11. K. *°draviḍā°*; N *śabarāṇām kirātānāṁ dramiḍādyāsu.*
12. K.N. *nāṭyayoge tu kartavyaṁ kāvyam.*
13. K. *jātiṣvetāsu sarvāsu śuddhāsu ca dvijottamāḥ*; N. *jātiṣvetāsu sarvāsu śubhāsu dvijasattamāḥ* II
14. K.N. *śaurasenaṁ* (N *śaurasenī*) *samāsṛtya bhāṣā kāryā tu nāṭake.*

māgadhyavantijā prācyā śaurasenyardhamāgadhī l
bāhlīkā dākṣiṇātyā ca sapta bhāṣāḥ prakīrtitāḥ ll 47 ll

śakārābhīracaṇḍālaśabaradramilāndhrajāḥ[1] l
hīnā vanecarāṇāṁ ca vibhāṣā nāṭake smṛtā ll 48 ll

māgadhī tu narendrāṇāmantaḥpurasamāśrayā[2] l
ceṭānāṁ rājaputrāṇāṁ śreṣṭhināṁ cārdhamāgadhī ll 49 ll

prācyā vidūṣakādīnāṁ dhūrtānāmapyavantijā l
nāyikānāṁ sakhīnāṁ ca śurasenyavirodhinī[3] ll 50 ll

yaudhanāgarakādīnāṁ[4] *dākṣiṇātyātha dīvyatām* l
bāhlīkabhāṣodīcyānāṁ khasānāṁ ca svadeśajā ll 51 ll

śakāraghoṣakādīnāṁ[5] *tatsvabhāvaśca yo gaṇaḥ* l
śakārabhāṣā yoktavyā cāṇḍālī pulkasādiṣu[6] ll 52 ll

aṅgārakārakavyādha[7] *kāṣṭhayantropajīvinām* l
yojyā śakārabhāṣā[8] *tu kiṁcid vānaukasī tathā* ll 53 ll

gajāśvājāvikoṣṭrādighoṣasthānanivāsinām[9] ll
ābhīroktiḥ śābarī vā drāmiḍī vanacāriṣu[10] ll 54 ll

suraṅgākhanakādīnāṁ sandhikāraśvarakṣatām[11] l
vyasane nāyakānāṁ cāpyatmarakṣāsu[12] *māgadhī* ll 55 ll

na barbarakirātāndhradramilādyāṣu[13] *jātiṣu* l
nāṭyaprayoge kartavyaṁ kāvyaṁ bhāṣāsamāśritam[14] ll 56 ll

1. K. *°śsabarā° sacaradraviḍodrajāh*; N. *°dramiḍaudrajāḥ*.
2. K.N. *nivāsinām*.
3. K. *ca sakhīnāṁ ca sūrasenāvirodhinī* ll
4. K.N. *yodha°*
5. K. *śabarāṇāṁ śakādīnāṁ*; N. *śakārāṇāṁ śakādīnām*.
6. K. *pukvasā°*; N *pucchasā°*
7. K. *aṅgārakāravyādhānāṁ*.
8. K.N. *śabara°*
9. K.N. *gavā°*; K. *kauṣṭrā*.
10. K. *drāviḍī draviḍādiṣu*; N *dramiḍādiṣu*.
11. K. *saunḍikāraśca rakṣiṇām*; N. *auḍrikānāśca rakṣatām*.
12. K.N. *syād*.
13. K. *°draviḍā°*.
14. K. *samāśrayam*.

gaṅgāsāgaramadhye tu ye deśāḥ saṁprakīrtitāḥ l
ekārabahulāṁ[1] *bhāṣāṁ teṣu tajjñaḥ prayojayet* ll 57 ll

vindhyasāgaramadhye tu ye deśāḥ śrutimāgatāḥ l
nakārabahulāṁ teṣu bhāṣāṁ tajjñaḥ prayojayet[2] ll 58 ll

surāṣṭrāvantideśeṣu vetravatyuttareṣu ca
ye deśāsteṣu kurvīta cakāraprāyasaṁśrayām[3] ll 59 ll

himavatsindhusauvīrānye janāḥ samupāśritāḥ[4] l
ukārabahulāṁ tajjñasteṣu bhāṣāṁ prayojayet ll 60 ll

carmaṇvatīnadītīre[5] *ye cārbudasamāśrayāḥ*[6] l
okārabahulāṁ[7] *nityaṁ teṣu bhāṣāṁ prayojayet* ll 61 ll

evāṁ bhāṣavidhānāṁ tu kartavyaṁ nāṭakāśrayam l
atra noktaṁ mayā yattu loādgrāhyaṁ buddhaistu tat[1] ll 62 ll

Translation

1. Thus I have briefly described Sanskrit recitation; I shall now explain the characteristics of Prākrit recitation.
2. It is dispersed and is devoid of the merits of refinement; the Prākrit-recitation should be known to be adapted to diverse situations.
3. It should also be known that in a dramatic representation, in brief, it is of three kinds : that is where the words are the same (as in Sanskrit), divergent and of local usage[9].
4. Expressions containing words like *kamala-*, *amala-*, *reṇu-*, *taraṅga-*, *lola-*, *salila-* etc., found in Prākrit works occur likewise as in Sanskrit.

1. N. *makāra*°.
2. 58 is wanting in N.
3. K.N. *bahulāmiha.*
4. K.N. *ca deśāḥ samāśritāḥ.*
5. K.N. °*nadīpare.*
6. K. *sāmāśritāḥ* l
7. K. *takāra*°; N *ukāra* (or *ḍakāra* ?)
8. In N. a blank space marks the end of the section.
9. The grammarians call the three categories of words by the names *tatsama, tadbhava* and *deśya.*

5. When sounds forming words affect modifications in conjunct consonants or in vowels or sustain loss and that often in the middle of words, such words are corrupt. Thus[1] :

6. The sounds that (in the alphabet) are followed by *e* and *o* and the one that follows the *anusvāra* do not exist in Prākrit; and such is the case with the sounds standing between *va* and *sa* and with the final sounds of the guttural, palatal and dental series[2].

7. *ka, ga, ta, da, ya* and *va* drop in Prākrit and their meaning is conveyed by the vowels. On the other hand, *kha, gha, tha, dha* and *bha* become *ha* without change in the meaning (of the word).

8. Placed before or after (another consonant) a *ra* is not preserved in Prākrit, except in the words of the type, *bhadra-, vodraha-, padra-,* (?), *hrada-, candra-,* (or according to the chāyā *bhadra-* etc. and *dhātrī-*)[3].

1. Below is given the chāyā of these Prākrit verses as given in the ·d. GOS.

eokāraparāṇi ca aṁkāraparaṁ ca pādasaṁkhyayā nāsti l
vasakāramadhye ca kacavargatavarga nidhanāni ll 6 ll

prāpnuvanti kagatadayavā lopamardhaṁ ca teṣām vahonti svarāḥ l
khaghathabhāḥ punaḥ hatvamupzyānti ardhaṁ ca muñcamāmāḥ ll 7 ll

uparisthodhaḥstho vā rakāraḥ prākṛte nāsti l
muktvā bhadra-codraha-hrada-draha-chandra-dhātrī-śabdeṣu ll 8 ll

khaghathadhabhānāṁ hakāro mukha-megha-katha-vadhū-prabhūteṣu l
kagatadayavānāṁ nityaṁ dvitīye sthitaḥ svaro bhavati ll 9 ll

It may be noted that the 8th stanza does not represent exactly the Prākrit-texts that we have now. For the stanza No. 7, see below § 316 f.

2. That is to say *ai, au,* the visarga *ṣa* and *śa, ṅa, ña,* and *na* (cf. Hc. I, 1). Evidently we do not find *ṛ, ṝ, ḷ, ḹ*. To remove this lacuna the commentary of Abhinavagupta paraphrases *pāae=pādasaṁkhyayā=* the quarters". But it is not acceptable. It is more reasonable to conclude that this grammar is not complete. This stanza occurs of course without being mentioned as a citation in a treatise on Prākrit prosody composed by Nanditāḍhya and edited by H.D. Velankar (Annals of the Bhandarkar Oriental Research Institute, XIV, 1932-33, pp. 1-38), v. 4 : *eokkāraparāiṁ aṁkāraparaṁ ca pāie natthi* l *vasayāramajjhayāṇi ya kaccavaggatavagganihāṇāiṁ.*

3. Cf. HC. II, 80, 81.

9. *kha, gha, tha, dha* and *bha* (except eventually) become *ha*[1] in *mukha-, megha-, katha-, vadhū, prabhūta-*; (of a group consisting of) *ka, ga, ta, da, pa, ba* the consonant that is in the second place is retained[2].

10. It should be known that *ṣa* always becomes *cha* in cases like *ṣaṭpada* etc. In the final (syllable) we have *ra* in the word *kila*, and the word *khalu* becomes *khu*[3].

11. The *ṭa* becomes *ḍa* in the words like *bhaṭa-, kaṭaka-, kuṭi-, taṭa-*, and etc.[4]; *śa ṣa*, throughout become *sa*: for example *visam* (=*viṣa-*), *saṁkā*, (=*śaṁkā*).

12. The non-initial *ta*, of words like *itara-* etc., becomes *da*, indistinctly pronounced. The *ḍa* of *vaḍavā* and *taḍāga-* etc. becomes *la*[5].

13. A *dha* placed in a word like *vardhana-* [that is to say in contact with a *ra*] becomes *ḍha*; in a dramatic representation *na* becomes *ṇa* in all positions.

14. *āpāna* becomes *āvāṇa*, the *pa* assuming the nature of *va*[6]; in addition in words like *yathā, tathā*[7] etc. the consonant *tha* becomes *dha*.

15. It should be known that *paruṣa* becomes *pharus*, because of the change of the consonant *pa* into *pha*[8]; *mṛta* is pronounced as *mao*, so also *mṛga-*.

16. The diphthong *au* occurring in *auṣadha-* etc. becomes *o*; in addition in *pracala-, acira-, acala-*, etc. *ca* may become *ya* too.

17. Such is the treatment of sounds used singly in Prākrit; now I proceed to formulate rules for modification of their groups.

18. The groups *śca, psa, tsa* and *thya*[10] become *cha*; similarly

1. *mottūna* of the preceding stanza has been omitted here.
2. Allusions to the assimilation of the groups : ex-*bhukta-*>*bhutta*, *utpala-*>*uppala*, etc. But *ya* and *va* do not have the same line of treatment (cf. II, 77, 79). It is why we have corrected the text here.
3. Cf. Hc. I, 265; II, 186, 198.
4. Cf. Hc. I, 195, Pkt. *bhaḍo, kaḍaa-, kuḍī, taḍam.*
5. Cf. Hc. I, 202.
6. Cf. Hc. I, 231.
7. Which become *jaha* and *taha.*
8. Hc. I, 202.
9. Should we assume here the extension of the Māgadhī palatals to Prākrit ? Cf. Pischel, *Gramm.* I § 217.
10. Hc. II, 21.

bhya, *hya*, *dhya* become *jha*[1]; *ṣṭa* becomes *ṭṭha*[2], *sta* becomes *ttha*[3]: *sma* becomes *mha*[4]; *kṣṇa* and *ṣṇa* become *ṇha*[5] and *kṣa* is changed into (*k*) *kha*[6]"

19. So *āścarya* should be pronounced as *acchariaṁ*; *niścaya-* as *nicchayaṁ*, *utsāha-* becomes *ucchāho* and *pathya-* becomes *pacchaṁ*.

20. *tubhyam* becomes *tujjhaṁ*, *mahyam* becomes, *majjhaṁ*, *vindhya-*, *viṁjho-*, *daṣṭa-*, *daṭṭho* and *hasta-*, *hattho*.

21. *grīṣma* always becomes *gimho*, *slakṣṇa-* becomes *saṇhaṁ*, *uṣṇa-* becomes *uṇhaṁ*; *yakṣa-*, *jakkho*; *paryaṇka-* becomes *pallaṁku*.[7]

22. Metathesis takes place in the group *hma* of the words like *brahman-*, etc.;[8] in *bṛhaspati* [the group] *spa* becomes *pha*[9]; *yajña* becomes *janno*[10], this be known; *bhīṣma-* (becomes) *bhimho*.

23. Whatever be the preceding or the following (different consonant), the guttural, once freed from a group, remains intact in theatrical representations[11].

24. This must be known about Prākrit and about Sanskrit; henceforward I shall explain classification of dialects (*deśabhāṣā*).

25. In dramaturgy, the language (*bhāṣā*) is of four types, let this be known, according to the case, whether the recitation is in Sanskrit or in Prākrit.

1. Hc. II, 26.
2. Hc. II, 34.
3. Hc. II, 45.
4. Hc. II, 74.
5. Hc II, 75; the text adds also *hṇa*<*ṇha*; but since the stanza has one more syllable, I think this exceptional treatment for which the following stanzas do not contain an example may be omitted.
6. Hc II, 3.
7. The last example does not correspond to a treatment explained before; but cf. Hc II, 68. As regards the Apabhraṁśa termination *-u-*, it is embarassing; besides the following verses do not have examples·
8. Cf. Hc II, 74.
9. Hc II, 69 admits some other treatments of this word; it is curious that this is exactly the word that has been given as an example in the normal treatment *sp*>(*p*) *ph*. Probably this text is to be corrected (*satvam* ?).
10. Several MSS have *jaṇṇo* which would correspond better to the general treatment *n*>*ṇ* taught by Bharata (V, 13). On the other hanp the preservation of the duplicated dental *n* is not unacceptable.
11. Allusion to cases of the type of these quoted by Hc II, 2 ?

26. The superhuman language (*atibhāṣā*), the noble language (*āryabhāṣā*), the common language (*jātibhāṣā*) and the language of other species of animals (*yonyantarībhāṣā*); such are the languages that are known in theatrical works[1].

27. The superhuman language is known as of the gods; the noble language is that of the kings. This implies a cultured recitation (that is Sanskrit) and it is properly established according to rules.

28. The common language is spoken in practice of theatrical performances in two styles: it contains words from the Mleccha dialects and is based on the usage of India.

29. As regards the language of animals of other species, it has its origin in the speech of domestic or wild animals as well in that of different birds; it is established by the theatrical canons[2].

30. The recitation based on the common language is done in two fashions in Sanskrit or in Prākrit, according to the usage of the four castes.

31. For brave and courageous heroes, for (courageous) and spirited, as well as for the noble and courageous, for the courageous and calm, the recitation should be prescribed in Sanskrit.

32. But even of all these heroes, if the role so demands, the language should be Prākrit[3].

33. For those (of these heroes) who have been maddened by wealth and power, or who are overwhelmed with poverty, or who have not received high education, Sanskrit should not be employed.

1. Abhinavagupta says that certain commentators mention abundance of the Vedic words as a characteristic of the *āryabhāṣā*: *vaidikaśabdabāhulyād āryabhāṣāto vilakṣaṇatvamasyā ityanye.*

2. Or according to one teacher of theatral art ? Abhinavagupta comments: *paśupakṣiprabhṛtīnāṁ yad rutaṁ tat nāṭyaprayoge kutrāpyavasare sambhāvyamityāha nāṭyadharmīti.*

3. Abhinavagupta cites as an example of this limitation Arjuna speaking Prākrit when he is disguised as Bṛhannalā : *arjunasya bṛhannalārūpeṇa pracchannasya kāraṇānyāharate.* It may be conjectured that here he allude to the *Pañcarātra* of Bhāsa, where actually Arjuna, in the guise of Bṛhannalā, speaks some words in Prākrit. The moment he starts speaking about the battle in which he had participated, King Virāṭa asks him to speak in Sanskrit: it is not fit to be described in Prākrit: *ūrjitaṁ karma saṁskṛtamabhidhīyatām* (Act II, 33/34).

34. For those, who have assumed a false appearance, for the monks, for the anchorites, for the religious beggars and for the jugglers, Prākrit should be the language.

35. In the same manner for the keeper of idols, for ascetics, for lunatics, for infants, for those who are possessed of evil spirits, for women, for men of lowly castes as well as for eunuchs Prākrit should be prescribed.

36. But for the (Brāhmaṇas) who have renounced the world, for saints, for disciples of the Buddha, for holy men, for theologists, for educated Brāhmaṇical students, Sanskrit should be employed.

37. For the queen, for the courtesans as well as for the female artists, one should assign Sanskrit recitation in accordance with the time and situation.

38. About matters relating to peace and war, to the modes of cultured conversation, to the course of planets and stars and also to the cry of animals;

39. Let this be known, that all this,—and also what is suitable or unsuitable for poetry—the spouse of the king knows (by tradition); this is why on occasions she should recite in Sanskrit.

40. For the amusement of everybody, agreeable to the usage, based on the practice of art, Sanskrit recitation should be assigned to the courtesans.

41. For acquiring practice in the art and for amusing the king, Sanskrit language is prescribed for female artists in theatrical treatises.

42. Established by tradition, the language of all the Apsaras is pure (that is Sanskrit) on account of their intimacy with gods and because the popular usage conforms to this rule.

43. It is known that recitation of the Apsarases may be done in Prākrit; when they are on the earth voluntarily, the (recitation) of the human being should be determined according to the exigency of their part.

44. In theatrical performances one will never assign recitation to the communities, such as the Barbars, the Kirātas, the Āndhras, the Dramilas, etc. in their own tongue.

45. But in respect of all the pure communities, to the best

of the Brāhmaṇas, in poetry, a language based on Śaurasenī should be assigned.

46. Or the drama-writers at their option will make use of local languages—because in a piece of theatre poems are taken from different regions.

47. Māgadhī, Āvantī, Prācyā Śaurasenī, Ardhamāgadhī, Bāhlīkā and Dākṣiṇātyā are the seven widely known languages.

48. Of the Śakāras, of the Ābhīras, of the Caṇḍālas, of the Śabaras, of the Dramilas and the Āndhras, as well as of the inhabitants of the forests, the lovely dialects are known as *vibhāṣā*[1] in dramatic works.

49. Māgadhī is the language assigned to the royal harems; Ardhamāgadhī is the language of servants of princes and of the guide-chiefs.

50 Prācyā is the language of buffoons, but that of the knaves it is Āvantī. Śaurasenī is suitable for heroines and their friends when they are not in difficulty.

51. Dākṣiṇātyā shall be assigned to the soldiers and city-guards; to gamblers Bāhlīkā; to the people of the North and to the Khasas, the dialects of their country.

52. To the Śakāras and to the public announcers—as to all the people of their class, Śākārī should be prescribed, and Cāṇḍālī to Pulkasa, etc.

53. For charcoal-makers, hunters, wood-cutters or for the mechanic Śākārī should be prescribed or sometimes the dialact of the inhabitants of the forest.

54. For those who live in camps among elephants, horses, ship, goats, camels etc. Ābhīrī or Śābarī is suitable and Drāmiḍī for those who live in forest.

55. For those who dig underground passages etc., for those who pierce holes in walls and guard horses (this should be) Māgadhī and also for the heroes when there is the question of protecting life in danger[2].

1. Abhinavagupta tries to define the words *bhāṣā* and *vibhāṣā*: *bhāṣā saṁskṛtāpabhraṁśaḥ* l *bhāṣāpabhraṁśastu vibhāṣā*—"a *bhāṣā* is a corruption of Sanskrit and a *vibhāṣā* is a corruption of a *bhāṣā*.

2. Because while speaking Māgadhī, he cannot be recognized, so means Abhinavagupta : *vyasanaṁ kasyāṁcitāpadi jātāyāṁ mā māṁ loks jñāsyatītyabhiprāyeṇātmano rakṣārth, aṁ nāyakopi māgadhyā vyavaharet.*

56. =44

57. As regards the people who are said to be living in the regions lying between the Gaṅgā and the sea, one who knows them should employ the language abounding in the sound *e*.

58. For the people who are known to be living between the Vindhya-mountains and the sea, one who knows it, should use the language abounding in the sound *na*.

59. For people inhabiting Surāṣṭra, the country of Avantī, as well the region lying to the north of the Vetravatī (Betwā), one should fashion a language abounding in *ca*.

60. For the people who live in the Himalayas, in Sindh and in Sauvīra, he who knows it will cause to be employed a language that abounds in the sound *u*.

61. As regards the people living in the region of the Arbuda-mountains (Mount Abu), on the banks of the Charmaṇvatī (the Chambal), one should always make them speak in a language abounding in the sound *o*.

62. Thus should take place the allocation of languages in dramas; whatever has not been said here, the intelligent persons will be able to learn from popular usage.

311. The reading of this passage, whatever be the mode of interpretation of certain difficult verses, leaves an impression of extreme inaccuracy. The classifications without ever coinciding overlap. The fragment of grammar commencing with the brutal *yathā* after stanza 5 appears to have a very weak connection with what precedes or follows it: at every instant one would have the tendency to declare it to be an interpolation, in case the total number of these "interpolations" would not finally have constituted an obstacle to this often idle expedient. As always, the problem of validity of the text of the Nāṭyaśāstra on the whole is represented the moment

1. With the verses 4 and 5 this fragment alone is in the āryā metre in the whole adhyāya. It is true that in the Nāṭyaśāstra this metre is employed most frequently, next to the śloka, but a comparative study of passages in different metres has not as yet been made, and this may lead us to some surprising conclusions. However, it would be worth the labour to examine carefully the titles of the adhyāyas; the adhyāya XVII is called, for example, in the Kāvyamālā edition, *kākusvaravidhāna*. This title suits only the concluding stanzas of the adhyāya (103-150 of the GOS edition).

one touches upon a passage whatsoever of this work.

312. Let us leave aside for the moment the fragment of grammar that is in Prākrit and in Sanskrit and let us try to analyse the classification of languages and dialects.

313. By the side of Sanskrit, and on the same plan, so to say, is named first of all Prākrit : it is to Prākrit, without other specification, that the fragment of grammar is related. Then we pass on to the dialects, without lien appearing clearly : *deśabhāṣā* (stanza 24). Consequently one will be inclined to conclude that like Sanskrit, Prākrit is a language common to the whole of India. Now the difficulty—*bhāṣā* (stanza 25), that does not appear to have been identified with the *deśabhāṣā* of the preceding stanza, is divided into four varieties (*atibhāṣā*, *āryabhāṣā* *jātibhāṣā*, and *yonyantarībhāṣā*), about which the least that can be said is this that they are badly in accord with the classification of *bhāṣā* and *vibhāṣā* of the stanzas 47-48. But before we come to *bhāṣā* and *vibhāṣā* we come across Śāurasenī, which would be the language of "pure" people (verse 45). Lastly we learn that the number of *bhāṣās* is seven (Māgadhī, Āvantī, Prācyā, Śaurasenī, Adhamāgadhī, Bāhlīkā, and Dākṣiṇātyā) like the *vibhāṣās* (Śākārī, Cāṇḍālī, Śābarī, Drāmilī, Āndhrī, and the "lowly language" of the inhabitants of the forest.

314. Lastly the stanzas 57-61 state the dialectical peculiarities of the inhabitants of the different countries of India.

315. Although the details are full of troubles, there remain two facts that are very important and they emerge from these stanzas of the Nāṭyaśāstra.

1. Bharata knows and authorises use of a large number of dialects. In addition to all those that he mentions, he leaves the possibility of employing some others (cf. v. 46). Since our text is attested by Abinavagupta's commentary, this multiplicity of dialects on the stage is certainly anterior to the 10th century A.D.

2. Among all these dialects, there is no place for Māhārāṣṭrī; and there never occurs the question of distinguishing the dialects of prose from that of poetry.

This may serve to demonstrate that in the age of Abhinavagupta the practice of inserting in dramas *gāthās* in

Māhārāṣṭrī for the characters speaking Śaurasenī was not current. But this does not constitute proof, as J a c o b i would like, that Māhārāṣṭrī was unknown in the north of India[1], and that it was foreign to the stage. For the purpose of affirming this it would be necessary to demonstrate that Prākrit studied at the end of the adhyāya XVII, the Prākrit with which is related the grammar and in which a part of the grammar is written is not Māhārāṣṭrī. Now normally one calls Prākrit Māhārāṣṭrī. Even H ā l a (stanza 2 and *passim*) names *pāua* as the language in which he writes his S a t t a s a ī. M· G h o s h avoids this difficulty by assuming that for Bharata Prākrit means the Middle Indian Language[2].

316. Let us revert back to the text and try to see as to which language do the rules of grammar of the adhyāya XVII represent. Firstly there is the language in which are written in stanzas 6-9 the illustrative examples to the relevant rules. In case we accept the word *atthaṁ*, that occurs twice, as equivalent to *ardham* as given by the chāyā as well as in the commentary of Abhinavagupta, the stanza 7 is difficult to explain.

317. I do not know an example of *attha*<*ardha-*. So I think—and it is this conjecture on which is based my translation,—that in a very regular manner *attha*=*artha-*; in the second hemistich the chāyā *ca muñcamānaḥ* too would have to be corrected as *amuñcamānaḥ* (or as *amuñcantaḥ*).

318. Another form that is foreign to normal Prākrit is *lopaṁ* of the stanza 7 (the Nepal MS has the normal form *lovaṃ*). One hesitates to correct the text, notwithstanding the rule relating to dropping of intervocalic consonants, as it is formulated in the stanza 7 : *vaccaṁti kagatadayavā lopaṁ*. The dropping of *pa* is not prescribed here; elsehere there is no question of the treatment *p*>*v*.

319. Another exceptional form is *heṭāhutto* (**adhastāt-stha*, cf. *Pischel*, *Gram.* § 107); normally *heṭṭhā°* is found. *se*=*teṣām*; genitive plural, too is rare.

Hemacandra (III, 81) admits this in the commentary

1. H. J a c o b i, *Bhavisattakaha*, p. 83.

2. It may be assumed that NS uses the word "Prākṛta" in the sense of Middle Indo Aryan : Māhārāṣṭrī, a later phase of Śaurasenī: Journal of the Department of Letters of the Calcutta University, Vol. XXIII, 1933.

according to the teaching of a different grammarian. Caṇḍa alone (I, 17) expressly authorises it.

The text is too brief for enabling us to delineate the general characteristics of the language; so it is with these remarks on the details that we shall stop.

320. As regards Prākrit that these verses would teach here, the characteristies are :—

1. *ai, au, ḥ, ś, ṣa, ṅa, ña, na* do not exist (stanza 6);
2. (The intervocalic) *ka, ga, ta, da, ya* and *va* always drop;
3. *kha, gha, tha, dha, bha* become *ha* (stanza 7), but they may be even preserved in the words *mukha, megha, kathā, vadhū* and *prabhūta* (stanza 9);
4. *ra* in conjuncts drops; but it may be retained sometimes (verse 8) :
5. *ka, ga, ta, da, pa, ba*[1], when the first elements of a group, drop. This not only corresponds roughly with Māhārāṣṭrī, but this would be worse than the "emasculated stuff" that has been criticised by Beames : all the intervocalics, without exception, would drop and all the dental *n*s would become *ṇ*! By the side of this there is not a single word on the absence in Prākrit of *ṛ* and *ḷ*, nor on the change of vowels. This without speaking about the morphological characteristic that is as important as the disappearance of the duel and of the transformations of the declension and of the conjugation.

321. It is evident that we have before us a fragment of a text. From the very first words *eoāraparāṇi a*, one has the impression of a lacuna. This *a* (*ca*) would be understood better in case it was continuing an enumeration. Probably in the preceding verses the matter discussed was the disappearance of *ṛ* and *ḷ*, that in the alphabet stand before *ai*, and *au*.

322. The Sanskrit stanzas that follow this fragment in Prākrit (stanzas 10-23) do not serve to fill its lacunae. Even a superficial examination proves that they are completely independent. There are unnecessary reduplications :

1. Cf. note to the translation (stanza 9).

Abhinavagupta should have been very much accommodating and full of religious regard for Bharata, in case he had been able to comment upon these texts patiently, one after the other. The stanza 6 teaches that *śa* and *ṣa* do not exist in Prākrit and that dental *na* is no more found in it. The same thing is repeated in the stanza 11 (*satvaṁ ca bhavati ṣaśayoḥ sarvatra*) and in the stanza 13 (*sarvatra ca prayoge bhavati nakāropi ca ṇakāraḥ*).

323. The stanzas 8-9 treat the groups of consonants, indeed in a very brief manner; the stanzas 10-16 are exclusively devoted to single consonants[1] and the author explicitly informs us that he will be treating groups of consonants only after the stanza 17.

324. Even the style of the two passages is different; in the stanzas that are in Prākrit the rules have a very general bearing and the words are quoted only when exceptionally they go against these rules. On the contrary the Sanskrit stanzas illustrate the rules with examples that they carry simultaneously.

325. Nevertheless, the passage in Prākrit and that in Sanskrit are related to a dialect that does not differ from classical Māhārāṣṭrī. But none of the two can claim to be a real grammar. The Prākrit theory had not been postulated by Bharata. Probably this had not been the intention. The two fragments content themselves with the (incomplete) exposition of the phonetic rules. Could they not represent—in the idea of Bharata or in that of the interpolator or of the interpolators who inserted them—the advice that might have been tendered in literary Prākrit by the stage-manager to the actors playing on the scene? It was necessary for these actors to know Sanskrit; all that he should do for them is to offer them advice regarding pronunciation so that their pronunciation of Sanskrit may have the appearance of Prākrit for the spectators and still it remains understandable.

326. A few words from Deśī—the mostly known ones—should have probably been added in the last touching. The

1. With the parenthesis of the treatment of *au*>*a* in the stanza No. 16. The interruption is very much damaging for the purpose of renouncing the idea of an accident suffered by the text.

Prākrit of the dramas is really a travesty of Sanskrit. The best writers, Kālidāsa, Bhavabhūti do not make the impression that they are writing in a verilable dialect in the Prākrit portions of their dramas. They are content with honouring certain rules of phonetic correspondence between Sanskrit and Prākrit. "The Prākrits (of the dramas)", says Sylvain Lévi, "are nothing but special pronunciation of Sanskrit"[1].

327. This language, this literary Prākrit, that is so close to Sanskrit, was to be the language on the scene of distinguished ladies and men of certain culture, who could not claim the honour of being speakers of Sanskrit. It is not an accident that Bharata in the beginning of the adhyāya XVII had placed it on the same footing as Sanskrit. About these two literary and rigid languages, a variable number of dialects were employed at the option of the authors and the public, according to the place of representation and according to the type of audience. The dramas of the classical age do not give us and are not capable of giving us an image of what might have been a theatrical representation of ancient India.

328. It was necessary to be a linguist and yet a vagabond for writing in all these dialects, more or less real, spoken by the people in general, who had acquired different degrees of civilisation, that very often did not possess even a written literature. To write in a dialect, even in one's own dialect, is an inconvenient thing; the works of the Provensal poets or the Neopolitan ballads satisfy more the foreigners than the native people. But to play in dialects is a different thing : an actor easily succeeds in imitating the accents of different regions. This is the same single inexhaustible source of comic or picturesque elements.

329 We do not understand why in the past India had shaken off this habit, since she does not break it off today ?

330. I know nothing better for understanding the ancient drama than the description given by Mr. Suniti Kumar Chatterji of the contemporary Indian theatre. The correspondences are numerous and striking.

"At the present day, it is common to find Bengali dramas in which in addition to the Standard Colloquial of Calcutta,

1. *théatre indien*, p. 23 of the Appendix.

the Rāḍha or West Bengali dialect, the East Bengali dialect (there has also grown up what may be called the Calcutta stage East Bengali which is an attempt to imitate the speech of Dacca), Oriya and Hindustani feature; and a quaint mixture of Bengali and Hindustani, a sort of stage "little language" with many affectedly "innocent" touches, is commonly used in the drama as the speech of aboriginal jungle tribes, to emphasise upon their character as a simple and unsophisticated folk, living an idyllic life, and in their innocence speaking a childish mixture of Hindi and Bengali; the mixture of Bihari, Hindi and Bengali, (p. 17) used by the sweepers and labourers of aboriginal affinities from Chota Nagpur, is the basis of this stage speech. The Hindustani used is the *Bazar* form of it, the Bengali writer usually not being conscious of the existence of a purer type of the language. In some popular Bengali farces and comedies, songs and sometimes whole scenes are in this dialect, or in an artificial blend of Bengali and Hindustani. Such scenes are common enough in the writings of authors like Girish Chandra Ghosh and Amrita Lal Bose, the two most famous names in the history of the Bengali stage and drama. Scenes and passages from the printed works of these writers will furnish good specimens of this dialect. This practice the modern Bengali drama took over from the papular *yātrā* plays; these usually had comic preludes and close-ups, called *saṁ* (pron. *shong*) in Bengali (=*swāng* of Hindustani) as well as comic scenes, in which some of the characters might use Hindustani. Thus a common scene, as a *prastāvanā* to a *yārtā*, play of the old type, on a theme from the Rāmāyaṇa or the Mahābhārata or the Purāṇas would introduce the king's sweepers (*methar* or *jhāṛūdār*) named Kāluā and Bhuluā, who would exchange repartees with the king's officials : there would be dancing and singing, and the conversation would be in Hindustani as well as Bengali"[1]

331. Nothing is wanting, neither the dialects of the savage people, the *hīnā vanacarāṇāṁ vibhāsā*, nor the artificial mixture of languages, that astonishes us so much in the world of grammarians like that of Mārkaṇḍeya[2].

1. S. K. Chatterji, *Calcutta Hindustani, A Study of Jargon Dialect*: Lahore, Mercantile Press, 1931, p. 16 sq.

2. Cf. Mk. XI, 1· *āvantī syān mahārāṣṭrīśaurasenyostu saṅkarāt*; XIV, 1: *cāṇḍālī māgadhīśaurasenībhyāṁ prāyaśo bhavet*, etc.

332. This richness of dialects and the liberty in respect of their employment must have normally been limited to the written literary dramas. But the popular theatre had in all the ages in India to carry the dialects to the scene, and above all the different accents of the people of the peninsula. We still understand now that in the Commedia dell' Arte, the Doctor[1] speaks the dialect of Bologne, the university

1. Constant Mic. *La comedia dell' Arte*, in the editions of plèiade, Paris, 1927 (p. 30, P. Martelli, *Lettre Recanati*) : In his Bologne-dialect (the doctor), strongly comical for other Italian ears, on account of its coarseness, lends a free drive to his verbiage full of discourses out of context and marked by an abundant gesticulation. Your trousers are not less comical...The dialect of Venice, rich in light diction, will provoke all thes pectators of Toscan to laugh. Finochio, this cheat, who would cling to a heap of straw so that he may not be drowned—his dialect of mountaineers of the vicinity of Bergame—which is not more beautiful—his costume white and green, his flattened cap—his mask that made him appear like a marmot—all this evokes laughter. But what to say of other inhabitants of the plain of Bergame ? His black and round mask......this special dialect of "Zani" (=Skt. *ceṭa*)...all this was rejoiced and will be rejoiced greatly by the people."

(p. 32. *Les Dialects*): "this diversity of colours had still been emphasised by the different dialects employed by the actors. This theatrical usage goes back to the days of the Romans, who in Atellanes laughed at the language of the Osques, that sounded so rough to Latin ears. The Italians, since the middle age, were conscious of the difference of the dominent influence reigning over the diverse regions of their country...They used to ridicule the inhabitants of Bulogne who believed to be knowing every thing better than others and they in a way caricatured the Doctor of Bulogne. Towns-folk used to make fun of the stupidity and vulgar language of the peasants and in particular of the villagers of the neighbourhood of Bergame and they took pleasure in finding again their synthetised type in the Zanis... A language, that has affinity with our mother tongue, always appears comical to us(33), because it creates in us the impression of a sort of distortion of our proper tongue (the inhabitants of Paris find the peculiarities of the dialect of the people of Marseilles and Auvergne very funny). The Italian actors felt these, but they did not take into consideration the amusing effects that they could evoke on the scene from this confusion of the languages. But in reality this process that consists in emphasising character of a type by a particular language, had a very profound significance, because the pronunciation revealed upto a certain point the spirit of the characters. Let us take for example the pronunciation of the Pantalons of Venice, the dwarf old voluptuous fellow, weakened by his sedantary existence of an enriched trader: the dialect of Venice is distinguished by its softness and by a certain delicate sonority: the letters *r*, *t*, and *d* do not occur, *c* and *g* are changed into *s* and *z*. For "Canal-Regio" the people of Venice pronounce "canaleïo"; in lieu of "giudecca"—"zudea"; the termination "ato" is modified into *ao*; and the manner of hissing, "speech of bird", as described by Ph. Monier, suffices already to characterise the spirit of the people of Venice. It suffices, at times to hear just two words for grasping the idea of a certain person in accordance with his pronunciation. Thus for example when Zani says "Macaru et sbiuffdei" in lieu of "Maccaroni raffioli" one immediately imagines of an uncultured dolt.

town par excellence, and that rich and old Pantalone, represents the Venitian middle class towards the beginning of decadence of Venice; but it is so because we know the

"The different dialects had their place in the literary comedy. (On the dialects in early Italian dramas and in the works of the predecessor of the improvised comedy, *Ruzzante*, see the excellent work of M. Alfred Mortier; *Ruzzante* (2 vols., Peyronnet, Paris 1925). In addition to the comedies cited by A. Mortier, I refer further to the drama *Il Sacrificio* or *Li Ingannati*, played by the academiciens Intronrati in 1531, in which appears a Spaniard "Giglio", who speaks an Italo-Spanish jargon. In the comedy *La Paca* of M. Marinegro (Venise, 1561), there are a Greek, two inhabitants of Bergame, a Brave, who speaks one dialect, and two characters of Malamocco and of Frulan (small localities in the vicinity of Venice).

"Very curious in this context is the comedy of V. Verucci. *Li diversi Linguaggi* (Venice 1609), where they speak French, Venician, Bergamasque, Romani, Sicilian, Bolonese, Nepolitan, Florentan and Peruginan. Sometimes Bohemian and Jewish jargons are brought in further. (The question of the comic effect or, speaking in a more general manner, about the scenic effect that this admixture of languages and dialects was to provoke, had not been till now studied in particular. However, we find certain data on this topic in the book : Geschichte der Macoronichen Poesie. (1829).

"Although it was necessary that the audience as a whole understood what was being spoken, still a few of the peculiarities of different dialects were made agreeable. Perrucci, with the intention of avoiding the risk of not being understood, recommends that the popular dialect of Bologne should not be used (34) when one is to play the part of the doctor in a region far away from Bologne, such as Naples or Palerme, but he permits mixture of this dialect with expressions from the dialects of Toscane, in the manner as is done by educated persons of Bologne... (Perrucci says) "one plays equally (35) the rôles in some other corrupt Italian dialects" (*linguagi stravolti d'Italia* (= Skt. *apabhraṣṭa*)."

P. 42 : "according to tradition it was the people of Bergame who manifested the greatest aptitude for this profession: they spoke a dialect that was sufficiently harsh in which certain amount of nonsense created humour and fun (Most of the buffoons of the court came from Bergame, Venice or Padua (Burckhardt, *Die Kultur der Renaissance*)."

"Besides it is possible that the model of the Bergamasque silliness was inherited by the towns people of Venice, for ridiculing the simple and innocent people who left their camp and came to Venice in search of employment."

P. 43 : "The Zani does not necessarily come from Bergame and does not always speak Bergamasque: according to Perrucci the first Zani can employ any dialect, but ordinarily he is an originaire of Milan, Bergame, Naples or Sicily or of other regions famous for their cunning, because the fineness of a composite language suiting to the doltishness is appropriate for the people of Naples and Bergame...the second Zanis speak different dialects: in Lombardy and in most parts of the country of Italy, they are made employ the dialect of the inhabitants of the valleys lying in the vicinity of Bergeme."

The description of Perucci (p. 45) of the two Zanis corresponds to the rules of the prescribed in the treatises on Indian dramatic art regarding the *viṭa* and the *vidūṣaka*.

history and the life of Italy. The allocation of the diverse dialects to different characters in the *Nāṭyaśāstra* and in other dramatic treatises and the rules of the Prākrit grammarians too would become clear to us in case we had before our mind the picture of the life of the people of ancient India.

333. *The dhruvās.* In addition to the grammatical fragment of the adhyāya XVII, the *Nāṭyaśāstra* gives a different specimen of Prakrit : the *dhruvās* of the adhyāya XXXII. It relates to the initial strophes of the songs meant to be sung in the course of theatrical representations. The details of the execution are not known to us. In the opinion of J a c o b i they did not form part of the drama, but of the concert that accompanied[1] it. However, it may be remarked that B h a r a t a explicitly insists on the lien that should exist between the *dhruvās*, the characters and the situations[2].

334. The *dhruvās* are in syllabic metres. This already suffices to distinguish them clearly from the *gāthās* of the Māhārāṣṭrī lyric. Although a major part of the text of the adhyāya XXXII is difficult to be understood and to be translated and rightly it would be better to await the publication of this adhyāya and of the commentary of A b h i n a v a g u p a in the GOS, this fact is, in any case, at present beyond the domain of our discussion.

335. From the exposition of B h a r a t a this conclusion clearly follows, rather it is confirmed, as already noted by J a c o b i on the basis of a passage of the *adhyāya* XV of the *Nāṭyaśāstra*.

336. Having enumerated all the syllabic metres and before beginning to describe the quantitative metres, B h a r a t a emphasises the existence of the *dhruvās* and announces that they will be treated separately : GOS XV, 192-194 (=KM XV, 143-145).

evametāni vṛttāni samāni viṣamāṇi ca 1
nāṭakādyeṣu kāvyeṣu prayoktavyāni sūribhiḥ 11

(1) H. J a c o b i, *Über die ältesten indischen Metriker und ihr Werk*: *Grierson Commemoration Volume*, Pt. II; p. 239 (Indian Linguistics, III, I-VI, 1933).

(2) Cf. *Nāṭyaśāstra* (ed. Kāvyamālā) XXXII, 351-352:
evaṁ bhāvān viditvā tu dhruvā kāryā prayakṛbhiḥ 1
vastuprayogaṁ prakṛtaṁ rasabhāvāśṛtaṁ ca yat 11
deśaṁ kālam avasthāṁ ca jñātvā yojyā dhruvā budhaiḥ 1

santyanyānyapi vṛttāni yānyuktānīha piṇḍaśaḥ[1] l
na ca tāni prayojyāni hataś obhāni tāni hi ll
yānyatra pratiṣiddhāni gītake tāni yojayet l
dhruvāyoge tu vakṣyāmi teṣāmeva vikalpanam ll

"These are the syllabic metres with equal and unequal feet (*pāda*), that should be employed by experts in the dramas and other poetical works. There are also other syllabic metres that are mentioned here collectively, but they should not be employed on account of their being devoid of beauty. Those that are prohibited here may, (however), be employed in songs : I shall give my exposition of this in connection with the discourse on the *dhruvās*".

337. The language of the *dhruvās* appears to be Śaurasenī.

bhāṣā tu śaurasenī syād dhruvāṇāṁ samprayojayet l
bhāṣā caiva tu kartavyā māgadhyā narkuṭaṁ tathā ll
divyānāṁ saṁskṛtagānaṁ pramāṇaistu vidhīyate l
ardhasaṁskṛtameva tu pārthivānāṁ ca yojayet[2] ll

"In case the language should be Śaurasenī, it should be employed for the *dhruvās*; but in case one employs Māgadhī (one should make use) of a *narkuṭa*. To the divine beings the authorities allocate Sanskrit songs, and for the human beings semi-Sanskrit should be employed".

338. It appears to us that in the face of this affirmation, the language of the *dhruvās* cannot be considered to be a "pre-classical literary Prākrit", as has been done by J a c o b i[3], who wanted to see in it the language that in the theatrical usage preceded Māhārāṣṭrī lyrics, of which Bharata had not taken any notice.

1. *piṇḍaśaḥ* is attested by the Nepal manuscript: the Kāvyamālā edition has the lectio facilior *paṇḍitaiḥ*. Cf. *iti piṇḍārthaḥ*, *Alaṁkāra-sarvasva* (K. M. 35), p. 118.

2. Ed. Kāvyamālā XXXII, 390-391.
bhāṣādiśaurasānāṁ dhruvāyāṁ saṁprayojayet l
yadāpi māgadhī yatra kartavyaṁ narkuṭaṁ tathā ll
divyānāṁ saṁskṛtaṁ gānaṁ pramāṇaistu vidhīyate l
ardhasaṁskṛtamevaṁ tu mānuṣāṇāṁ prayojayet ll

3. H. J a c o b i, *Bhavisattakaha*: Abhandl. der Königl. Bayer Akad; Philos.-Philol. Klasse XXIX, Bd. 4 Abh. Munich, 1918; p. 84*-86.*

339. In case we so like, we may call this language "Pre-Śaurasenī" in lieu of Śaurasenī, but we have no authority to put aside the affirmation of Bharata. And while using this name, we would admit the existence of a classical Śaurasenī, codified posterior to the language of the *dhruvās*, a thing that does not correspond to the reality. The Śaurasenī of the dramas and the language of these *dhruvās* are sufficiently similar and present in addition a good number of contradictions in common. Since it is possible that many of these accidents might have been due to diversities of manuscripts of the *Nāṭyaśāstra* and of the dramas, the linguistic discussions on these points of detail have a very weak philological foundation.

340. In 1918, in the introduction to the *Bhavisattakaha* (pp. 84-86) J a c o b i had examined this language of the *dhruvās*; but he did not have before him a text other than that of the Kāvyamālā edition and a certain number of his conclusions have been rendered inacceptable on this account. Forty years later Manomohan G h o s h[1] has published the *dhruvās* of Bharata on the basis of his studies of two manuscripts of the *Nāṭyaśāstra* as well as on that of the editions of the Kāvyamālā and of the Kashi anskrit Series of Chowkhamba[2]. But G h o s h did not know of or he did not like to take into account the study of J a c o b i : he too did the same work on his part for the purpose of arriving partly at the same conclusion regarding the details.

341. J a c o b i does not consider the language of the *dhruvās* to be Śaurasenī; probably the affirmation of Bharata in this regard did not strike him. However, he admits that Śaurasenī and the language of the *dhruvās* have some points in common :

1. The replacement of the intervocalic *t* by *d*;
2. The suffix of the absolutive—*iya*;
3. The form *sadisa* (Skt. *sadṛśa*)

342. But two characteristics of the language of the *dhruvās*, for J a c o b i, would belong to Māhārāṣṭrī :

1. Manomohan G h o s h, *Prākṛta Verses of the Bharata-Nāṭyaśāstra*; Indian Historical Quarterly, VIII, 1932.

2. I have not succeeded in procuring this edition in full of the *Nāṭyaśāstra*, published in 1929. According to M. G h o s h it was probably based on th^ collation of five MSS which were not described elsewhere.

1. The affix of the locative singular *-mmi* employed for the thems in *-a*, occurring simultaneously with the more frequent forms in *-e*;

2. The presence of the absolutive in *-ūṇa* by the side of that in *-iya*.

Ghosh does not doubt that the language of the *dhruvās* should be Śaureseni. It, however, differs in his opinion from the Śaurseni of the dramas on account of the following characteristics :

1. Frequent preservation of the infix *-aya-* of the verbs of 10th conjugation, of the causative and of the denominative :

2. Preservation of the intervocalic *c*;

3. Preservation of the intervocalic *v*;

4. Preservation or suppression of the intervocalic *g*, *j* and *d* without an apparent rule.

343. The two objections of Jacobi about the identification of the language of the *dhruvās* with Śauraseni are not decisive; they would serve rather to demonstrate a certain incoherence or instability in this language or in the tradition of the text of the *Nāṭyaśāstra*, but they would not demonstrate its relationship with Māhārāṣṭrī. Besides the Śauraseni of the dramas does not behave differently.

344. The "oriental grammarians" (Pu IX, 46; Mk IX, 62; RT 11, 1, 14) teach, it is true, that Śauraseni employs the affix *-e* to the exclusion of *-mmi* for the locative singular of the themes in *-a*, but this rule is not followed with rigour in the texts : Rajaśekhara constantly employs the termination *-ammi*; Hillebrandt (Introduction to the edition of the *Mudrārākṣasa*, p. 11) admits that the readings like *cāṇakkammi akaruṇe* are found in the best manuscripts. It is possible that these forms are wrong, as wanted by Pischel and Sten Konow[1]. The question has no importance here, but in any case it has to be recognised that the language of the *dhruvās* does not behave in this regard differently from the Śauraseni of the dramas.

345. The same for the affix *-ūṇa* of the absolutive employed concurrently with *-iya*. Here we have also the authority

1. Pischel, *Gramm.* § 366a; Sten Konow, *Introduction to the edition of the Karpūramañjarī*, HOS, pp. 202-203.

of Hemacandra who permits the absolutive in -*ūṇa*[1] for Śaurasenī. And the texts on this point do not cantradict the grammarians[2].

346. The remarks of Ghosh would, in the opinion of the author, serve to show the archaic character of Śaurasenī of the *dhruvās* and to fix the date of their composition to a period anterior to the 3rd century of the Christian era.

347. Now the preservation of the infix -*aya*- in place of -*e*- is not an unknown fact in the Śaurasenī of the dramas[3]. Moreover, it is not accurate to say that the intervocalic -*c* was always preserved in Śaurasenī of the *dhruvās*. The same Ghosh, who had formulated this rule, retains in the text the form *sahayarī* (XXIX=KM XXXII, 120) explained it in his index as *sahacarī*, *saharaya*-(XXXVII=KM 135) for *sahacara*-=and *viaradi* (LXXXVII=KM 236) for Skt. *vicarati*.

348. As regards the preservation of the intervocalic *v* it is not amazing. Even in the lyrical Māhārāṣṭrī the dropping of *p*, *b*, *v* is not so frequent as that of *k*, *g*, *c*, *j*, *t*, *d*[4]. That *mādhavaṁ* (XXIV=KM 110) and *kusumavadī*) (XXVII=KM 116)—the only two examples, according to Ghosh[5], of intervocalic *v* in the Śaurasenī of the *dhruvās*— do not exhibit dropping of this phoneme; it is a fact that may have analogies in any passage of the Śaurasenī of the dramas.

349. As regards the last argument, the retention or suppression of *g*, *j*, *d* it seems that we need not linger on here. Even in the opinions of the grammarians the dropping of the intervocalics is not observed in Prākrit as a constant rule : Vararuci (II, 2) says, *prāyo lopaḥ*, "generally they drop", and Bhāmaha comments *prāyograhaṇād yatra śrutisukhamasti tatra na bhavatyeva* : "on account of "generally", it is to be understood that dropping does not take place if the (consonant) is agreeable to the ear".

1. Hc. IV, 271; *ktva iadūṇau*.

2. Cf. Pischel, *Gramm.* § 584.

3 Cf. Pischel, *Gramm.* § 490.

4. Cf. Pischel, *Gramm.* § 186; A. C. Woolner, *Introduction to Prākrit*, Calcutta 1917, p. 11-12.

5. We ought to add at least *davavibhava*=*dravavibhava* given in the index, the index that the author has decidedly refused to utilize.

350. It is possible that the advancement in our acquaintance with Prākrit may one day enable scholars to formulate the rule of dropping of intervocalic consonants in the different dialects, but for the present, we are still far away from it, and it would be unjust to pity Śaurasenī of the *dhruvās* for its lack of consistency, since the Śaurasenī of the dramas and the lyric Māhārāṣṭri too may be accused in this regard.

351. In case the *dhruvās*, as says Bharata and as it is confirmed by an examination of the language, are in Śaurasenī, we are taken to this paradoxical conclusion : according to the *Nāṭyaśāstra*, the characters on the stage speak in a language akin to Māhārāṣṭrī and sing in Śaurasenī. We are simply obliged to accept this.

352. We should arrive at our judgment after we have examined all the pieces of information. These deductions from the statements found in the *Nāṭyaśāstra* are most misleading and perhaps in the last place they are such as take us to most fruitful reflection.

CHAPTER III

4. THE ORIENTAL GRAMMARIANS

PURUṢOTTAMA, RĀMAŚARMAN, MĀRKAṆḌEYA

41. The Eastern Grammarians—so called by Sir George Grierson, who had devoted an important part of his activity in studying them[1]—represent a well outlined group whereof the characteristics are quite clear. It is in fact a regular school that we have with the *Prākṛtānuśāsana* of Puruṣottama, *Prākṛtasarvasva* of Mārkaṇḍeya and *Prākṛtakalpataru* of Ramaśarman. The unity of the doctrine is so striking that it is convenient to study them together, the one almost always helping in the interpretation of difficult passages of the others.

42. *The Prākṛtānuśasana* of Puruṣottama is exclusively known from a MS preserved in the and Kathamandu Library. This manuscript in old Newariscript bears the date 385 of the Nepal era (1265 A.D.)[2]

43. In the introduction to my edition of this work, I have discussed the questions relating to the personality of the author and the state of the manuscript. I take the liberty to request reader to refer to the same.

44. I have no intention to repeat here what will be found in my edition of the sections on Māhārāṣṭrī in the work *Prākṛtakalpataru* of Ramaśarman that is actnally in the press.

45. As regards the *Prākṛtasarvasva* of Mārkaṇḍeya, the work is sufficiently known and it is not necessary to describe

1. *The Bṛhatkathā in Mārkaṇḍeya* : JRAS 1913, p. 391: *The pronunciation of Prākrit palatals* : JRAS 1913, p. 391-6; *Apabharaṁśa according to Mārkaṇḍeya* and "*Dhakkī*" *Prākrit* : JRAS, 1913, pp. 875-883; The *Prākrit Vibhāṣās* : JRAS, 1918, p. 489-517; *Paiśāchī in the Prākṛita-kalpataru*- IA XLIX, p. 114; *The Apabhraṁśa Stabakes* of *Rāmaśarman* (*Tarkavāgīśa*) IA, LI, PP. 13-28; LII, pp 1-8; 187-191; *Paiśāchi* and *Chūlikāpaiśāchika* (IA LII, pp. 16-17); *The Prākrit Dhātvādeśas according to the western and eastern schools of Prakrit grammarians* (Mem. Asiat. Soc. Beng., VIII, No. 2), Calcutta 1924; *The eastern school of Prākrit grammarians and Paiśācī Prākrit* (Sir Asutosh Mookerjee Silver Jubilee volumes, Vol. III, part 2, pp. 119-141), Calcutta, 1925; *The Śaurasenī and Māgadhī Stabakas of Rāma-Śarman* (*Tarkavāgīśa*) IA, LVI and LVII, Supplement.
2. [Edited, translated and annotated by L. Nitti– Dolci, Paris 1938].

it here in detail. It has now been carefully edited by Bhaṭṭanāthasvāmin, but this simple edition, wholly in Devanāgarī, without notes and an index, is not convenient for consultation[1]. Two MSS of this work are preserved in London : Pischel had consulted them for his grammar (cf. § 40) : but unfortunately they are very badly preserved, so much so that he could not utilize all the data provided in Mārkaṇḍeya.

46. It suffices to read the masterly introduction of Jacobi to his edition of the Bhavisattakaha[2] for verification of a major part of what he was able to derive from the edition of the *Prākṛtasarvasva*.

47. The importance of Mārkaṇḍeya had been recognised early by Sir George Grierson. In addition to the printed edition and the two London MSS, he had succeeded in procuring its three other MSS; on the basis of these he wanted to prepare his critical edition of the Prākṛtasarvasva[3]. We hope he has not renounced this project ; Mārkaṇḍeya, edited by G.A. Grierson could change the orientation of Prākrit philology, dominated since long by Hemacandra and Pischel. There still remain to work according to them, due to them and necessarily also against them.

48. The date of Mārkaṇḍeya is confirmed by that of his patron Mukundadeva, king of Orissa. In fact at the end of his grammar he says :—

srīmadvīramukundadevanṛpatau dohstambhakumbhīnasa-
krīḍāgrastasamastaśātravakulaprāṇānile dharmataḥ ।
śāsatyutkalamedinīṁ raghupatau sākṣādayodhyāmiva
grāme vīravarapratāpanṛpateḥ pūrṇo nibandho navaḥ ॥

"When the illustrious hero, King Mukundadeva, whose strong arms, while sporting, have absorbed like snakes the winds the air of life-breath of all families of enemies, was ruling according to law over the land of Orissa, like the chief

1. *Prākṛtasarvasva of Mārkaṇḍeya Kavīndra* by Bhattanatha Svamin : Granthapradarśinī Series, Vizagapatam, February-June, 1912.

2. Abhandl. der Königl. Bayerisch. Akad. der Wissenschaften, Philosophisch—philologische und historische Klasse, XXIX, Bd. 4. Abh. Münich 1918.

3. JRAS, 1918, p. 503.

of the Raghus himself over Ayodhyā, in Village of Vīravarapratāpa King this new work was completed.

49. One King Mukundadeva ruled in Orissa from 1664 to 1692 according to the calculation of Sterling, that has been generally accepted since Aufrecht down upto R.D. Banerji, the most recent historian of the country[1]. He has been identified with the patron of Mārkaṇḍeya. But, as remarked by Grierson, there are in the history of Orissa other kings of this name. The date remains uncertain consequently. In any case Mārkaṇḍeya could not be very ancient; the same Grierson attests that "his village Bīrpratāpapura or Biropura is well-known and there is still a plot of land that is associated with his name[2].

410. I, however, add with all necessary reservations, that there are two facts that would appear to place Mārkaṇḍeya in an age earlier than the 17th century A.D.

1. As remarked by Pischel (*Gramm.* § 40), none of the authors cited by Mārkaṇḍeya belong to a period posterior to Śaka-Saṁvat 964 = 1042—43 A.D., excepting Vasantarāja, for whom the date 15th century is outright uncertain.

2. Mārkaṇḍeya (V, 131) attributes to himself the authorship of a saṭṭaka, a dramatic work entitled *Vilāsavatī*. Now a drama of this name is cited in the Śāhityadarpaṇa[3] *sandhicatuṣṭayavatī yathā vilāsavatī* "an example (of *nāṭyarāsaka*)[4] with four junctions in action is the Vilāsavatī".

411. Having been given that Viśvanātha, the author of the *Sāhityadarpaṇa*., certainly lived before the 14th century A.D. Mārkaṇḍeya would have to be placed before this date.

412. We need not at all insist, however, on the insufficient force of these arguments : the first one would, moreover, go to demonstrate that Mārkaṇḍeya prefers to cite works already old, so to say that are classical and stand only on a reconciliation of two names devoid of all contents.

413. The three Eastern grammarians study the same languages

1. Catalogus bibl. Bodl. pars I : Oxford, 1859, p. 181; *History of Orissa*, Vol. II, Calcutta, 1931, p. 43.

2. A private letter addressed to M. N.B. Divatia : Annals of Bhandarkar Oriental Research Institute, XIV, 1932-33, p. 108.

3. VI, 543; Ed. Bibliotheca Indica, Calcutta, 1851, p. 202.

4. And not of *saṭṭaka* !

and group them into four main sub-divisions : *bhāṣā, vibhāṣā, apabhraṁśa* and *paiśācika*. Among the *bhāṣās* they reserve a particular place to Māhārāṣṭrī, the study of which serves as the foundation for that of others. It is so possible, as we have already said, to discuss together their teaching. However, before we take up this summary discussion, we would like to examine the citations that are found in particular in the *Prākṛtasarvasva* and in the *Prākṛtakalpataru*.

414. In case all these could have been identified, we could have a picture of our literary acquaintances in Prākrit upto the 17th century. But unfortunately many of the examples remain unidentified, particularly in Rāmaśarman. Some other pieces of information too are silent for us, since we do not have the works in questions. But even with these reservations, the list of the sources of the Eastern grammarians is important.

415. Śākalya is the teacher most often cited by the Eastern grammarians[1]. None of the other Prākrit grammarians make any reference to him. We know nothing either about his time or work, since he cannot be identified with the ancient compilator of the Padapāṭha of the Ṛgveda, quoted by Pāṇini. His full name according to RT is Śākalya Māṇḍavya[2]. Mārkaṇḍeya refers to him four times : once in the introductory verses :

> *śākalya-bharata-kohalā-varacuci-vasantarājādyaiaḥ* l
> *proktān granthān nānālakṣyāṇi ca nipuṇàmālokya* ll
> *avyākīrṇaṁ viśadaṁ sāraṁ svalpākṣaragrathitapadyam* l
> *mārkaṇḍeyakavīndraḥ prākṛtasarvasvamārabhate* ll

"After having minutely studied the works of Śākalya, Bharata, Kohala, Vararuci, Vasantarāja etc. as well as the different examples (furnished by the texts) Mārkaṇḍeya, prince of poets, begins, (here) the "Wealth of Prākrit", that is a well-arranged and substantial resumé written in short verses."

416. These verses are in the Āryā metre that permits of

1. Cf. Pischel, *De gramm. pr.* pp. 2-3; *Gramm.* § 31.

2. Consequently to be corrected RT I, VIII, 43 in the ed. of *Dhātvādeśas* by Grierson.

great possibility of displacement of words. The initial position of Śākalya in the compound word is important. Mārkaṇḍeya wanted to accord to him a more important position than even to Vararuci ? The small number of quotations that he has taken from him appear to stand in contradiction to this preferential status. Was this a name more illustrious than others? It would be astonishing in presence of Bharata. Did Mārkaṇḍeya want to place the names in a chronological order ? This last hypothesis appears probable and in this case we should understand that Mārkaṇḍeya indentifies the Prākrit grammarian and the author cited by Pāṇini.

417. The three other citations from Śākalya correspond to well-defined facts : Mk V, 30 (= Vr V, 24) *āditau bahulam.*

418. According to Vararuci the feminine suffixes *-ā* and *-ī* are interchangeable : ex. (from the edition Bhāmaha-Cowell) *sahamāṇā* and *sahamāṇī*, *haladdā* and *haladdī*, *suppaṇahā* and *suppaṇahī*, *chāhā* and *chāhī*. Mārkaṇḍeya restricts this freedom of choice in the commentary: *kvacidādeva* 1 *piā* 1 *vallahā* 1 *asahaṇā* 1 *ahaṇā* 1 *māṇiṇī* 1 *māṅaṁsiṇī* 1 *halantādīd eveti śākalyaḥ.*

"There are cases in which the suffix *-ā* is exclusively used. Ex. *piā* etc. The themes in consonants on the other hand have the feminine only in *-ī* says Śākalya; ex. *māṇiṇī*, *maṇaṁsiṇī* etc."

419. Vasantarāja in his commentary restricts also the rule of Vararuci (V, 24) ; he says that there are cases where the suffix *-ā* is exclusively used and there are others where only *-ī* is employed. Others make this choice depend on the theme.

ityevaṁ vyavatiṣṭhante bahulagrahaṇāt pare ll

This is the doctrine of Śākalya himself, as it is cited by Mārkaṇḍeya, as far as at least the consonantal themes are concerned. MK (V, 96) *śākalyasyāta in mate* "In the opinion of Śākalya in the place of *-ā-* (of the themes *tujjha-* and *-tumha* pronoun of the second person before the termination *-su* of the locative plural) one says *-ī-*". *tujjhisuṁ*, *tumhisuṁ*. However, Mārkaṇḍeya adds that this opinion is not approved by many other grammarians :— *etattu na bahusaṁmatam.*

Mk IX, 109, *hośca sākalya-mate syāt*:—"In Śaurseni according to Śākalya the root *bhū*," to be" becomes "*ho*" too. Ex. *hodi* beside *bhodi*. Cf. RT II, 2, 25.

Rāmaśarman cites Śākalya eight times in his text. RT I, V, 19 *śākalyamāṇḍavyamate hakāraḥ*.

"In addition to the suffixes *-alla* and *-ella*) we should also consider that according to Śākalya-Māṇḍavya, the suffix *-ha* too (does not change the signification of the word to which it is affixed)". Cf. Mk. IV 48 *svārthe ca haśca*.

RT I, V, 23 *ktvārthe<tumam. śāsati>kepi dhīrāḥ*
śākalyamāṇḍavyamate vilokya l

"Certain scholars, in agreement with the doctrine of Śākalya-Māṇḍavya, teach also the employment of the infinitive in the sense of the absolutive, "cf. MK. IV, 48.

RT I, VI, 25 *śākalyamāṇḍavyamate tu tumbhe* :" according to Śākalya-Māṇḍavya one may say also *tumbhe* (in the accusative plural of the pronoun of the second person)".

RT I, VII, 14, *śākalya<māṇḍavya>mate tu eva*
bhavya [*kta*]*-tuṁ-ktvāpara editau ca* ll

In the opinion of Śākalya-Māṇḍavya in the future the verbal forms in *-ta* of the infinitive and absolutive the thematic vowel may be *-i* or *-e*". Cf. MK. VI, 7

RT, I, VIII, 14......*'tha bhidi-cchidorndo bhede ca śākalya-mate tayoḥ syāt*.

RT I, VIII, 42 *dhātu-svarūpāṇyapaāṇi pakṣe*
śākalya<māṇḍavya>matānugāmi[1] l
kātyāyanasyāpi mate tathaiva
jñeyāni lakṣyānubhavakrameṇa ll

"The other particular forms of the roots may be deduced from the teaching of Śākalya-Māṇḍavya : but accordidg to Kātyāyana, they should be learnt from the texts".

RT II, 25=Mk. IX, 109
bho-ho-ca śākalyamate bhuvaśca.

1. I would correct it as *ānugāni*.

420. Puruṣottama cites Śākalya only once, in case I understand the text well :

Pu VI, 14 *ssaśca śākalyasya* (MS *śākalyesya*) "[In addition to *-hi* the affix of the future] there is also *-ssa-* according to Śākalya".

421. So it is to Śākalya that we should attribute the extension of the affix *-ssa-* of the future of the first to the other persons (Cf. § 479).

422. All these facts attributed to Śākalya by one or the other Eastern grammarian are extraneous to the doctrine of Vararuci. Besides they are on the whole very precise : one of them corresponds to a particularity of Śaurasenī. And, in case I have well understood RT I, VIII, 42, Śākalya probably had composed a very important list of *dhātvādeśas*. So Śākalya had written a grammar of the principal Prākrit and of Śaurasenī. For other dialects we do not have the same certitude : however, we must keep in mind the fact that Rāmaśarman and Mārkaṇḍeya very often cite opinions of the grammarians without mentioning their names : *iti vadanti, iti kecit, iti kaścit*, etc. Thus for example we have seen that RT I, V, 23 attributes to Śākalya a rule that Mārkaṇḍeya cites without naming its author. So it is possible that a certain number of other anonymous citations may possibly be attributed to Śākalya.

423. The notion of a literary proprietorship being unknown in India, the question of citations from the works should be examined after we have divested our mind in this regard. I have the impression that at least in respect of the grammatical sūtras the Indians never cite their contemporaries or their immediate predecessors by naming them and they reserve the honour of mentiening by name for the "classical ones"[1].

424. Puruṣottama in his commentary on the *Aṣṭādhyāyī*, when he comes by a grammarian's name cited by Pāṇini, he often tries to justify this unusual favour. The justification, almost constant, is this : Pāṇini names him for showing him honour[2]. In case the Eastern grammarians name Śākalya, it is probably

1. This would also have the value of an explanation for the antiquity of the quotations of Mk. (cf. § 410).

2. *Bhāṣāvṛtti* on Pāṇ. VIII, 4, 51 that mentions Śākalya: *ācāryapādānāṁ pūjārtham*, ibid upon Pāṇ. VI, 1, 92, *āpiśaligrahaṇaṁ pūjārtham*, etc.

also to render him some honour. Next to Vararuci, whose work has been completely included in their writings, it is Śākalya whom they respect the most. It is possible that a chance in research may one day confront us with the text of Śākalya, but even from now it may be affirmed that Śākalya had composed a grammar of the principal Prākrit and of Śaurasenī and that had been one of the sources of the Eastern grammarians and that in case Pu VI, 14 is to be understood, as it has been understood by me, he is anterior to the 13th century A.D.

425. While Mārkaṇḍeya never cites Vararuci by his name, Rāmaśarman has referred to him twice in his text : once on the occasion of the lists of his *dhātvādeśas* and once in connection with a particular verb. We need not mention the commentary, that I leave aside intentionally, since I do not consider it to be a work of the author of the *Prākṛtakalpataru.*

426. The citation in RT is the following :—

RT I, VIII, 5 *jambhāa uktaḥ khalu jṛmbhateḥ ṣyāt kātyāyanenośita eva jambhā,* "In place of the root *jṛmbh-* (to yawn) one ought to read *jambhāa* : but Kātyāyana wants that one should say *jambhā.* Now in the edition Bhāmaha-Cowell it is the form *jaṁbhāa-* that is given (VIII, 4), while the *Prākṛtasañjīvanī* gives the reason to Rāmaśarman with *jaṁbhā* (VII, II). Rāmaśarman, however, is too late a writer to be considered to arbitrate in case of a difference between Bhāmaha and Vasantarāja. It is also astonishing that he twice quotes in this manner Kātyāyana in his book on *Dhātvādeśa,* whilst he does not mention his name anywhere in the whole work. I believe that Rāmaśarman is above all a poet (although a bad poet) and that he had intended to include in a verse the names of the *Eastern grammarians.* So it is probable that he did not ever bother to go up to his source upto Vararuci within the space, and that he does not take into account what his grammar owed to him. Who knows about the chance in reading that provided him with two isolated citations that he included in his work without caring much about the source ?

427. Rāmaśarman does not introduce many of the proper names in his work, nor does he mention several other works

and several authors. In the beginning alone he cites Setubandha.

428. In the stabaka on Śaurasenī he names Kapila and Śūdraka, in that on Paiśācī, Haraiśaṅkara; moreover, he explicitly quotes the drama Mālātīmādhava[1]. At the end of the stabaka on Apabhraṁśa he speaks about an "old poet": it is in his work that scholars are to find out examples of certain particular forms in Apabhraṁśa. Grierson thinks that this old poet possibly was Piṅgala.[2]

429. Puruṣottama cites a single name other than Śākalya. This is Hariścandra, from whom he borrows a sentence that Mārkaṇḍeya utilizes for the some occasion. It is in connection with Ṭākkī, a *vibhāṣā*, of which the characteristics remind us of those of Apabhraṁśa and what for Hariścandra is in fact is an Apabhraṁśa[3].

430. Mārkaṇḍeya on the contrary cites a large number of works and authors either for confirmation or for contradiction of their opinion or for borrowing from them examples in support of his sūtras. In two cases he shows scruples in respect of accuracy that are not very frequent in the writings of Indian philologists. Except for this there is nothing that may merit his being studied and published in Europe.

431. In the passage that he cites on the subdivision of languages, for example (Intro. 4), he leaves the form *kaikaya*, as he finds in text (Introd. 8; XIX, 1, etc.). But in any case he knows to utilize the evidence of prosody for correctness of a form like *uaṇīā* (*upanīta* with shortening of the ī, cf). Pischel, *Gram.* § 81) of the *Setubandha* (IV, 63)[4].

432. He criticises the forms, but he does not rectify the withauthority. One cannot help but appreciate the rigour of his argumentation in relation to the verbal affixes *-te* and *-ti* :

1. RT II, 1,28 : *kapilasya tavya-ktayor gatiḥ syād matamatra tasya*: II, 1, 29—*spṛśateśchubaśca* l *chippa-cchībaścāsya nirūpitau dvau bhāvepi karmaṇyapi śūdrakasya*. The authority of Kapila too is quoted in respect of the same forms *gahidaṁ* and *gahidavaṁ* by Mārkaṇḍeya (IX. 130, cf. § 435). The name of Śūdraka is found only in the *Prākṛtakalpataru*: RT III, 3, 19 and 20.

2. RT III, 1, 31 :—*tatradāharaṇaṁ purātanakaveḥ kāvyeṣu bodhyaṁ budhaiḥ* cf. Grierson IA, LII, 1923, p. 16-17.

3. Pu XVI, 10 : *hariścandrastu imāṁ ṭakkabhāṣāṁ apabhraṁśamicchati na prākṛtam* ; Mk XVI, 2 : *hariścandrastvimāṁ bhāṣāmapabhraṁśa itīcchatī* (cf. § 4102).

4. Mk I, 6 :—*atra dīrghatvaṁ cenmātrādhikye chandobhaṅgaḥ*.

Mk. VI, 4 *letiṅor ediṇau smṛtau* ll *paḍhaï* l *paḍhae* ll *vaṭṭae* l *vattaī* ll "*prāyaḥ kaga*—(II-2)" *ityādinā talopenaiva siddhyati kiṃanena sūtreṇeti na vācyam* l *tasya prāyikatvāt paḍhadi paḍhade ityādyaniṣṭasiddheḥ* l *nāṭakeṣu tathā dṛśyata iti cet mahārāṣṭrītarāsu bhāṣāsu tathā siddherna viruddham* l *rājaśekharasya mahārāṣṭrī prayojyeṣu ślokeṣvapi dṛśyata iti cenna tasyaivāvimṛśyakāritvaṁ nāparādhonuśāsanānām* ll

"In place of the affixes of the third person singular *-te* and *-ti*, one employs *-e* and *-ī*. Ex. *paḍhae paḍhaī*, *vaṭṭae vaṭṭaī*. Now the forms are obtaiend already by dropping of the *-t* (II, 2); what is the purpose of the present sūtra? The objection is not valid. Because one should avoid the possibility forms like **paḍhadi*, **paḍhade*, that one could do in case the rule (for the dropping of the *-ta*) were not obligatory. But can these forms be objected to, although they are, actually found in dramas. "Yes", would be our reply, because there is nothing against their correctness except in Māhārāṣṭrī. But Rājaśekhara has used them even in Māhārāṣṭrī verses. There he has done so through inadvertance, but there the fault does not lie with the rules".

433. I believe it is difficult to make use of the P r ā k ṛ t a-s a r v a s v a before we have acquired some degree of confidence in its author. Possibly Mārkaṇḍeya was a man of great learning and of high integrity—a quality that is very much important for a philologist. The examples that he gives of his rules are appropriate and varied. Certainly they must have been based upon his vast amount of study[1]. On this account he deserves to be studied closely.

434. First of all we shall examine the authorities referred to by him in his text before we pass on to the passages cited in support of a particular form.

435. In addition to Śākalya and Bharata (cf. § 415 and §33) Mārkaṇḍeya cites by name in his introduction Bhāmaha Vasantarāja[2], Kohala[3] and Pāṇini. Besides the same

1. The same favourable judgment in respect of the citations of Mārkaṇḍeya has been expressed by G. A. Grierson :—*The Eastern School of Prākrit Grammarians,*, etc. Asutosh Mookerji Silver Jubilee Volumes, III, 2, p. 122.

2. Other reference to Vasantarāja, Mk. VII, 34.

3. Other reference Mk. XII, 1.

Mārkaṇḍeya attributes an other citation to Kapila (IX, 130, cf. RT II, 1,28). It is questionable if this name is to be corrected as Kohala ?

436. Daṇḍin is cited by name only once (Intro. 9= Kāvyādarśa I, 34); another citation too has been borrowed from him (Intr. 8— Kāvyādarśa I, 102).

437. Bhojadeva too is named once: the citation, however, does not occur in the *Sarasvatīkaṇṭhābharaṇa*.

438. We find here mention of Aniruddhabhaṭṭa (XII, 38), Hariścanadra (XVI, 2), and Bhagīratha Vardhamāna (XIV, 3; XVII, 13). We have no knowledge of the grammatical or rhetorical works that may be attributed to them.

439. A demi-śloka taken from the *Pāṭhaśikṣā* (II, 2) is also quoted; it has not been possible for me to identify the passage as yet.

440. Grierson[1] has traced a *kārikā*, quoted by Mārkaṇḍeya IV, 64 in the context of the import of the word *vibhāṣā*, in the commentary of the Laghukaumudī on Pāṇini III, 3, 113, There it is attributed to the *Sārasvata*. In fact it is a definition of the *caturvidhaṁ bāhulakam* that is well anterior to the Laghukaumudī; Hemacandra I, 2 cites its first hemistich.

441. Some others of these *kārikās* could be identified with the help of works that we possess, but the research in this line is very difficult on account of lack of an index.

442. This list of authorities, however, would not be complete, if we leave aside the quotations from anonymous writers. Like almost all the Indian grammarians, Mārkaṇḍeya often refers to the opinion of a predecessor without naming him : *iti kaścit, iti kecit, ityanye*, etc. The *Prākṛtasarvasva* contains nearly forty of such citations; about fifteen of them have a general bearing and they either define a dialect (cf. Mk XIII, 9) or establish an exact value of a technical term (cf. IV, 64); on the contrary twenty-five of them appear to have in view particular sūtras of one or of some other grammarian. We cannot fail to note twenty-two of these citations relate to Māhārāṣṭrī, three only to the aggregate of the other dialects. Moreover, two of these last ones (Mk. XI, 8 and 20) are

1. JRAS, 1918, p. 489.

preceded in the edition of the *Granthapradarśanī* series by an asterisk that may probably be indicator of a doubt of the editor with regard to the authenticity of the passage[1].

443. So in reality only in the part concerning the dialects other than the principal Prākrit there is a single citation that appears to refer to an other grammar[2].

444. The same is true about the treatment of Hemacandra as well (see § 611 ff.) The explanation given by him holds good about Mārkaṇḍeya too. The grammar of the principal Prākrit is fixed and traditional and it regulates a written and literary language, i. e. of the Māhārāṣṭrī lyric.

445. The undisputed authority, the founder of this grammar is Vararuci. About him are grouped the commentators and the disciples. Whenever Mārkaṇḍeya or Hemacandra cites in respect of a form the opinion of an anonymous grammarian (*itī kaścīt, iti kecit*) they he it in this manner only when his own opinion contradicts or supplement or interprets in a different fashion the relevant sūtra of Vararuci.

446. From what has been said above we are able to mark the weakness of some of the arguments of Th. Bloch (cf. §614ff.), who has tried to find out in Hemacandra a proof of his knowledge of Vararuci by depending justly upon these anonymous references. Vararuci was taken in his *entirety* into the grammar of Hemacandra, while the discussions and citations are related to his controversies about teaching only.

447. We ought to know well the Indian methods to guard ourselves against drawing conclusions unkown to their systems.

The absence of a reference to a preceding authority is never a proof of originality of the passage in question.

The argument *ex silentio* is not valid. In case we do not remember this we shall be exposed to commission of more serious errors.

In case Hemacandra and Mārkaṇḍeya do not refer to their predecessors in respect of the dialects other than the principal

1. The edition does not contain a preface and the value of the signs is not determined.

2. Mk. XX, 9 *ddhasya tthaḥ kvaciditi kecit*" "(in Śaurasena Paiśācī) in place of the group *ddha*, according to the opinion of certain grammarians, one may have *-ttha-*; ex. *atthāsanaṁ* (Skt. *adhyāsana*—?)".

Prākrit, it does not prove that there did not exist any such ones. On the other hand there is the strong probability that they have borrowed the most in this domain. We are in a position to demonstrate this with regard to Mārkaṇḍeya who is fully in accord with Puruṣottama likewise in respect of the external order and in that of the subject-matter of this part of the *Prākṛtasarvasva*.

448. For making their own views clear by an image, the Indian grammarians aim to depend upon the authority of their famous predecessors, exactly like the aristocrats proud of their family traditions : we, it is true, depend much upon our parents and grand-parents, but it is common to nobility and to people not of high birth"; whilst it is a rare privilege to be able to recognise in one's ownself (and on solid or weak basis) the physical and intellectual characteristics of a cross. When Mārkaṇḍeya mentions the names of Bharata and Vararuci in connection with Prākrit grammar it appears to him to add to his nobility.

There were possibly commentators or later-day grammarians belonging to the school of Vararuci, from whom he probably has derived his information, although he did not accord to them the honour of mentioning their names in his work.

449. As regards those who would have really been before him at every instant when he was writing his book, it was perhaps not elegant for this "Eastern grammarian" who probably was the common source of the *Prākṛtasarvasva*, of the *Prākṛtakalpataru* and of the *Prākṛtānuśāsana* of Puruṣottama to speak about them.[1]

1. Should we seek in this habit too the cause of the difficulty that is presented by the identification in the case of a large number of Indian citations (the citations from Bharata in commentaries and rhetorical treatises are burnings examples thereof) ? When a writer cites by name an author, we should not be suspicious about the accuracy of the quotation: he does not cite him on account of urgency of demonstration, but for elegance and for reminding the readers that the subject that interests him is not of yesterday. And we have to keep in mind that sometimes there is the tendency to exaggerate these titles of nobility, even though for this one may be obliged to solicit a few of the texts.

450. I have tried to identify the twenty-six anonymous citations given by Mārkaṇḍeya in the first eight books of the *Prākṛtasarvasva*; I could succeed in respect of only nine of them, but I have the impression that the others too would not have escaped, in case I could have utilized some other commentaries of Vararuci. Besides it is probable that their identification has possibly escaped me, although this might have been possible even with the materials that were at my disposal[1].

451 Perhaps one would be astonished at the coincidences between Mārkaṇḍeya and Hemacandra; the tradition concerning Hemacandra too explains them. Hemacandra is reported to have consulted a large number of works (cf. §69). One of his sources could likewise have been utilised by Mārkaṇḍeya. In any case we ought to reject outright the idea that Mārkaṇḍeya had ever utilized the grammar of Hemacandra, since the coincidences are of an extreme rarity in consideration of the very much increased number of independent innovations present in their works.

452. The independence of Rāmaśarman vis-a-vis that of Hemacandra cannot be easily demonstrated; the concordances are striking throughout the whole of the treatment of the principal Prākrit, and what is more revealing is that they exist where Rāmaśarman differs from Mārkaṇḍeya. Not only this is certain that Rāmaśarman and Hemacandra had utilised the common source, but at times one has also the impression that this was precisely the *Siddhahemacandra* that Ramaśarman had consulted[2].

453. The examples given by Mārkaṇḍeya are drawn from greatly varied and large number of works. Sometimes he

1. Mk. I, 7 (cf. Vas. I, 5; Hc. I, 139); Mk. I, 15 (cf. Vas. I, 11; Bhām. I, 12; Hc. I, 85); Mk. I, 21 (cf. Hc. I, 101); Mk. II, 2 (cf. Bhām. II, 2); Mk. II, 24 (cf. Bhām. II, 26); Hc. I, 236); Mk. III, 6 (cf. Bhām. III. 5; Hc. II, 83); Mk. IV, 60 (cf. Bhām. IV. 33); Mk. V, 90 (cf. Hc. III, 981); Mk. VII, 17 (cf. Hc. IV, 75). The following remain to be identified : Mk. II, 42; III, 30; III, 34; III, 40; III, 45; III, 75; IV, 20; IV, 33; V, 63; VI, 31; VII, 4; VII, 42; VII, 143.

2. Cf. for example in—

RT, I, 1, 3 (Hc. I, 165); I, 5 (Hc. I, 65, 98); I, 8 (Hc. I, 81); II, 13 (Hc. I, 261); II, 16 (Hc. II, 58); III, 2 (Hc. II, 78); III, 5 (Hc. II, 23); III, 14 (Hc. II, 68 and comm.); VI, 17 (Hc. III, 80); VII, 11 (Hc. III, 179).

himself mentions the source of the citation; in the list that follows these references, such cases are preceded by the figure 1.

454. The editor of the *Prākṛtasarvasva* has made the laudable attempt to identify the examples figuring there without mentioning their authors : all these identifications have been verified by me and they have been grouped under the figure 2.

455. The figure 3 indicates some citations that were located by myself.

456. However, there remain a good number of cases that are to be located still. Perhaps some of them will resist all efforts, either on account of being too short or too common or because we do not possess any more the works that contained them.

However, an European edition of Mārkaṇḍeya would certainly augment the number of identified citations by placing before readers more numerous and more current examples from Prākrit literature than what I have done.

457. Hāla (1) explicitly attributed to the *Saptaśatī* by Mk. : III, 32 (=H. 934); IV, 3(=H. 52); V, 33 (=H. 314), V, 90 C= H. 524); VI, 39 (=H. 609).

(2) Identified by the editor of the *Prākṛtasarvasva* II, 37 (=H. 8); III, 40 (=H. 9); III, 84 (=H. 696); IV 64 (=H. 71); IV, 64 (=H. 339); VII, 60 (=H. 182); VII, 107 (=H. 13); VIII 25 (=H.4).

(3) New identifications : IV, 54 (=H. 560); VIII, 6 (=H. 946); VIII, 12 (=H. 15).

Setubandha (1) I, 7 (=R.I, 3); I, 21(=R. IV. 63); I, 43 (=R. IV, 7), V, 65 (=R. III, 1); VI, 14 (=R. III, 3); VII, 26 (=R. I, 20); VII, 42 (=R. I, 8); VII, 102 (=R.

(2) I, 17 (=R. I, 34); III, 76 (=R. I, 14); IV, 58 (=R. III, 1); V, 69 (=R. IV, 23); VI, 46 (=R. II, 8); VII, 20 (=R I, 35); VII 28 (=R. I, 10); VII, 37 (=R. I, 38); VII 102 (=R. I, 39); VII, 153 (=R. I, 40); VIII, 2 (=R. I, 15); VIII 4 (=R. I, 38); VIII, 17 (=R. V., 4).

(3) IV, 39 (=R. II, 44).

Vākpatirāja. The absence of citations taken from the *Gaüḍavaho* is sufficiently astonishing, although the case may not be unique. As remarked by Pischel in another case as well (*Gramm.* § 13) the citations attributed to Vākpatirāja are not found in the *Gaüḍavaho*.

(1) V, 33; V, 107; VI, 48.

Śakuntolā[1]

(2) IX, 47 (= IV, 70/71) ; IX, 86 (= III, 59; XII, 24; XII 36 (cf. VI, 123).

Mālatīmādhava[2]

(2) II, 30 (= VI, 10) cited also by RT III, 3, 19.

(3) IX, 20 (= II 1/2)

Mṛcchakaṭika[3]

(1) XIII, 8. This citation is found neither in our edition of the Mṛcchakaṭika nor in the Cārudatta.

(2) XIII, 6 (= I, 18, p. 15).

Viṇīsaṁhāra[4]

(2) XII, 3 (= III, p. 33) ; XII, 38 (cf. III, p. 35)

Ratnāvalī[5]

(2) III. 76 (= II, 26, p. 24) ; VIII, 4 (= I, 15, p. 9) ; VIII, 13 (= II, 26, p. 24); IX, 148) (= II, p. 21); X, 4 (= III, p. 51); X, 6 (cf. II, p. 28); X, 9 (= II!, p. 46).

Karpūramañjarī[6]

(1) I, 50 (cf. I, II) ; III, 77 (= I, 24); V, 118 (cf. I, 32); VI, 48 (cf. II, 38); VII, 61 (= I, 17).

Bhaṭṭikkāvya

(1) I, 9 (= XIII, 4): I, 42 (= XII, 33); II, 42 (= XIII, 45).

Prākṛtapāiṅgala (Kāvyamālā No. 41).

(1) V, 34 Paiṅgala ?) not identified; V, 106 (= II, 5); XVII, 56 (= II, 142); XVII 56 (= I, 46) ; XVII, 57 (= II, 69).

2. XVII, 8 (= I, 5a); XVII (= II, 142). *Kāvyamālā* No. 24 1891.)

(2) III, 42 (III, p. 58); IV, 64 (= II, p. 54), IV, 64

1. Ed. Capeller, Leipzig, 1909.
2. Ed. Nirṇaya Sāgar Press, 1926.
3. Ed. Nirṇaya Sāgar Press, 1926.
4. Ed. Grill, Leipzig, 1871.
5. Ed. Lehot, Collection E. Senart, Paris, 1933.
6. Ed. Sten Konow, HOS.

(=III, p. 58); VII, 29 (cf. IV, p. 124); VII, 43 (cf. V, p. 189).

Rasagaṅgādhara (Kāvyamālā No. 12).

(2) VII, 137 (=p. 165)

Works that have disappeared, but of which the existence has been known.

Bṛhatakathā

(1) XIX 9

Vilāsavatī of Mārkaṇḍeya(?)

(1) V, 131; cf. p. 91.

Chalitarāma.

(2) IX, 151 (=Sāhityadarpaṇa 528 and Daśarūpa, Bibl. Indica, comm. III, 16).

Works totally unknown :

Śṛṅgārotkarṣa.

(1) 1, 50

Guṇapatākā

1, V, 65.

458. Excepting a passage of the Mṛcchakaṭika and another doubtful one from the Prākṛtapaiṅgalasūtra all the citations attributed exclusively by Mārkaṇḍeya to works that we possess have been already located. The result proves the accuracy of Mārkaṇḍeya and authorizes putting great weight to his testimony even in respect of the works that we no more possess.

459. Māhārāṣṭrī or principal Prākrit—The three grammarians of the Eastern School devote a major part of their works to the principal Prākrit. Their undisputed master is Vararuci, but there is no trace of the least effort towards discussion of his sūtras. Even as regards the external arrangement, Puruṣottama and Mārkaṇḍeya imitate Vararuci; they subdivide the grammar of the principal Prākrit into a eight sections, a thing that corresponds to the original divisions of the Prākṛtaprakāśa.

460. Rāmaśarman has adopted the same classification; besides he adds one *stabaka* on the reduplication of consonants. Taking for example the first *pariccheda* of the grammar of Vararuci and comparing it with the corresponding part of the works

of Mārkaṇḍeya and Rāmaśarman[1] one immediately is convinced of this fidelity of the grammarians of the Eastern School to the teaching of Vararuci.

461. The sūtras of the edition B h ā m a h a-C o w e l l are found all in the same form in Mārkaṇḍeya with the exception of :—

Vr. I, 7 *lavaṇanavamallikayor vena,*
cf. Mk. I, 9, *lavaṇasya vena samam.*
Vr. I, 11 *iti sadādiṣu.*
Mk. I, 14, *it sadi.*
Vr. I, 33 *ḷtaḥ kḷpta iliḥ.*
Mk. I, 39 *ḷtastu liḥ.*
40 *iliḥ kḷpte*

We have just to the refer to table of correspondences of the *Prākṛtasañjīvanī* with the edition Bhāmaha-Cowell (cf. §227) in order to see whether these are also the sūtras in which the two works differ.

Vr. I, 7 does not have a correspondence in the *Prākṛtasañjīvanī*; I, 11 has the same form as in Mārkaṇḍeya, that is to say that Vararuci authorises in the edition Bhāmaha—Cowell the forms *saï, taï, jaï,* (Skt. *sadā, tadā, yadā*), while in Vasantarāja, as in Mārkaṇḍeya, the rule authorises only *saï*[2] and Vr. I, 33 is presented in the *Prākṛtasañjīvanī* in the form *ḷtaḥ iliḥ*[3].

462. As regards Rāmaśarman he teaches exactly as taught by Mārkaṇḍeya, excepting in the stanza that corresponds to Mk. I, 14 in which he too, as in the edition Bhāmaha-Co-

1. The comparison should be limited to these two authors, since, as already indicated by the present writer in her edition, the Nepal MS does not contain the original of Puruṣottama, so far as it relates to the phonetics of vowels, of the single consonants and partly of groups of consonants.

2. It may be noted that according to Pischel, *Gramm.* § 113 this particular treatment of *sadā* is due to the accent. So it is probable that against Bhāmaha and Rāmaśarman (I, 1, 8) Vasantarāja and Mārkaṇḍeya are correct and that they are more faithful to Vararuci.

3. It is possible that the original rule of Vararuci had been *ḷta iliḥ* as in Vasantarāja: the single current word with *ḷ* being the root *kḷp*. Subsequently according to the Vārttika of Vasantarāja (I, 34) we are to think of *lkāra, liālo*. For this word Vasantarāja has imagined an adhikāra *vā* which would have its force on the sūtra : *veti vartate* l *sā ca vyavasthitavibhāṣā teneha na bhavati* l *liālo lkāraḥ* ll *lkārarkārayoḥ sāvarṇyāt ayuktasyāpi lkārasya riḥ* ll Bhāmaha has introduced *kḷpte* in the sūtra itself. Mārkaṇḍeya has explicitly separated the two treatments of the initial and medial. In any case only it was only he who had reproduced the teaching of Vararuci accurately —a thing that appears to me to be very much probable.

well, authorises the forms *jaï* and *taï*. RT I, 1, 8 *it syāt sadādau tu sadā yadā ca tadā.*

463. So it may be concluded that so far as it concerns the phonetics of vowels, the teaching of Vararuci has in its entirety passed into the work of the "grammarians of the Eastern School" The differences always indicate an uncertainty of the text of Vararuci. The grammarians of the Eastern School only continue the discussion of the commentators.

464. However, while reproducing faithfully the text of Vararuci, they sometimes desire to add there some rules. It is not surprising that they are merely the rules, that are presented in a different form, or they are placed differently or they are missing in one or the other Eastern grammarian. Since we do not possess the grammar of Puruṣottama, so far at it is relates to the phonetics of vowels, let us examine at this point the additions of Mārkaṇḍeya and Rāmaśarman to the grammar of Vararuci.

465. These are the sūtras of Mārkaṇḍeya that do not have their corresponding ones in Vararuci.

Mk. I, 5 *prathame prathayor yugapat krameṇa vodbhavati* ll *ata ityeva puḍhamaṁ* l *paḍhumaṁ* ll

RT I, V, 2 *utvaṁ mabhinne prathame krameṇa dvayośca vāto na punar dvayośca* l

Mk. I, 10 *lāvaṇyasya vikalpena* (s.e. *ot syāt*) *loṇṇam lāaṇṇaṁ* ll it is wanting in RT.

Mk. I, 22 *jīver vā syāt* ll (s.e. *id vā syāt*) *jiaï* l *jiaī* l; it is wanting in RT.

Mk. I, 27 *uparer vā* ll (s.e. *ad vā syāt*) *avari* l *uvari*; it is wanting in RT.

Mk. I, 29 *se dura ūt* (s. e. *ūt syāt*) *dūsaha dūsīlo* (but) *dug gamo dukkaro.*

RT. I, V, 5 *adurjanādau tu visarjanīyayutapasargasya vadanti dīrgham* l

Mk. I, 50 *maunamaulyorvā* (s. e. *aūt*).

cf. RT. I, I, 24 (the words *mauna* and *mauli* figure in the gaṇa *paurādi* : so the treatment *au*>*aū* is obligatory.

466. It may by remarked that of these six sūtras added by Mārkaṇḍeya to the teaching of Vararuci, three (I, 10; 22,

27) do not have a correspondence in Rāmaśarman[1]; one (I, 50) stands here contradicted and two (I, 5; 29) are placed differently; this detail is not immaterial, since the stabaka V of Rāmaśarman corresponds to the 4th pāda of Mārkaṇḍeya, the *saṅkīrṇavidhi* : here we find the rules on the sandhi, theory of the suffixes and the words that present an irregular treatment; in short all that remains to be said about the word Prākrit before passing on to the declension. Here when the influence of the adhikāras necessarily became weak, some new sūtras could more easily be introduced, without disturbing the established order.

467. Rāmaśarman on his part, in the first stabaka, further adds some rules that are not found in the first pāda of Mārkaṇḍeya; these innovations are neither numerous nor interesting :—

I, 1, 2; *sasyāśvayornityamihāpare* ca.

I, 1, 5 :—*nityaṁ ca padmādiṣu cāvikarṣe nir o vikalpena ca nirjhare ca.*

I, 1, 6 : *atorpitasvasti-vahitra- pakṣma cod vā* : cf. Mk. III, 26.

I, 1, 8 : *tadā kvacicchālmalimātrayoret.*

1, 1, 10 : *tu triṁśati vīsā viṁśatyāmapi ūhanīyaḥ* cf. Mk. IV, 5.

1, I, 10 (*na*) *vā tu pīṭhe* (s.e. *et syāt*)

The simple reading of these passages shows that Rāmaśarman is not a good grammarian. The words *sasya-* and *aśva-* follow the same ordinary rule of the words of which the group with a sibilant is reduced to a simple sibilant : they elongate the vowel; the prefix *nis-* does not become *o*, etc.

468. This too is interesting to remark that Rāmaśarman has for him the authority of Hemacandra all the times when he deviates from Mārkaṇḍeya. He must have certainly utilized either the grammar of Hemacandra, as we know it, or of his sources that provided him with the "non-Vararucian" material.

469. To sum up, so far as it concerns the phonetics of vowels of the principal Prākrit, the Eastern grammarians (in this case Rāmśarman and Mārkaṇḍeya) took upon themselves

1. The sūtra I, 22 is particularly foreign to the doctrine of Vararuci, who does not study the verbal forms in the phonetic part of his grammar (se § 134).

the task of faithfully reproducing the teachings of Vararuci : they made only some rare additions and these additions are only on points of details and they show the greatest independence from one another.

For the purpose of verifying this hypothesis let us now examine the teachings on conjugation in the Eastern grammarians (Pu VI, 1, 1-44; Mk, VI, 1-48; RT VII, 1-15) and in Vararuci (VII, 1-34) of the edition Bhāmaha-Cowell=VI, 1-34 of the *Prākṛtasañjīvanī*).

470. So far as it concerns Vararuci this portion of the text is firmly established : the *Prākṛtasañjīvanī* and the edition Bhāmaha-Cowell are identical in respect of the subject-matter and do not present any difference of forms except in the sūtras 2, 16, 25, 26, 27, 28 (cf. §277)

471. We are astonished to find that of the three Eastern grammarians Rāmaśarman is more faithful to the teaching of Vararuci, although it is he who does not hesitate to multiply the additions ordinarily.

472. I have the impression that the rigidity of the text of Vararuci and the unusual fidelity of Rāmaśarman are due to the same cause: it is difficult to make any alteration in respect of the conjugation; it is necessary to have sufficient knowledge of the sufficiently vast language so that everybody may become capable of to observing the particular treatment of a word. To put an equivalent to Skt. *arpita-*, *Pkt. oppio*, *appio* (RT I, 1, 6) in respect of a word that was not known to Vararuci or which had deliberately been avoided by him is not of serious consequences, but it requires a different authority for affirming as has been done by Mārkaṇḍeya (VI, 1), that in Prākrit sometimes the present has the force of the past or of the future. Rāmaśarman was obliged to depend on every occasion on the authority of Vararuci for explaining the conjugation in verses that are otherwise rather bad.

473. So it is not astonishing to affirm, by comparing Vararuci with the Eastern grammarians, that the 34 sūtras of the book on conjugation in the *Prākṛtaprākaśa* are found, although at times in a little different form, in Puruṣottama, Mārkaṇḍeya and Rāmaśarman. Here is a list of some of the divergences in respect of the details :—

1. Vr. VII, 2 *thāssipoḥ si se* is wanting in Mārkaṇḍeya.

Since this sūtra is preserved in RT and Pu, probably here we have a case of a lacuna in the manuscript of Vr. utilized by Mk; in fact on the sūtra VI, 5 Mk removes this lacuna in the commentary : *sesiṅostu kāryāntarābhāvāt paḍhasi paḍhase*, "in place of *-se* and *-si*, since there is no other operation, (*-se* and *-si* are preserved. Ex.) *paḍhasi*, *paḍhase*".

2. Vr. VII. 3 *iṭ mipor miḥ* (Pu VI, 7; RT VII, 2). Mārkaṇḍeya has one sūtra of a little obscure form : Mk. VI, 5 *er miḥ* ll *syāt* l *vaḍḍhāmi*...l *maṇṇe jāṇe tu saṁskṛtāt*. The commentary appears to authorize interpretation of this sūtra in the same manner as Vararuci : the affix *-mi* replaces the active and middle affixes of the singular". It is equivalent to excluding the ātmanepada affix *-e*. This has been used by Hāla, in addition to the survival of *jāṇe* and *maṇṇe* (Skt. *manye*) that have almost an adverbial value[1]. The commentary of Mārkaṇḍeya appears to allude to it.

Vr. VII. 6-7 recurs also in Pu in the book on *dhātvādeśa* (VII, 3), Likewise :—

Vr. VII, 9 is considered by Mk (VII, 173) and Pu (VII, 27) as a rule to be classed among the *dhātvādeśas*. RT (VII, 4) follows Vararuci.

Vr. VII, 21 and Vr. VII, 24 are wanting in Pu, but since we have his grammar preserved only in one single manuscript, that too is not provided with a commentary, it would be foolish to draw thence conclusions with regard to these lacunae. So I would not dare affirm that Pu did not teach *-jja*-and *-jjā-* as suffixes preceding the terminations, or *-hīa*-after a root ending in a vowel.

Vr. VII, 28-29 do not occur in the same form in Mk. However, Mk VI, 47, 48 say substantially the same thing.

Lastly the sūtras of Vr. on the modifications of the thematic vowels before verbal terminations or suffixes (VII, 30-34) were included by Mk in a single sūtra and in a very flexible meaning (VI, 7; *prāyeṇāta edidātaḥ śyuḥ*.

474. Consequently it may be affirmed that for conjugation as well the Eastern grammarians faithfully follow the teaching of Vararuci. Excluding Vr. VII, 21 and 24, that do not

1. Cf. Pischel § 457. The other examples of the first person in *-e* recur in the Śaurasenī portions of the dramas.

have correspondence in Pu, no sūtra of Vararuci is wanting in any Eastern grammarian.

This very clear result does not need a commentary.

475. Let us now examine the new items added by the Eastern grammarians in respect of the conjugation. Of them Mārkaṇḍeya has the distinction of having made the largest number of important additions (19 sūtras) : he is followed far behind by Puruṣottama (6 sūtras)[1] and Rāmaśarman (5 sūtras); so it is under Mārkaṇḍeya that we shall class the innovations :

Mk VI, 1 *laḍ bhūtabhāvinor vā syāt*, "the present may be substituted (in Prākrit) for the past and the future (including the conditional)".

Mk VI, 6 *laṭi miṅā il lug vā*, "the *i* of the termination *-mi* of the present may be dropped : Examples.

paḍhaṁ, *hasaṁ* (—*paḍhāmi*, *hasāmi*), cf. §. 670.

Mk VI, 9 *atonte tu vā prathame* (cf. Pu VI, 9) the themes in *-a* may also have the termination *-nte* in the third person (plural ātmanepada)."

Mk VI, 11 *ttha thatābhyām*.

"In the second person plural of the parasmaipada and ātmanepada the $\sqrt{as}$ "to be" may also become *ttha*".

Mk VI, 16 *akāsyakāsamau syātāṁ sthānekārṣīdakārṣamoḥ* "in place of *akārṣīt* and *akārṣam* may be substituted *akāsi* and *akāsaṁ*".

Mk VI, 18 *lṛṅarthe va* (s.e. *śatṛsānayor ntamāṇau*, "the present parasmaipada and ātmanepada participles too have sometime the force of the conditional"; cf. Pu VI, 32 ?

Mk VI, 19 *ata eva māṇaḥ syāt*, "the suffix *-māṇa* occurs only after a verbal theme in *-a*". Ex. *paḍhamāṇo padhanto*, but always *honto*, *dento*.

Mk VI, 22 *ssa ca* (s.e. *bhaviṣyati hiḥ*).

"In the future we find the suffix *-ssa-* too in addition to *-hi-*. Ex *paḍhissaī*; *hossaī*.

= Pu VI, 14; RT VII, 5.

1. Four of these sūtras correspond with those of Mk., and hence they are examined in the following lines. There remain VI, 6 and VI, 32 that present some difficulties in respect of the text and interpretation. Cf. the edition of Puruṣottama by the present author.

Mk VI, 23 *śatṛśānayorlugvā* (s.e. *ssasya*), "the suffix *-ssa-* of the future may disappear in the present participle of the parasmaipada and in the ātmanepada". Consequently we may say *hossanto* and *honto*, *paḍhissamāṇo* and *paḍhamāṇo*. This is an unintelligible sūtra. Here we do not have a case of dropping of *-ssa-* of the future and of having *honto*, but the problem concerns the form of the present participle. It may be that sometimes the present participle has the force of the future in Prākrit (cf. Mk VI, 1), but the actual reading of the sūtra of Mk appears absurd.

Mk· VI, 27. *ekavacanaṁ ca hitthā bhavet kṛñaḥ prathama-madhyamayoḥ* (s. e. *bhaviṣyati*, "the affix *-hitthā* too is employed to form the third and second persons of the singular of the future from the root *kṛ-*" So *kāhitthā·* = *kriyāt*, *kṛṣiṣṭa*, *kṛiyāḥ*, *kṛṣiṣṭhāḥ*.[1]

Mk VI, 32 *madhyame hirekācaḥ*. "In the second porson singular of the verbs having monosyllabic roots (= ending in a vowel), the termination of the imperative is *-hi*.

—Pu VI, 25; RT VII, 9-

Mk VI, 33 *ata uttarasya lopaḥ*.

"In case the verbal theme ends in *-a*, there may take place dropping of the termination of the second person singular imperative".

—Pu VI, 24 and RT VII, 9.

Mk VI, 35 *jjo jjāhi ca tiṅāṁ vā*.

"(The terminations) *-jjo* and *-jjāhi* may be employed in place of all the verbal terminations."

Mk VI, 38 *na jjā ntintvoḥ*.

"(The suffix) *-jjā-* is not used in the presence of the terminations *-nti* and *-ntu*". Ex. *dejjanti*, *dejjantu*.

Mk. VI, 39 *tṛṭi ca kartari yak asmād ihiśca*.

"The future too has a passive in addition to the active we add (to the suffix of the passive) *-ihi* for forming it= RT VII, 11.

1. The insertion of this sūtra VI, 27 disturbs the original order of Vararuci—Mārkaṇḍeya, by admitting that the following sūtra (28 *kāhaṁ dāhaṁ kṛdāñoḥ staḥ*) should be connected with the sūtra VI, 25 (*miñā sscṁ*) by a *maṇḍūkapluti* "jumping of a frog". Here we see the extent to which he was anxious for remaining faithful; he had no desire to disturb the tradtional order. For analogous examples, cf. Mk. I, 41 (where he prefers this expedient to the insertion of a *vā* in the same sūtra); V. 18, etc.

Mk VI, 42 *prāyeṇa vartamānepyetau ṣyātām*. Often we find also forms (with these suffixes of the passive *-īa-* and *-hīa-*) having the force of the present.

—RT VII, 12

Mk VI, 43 *purādiyoge ca* (cf. above)·

They are employed also with the adverbs like *purā* etc.

Mk VI, 46 *kvacidavaś'ca* (s.c. *ṇiṅaḥ*)

"The affix of the causative may also be *-ava-*".

Mk VI, 48 *āvaśca kṛti ṇakādau ca.*

"The affix of the causative may also be *-āva-* in the case of formations with the primary suffixes *-ṇak* etc. (that is to say that before the suffixes *-ṇak*, (*-a-*), *tṛṅ*, *tṛṅi* (suffix of the agentative *-tṛ-*), *-kta* (verbal suffix in *-ta*), *-ktavant* (the verbal suffix *-tāvat-*), *tavyaṅ anīyaṅ* (verbal suffixes indicative of necessity), *aṇaṭ ṅana* (suffix-*ana-*),*-tumam* (suffix-*tum* of the infinitive), *-ktvā* (absolutive-in *-tvā*), *yak* (suffix of the passive).

Of these innovations, Mk VI, 1; 18, 42 and 43 concern aspects of the syntax. We may perhaps add also VI, 23 of which the meaning remains ouscure to me.

476. We always have here the question of the use of the tenses : Mk VI, 1 teaches that in Prākrit the present may have the force of the past and of the future. Since he does not give any example and since he is alone to affirm this we are not able to know the phenomenon that he had in view when he made this statement[1].

Mk VI, 18, that perhaps has a correspondence in Pu VI, 32, is more explicit : The present participle, active or middle, may be used in the meaning of the conditional". Ex. *jaï paḍhanto tā paṇḍido honto*, "if he had read, he would have become cultured."; *jaï bhuñjamāṇo tā thippamāṇo*, "if he had eaten, he would have been satisfied".

477. The rule with analogous examples occurs also in Hc III, 180. It is also cited by the scholiast from the

1. Cf. however, A. Weber: Introduction to the first edition of the Saptaśataka of Hāla (Leipzig 1870), p. 63: Die Formen der Vergangenheit werden...direkt durch das Praesens selbst vertreten". The form of the past are...directly substituted by those of the present itself. Apparently it is a case of style common to several languages, rather a characteristic of Prākrit.

Setubandha[1] and from the *Saptaśataka*[2].

478. Mk VI, 42 does not quote examples. Mk VI, 43 cites two sentences that are provided by him with a translation into Sanskrit : *purā jāhīa* (*purā yāti*) and *evaṁ ettha purā vasīa chattā* (*atra purā vasanti chātrāḥ*). The two sūtras appear to satisfy a necessity. The forms in *-īa*, *-hīa*, understood as those of the past by the grammarians, did not actually exist. So some of their functions should have remained outside the definition *īa bhūte* (Vr. VII, 23). Cf. Pischel, *Grammar* § 466 on this point.

It may, however, be noted that these forms do not occur in the classical texts of the Māhārāṣṭrī lyrics.

479. The other additions made by Mārkaṇḍeya concern the peculiarities of morphology :

Mk VI, 6. The forms *paḍhaṁ* and *hasaṁ* are unknown to Māhārāṣṭrī lyrics, (cf. § 670).

Mk VI, 9. Vr does not teach the termination *-ante* of the ātmanepada in Māhārāṣṭrī. The texts provide him with the reason, because it is not attested except in a doubtful form *ucchāhaṁte* (H. 638).

Mk VI, 14. The form *ttha* of the second person plural of the present of the verb *as-* "to be" is very rare, as remarked by Pischel, *Gramm.* § 498). In any event, it is not found in the Māhārāṣṭrī lyric, which appears to justify the omission of Vararuci.

Mk VI, 16. These two aorists are unknown to Māhārāṣṭrī. Pischel, (*Gramm.* § 516) gives its two examples borrowed from Ardhamāgadhī.

Mk. VI. 19. It is difficult to decide if Mārkaṇḍeya was right in putting this limitation. In view of the situation that a great majority of roots in Prākrit end in *-a*, the absence of the middle participial forms in *-omāṇa-*, for example, does not prove any important thing. Pischel. (*Gramm.* § 476) explicitly attributes the form *homāṇo* to Māhārāṣṭrī, although

1. *Rāvaṇavaha* or *Setubandha* prākṛt und deutsch herausgegeben von S. Goldschmidt, Strassburg—London, Trübner, p. 285-11, 80 *daṭṭhuṁ tumaṁ ti hontaṁ jai ettāhe vi jīviaṁ vialantaṁ* ll commentary- *bhavada-bhaviṣyat*/ *vigalad vyagaliṣyat* l *tṛṅarthe śatṛ vaktavyaḥ* ll

2. Cf. Hāla 26 and comm. in the first edition of Weber (Leipzig, 1870).

it is not attested in Hāla or in any of the two principal epical poems.

Mk VI, 22. This extension of the suffix *-ssa-* of the future to persons other than the first appears to be unjustified so far as it concerns classical Māhārāṣṭrī. After going through §§ 520-534 of the grammar of Pischel, we do not find the forms such as *bhaṇissaï*; whilst they are abundant in Śaurasenī (*bhaṇissadi*) and in other dialects. This is the usage of Hāla who has *bhaṇissaṁ* (12, 347) against *bhaṇihii* (858, 918 etc.); *hossaṁ* (743) against *hohii* (187, 225, etc.); *karissaṁ* (743, 882) against *kāhisi* (80, 90, 683); *jāṇissaṁ* (749) against *jāṇihisi* (528, 643) etc. I have found only one exception as yet: *samāgamissaï* (962), that occurs in the second edition of the recension of Teliṅga in a stanza, but that is cited elsewhere in the *Kāvyaprakāśa* of Mammaṭa, where the still more aberrant form *samāgamissadi* is found[1]. Consequently we are authorised to suspect its authenticity.

Mk VI, 27. The form *kāhitthā* is unknown to classical Māhārāṣṭrī

Mk VI, 32-33 Here at least at one place, Vararuci appears to be wrong. There is no doubt that Prākrit has, beside the termination *-su*, also *-hi* employed in the second person singular imperative of the roots ending in a vowel and the termination zero for the themes ending in *-a* (example *hohi* (Hāla 259, *kuṇa* Hāla 152 etc.) But this omission of Vararuci may be justified by supposing that these two rules were contained for him in the sūtra *śeṣaḥ sāṁskṛtāt* (X, 18).

Mk VI, 35 and 38 are difficult for the purpose of a critical study on account of absence of examples in the text. **dejjanti* and **dijjantu* do not exist. Mārkaṇḍeya himself is the author of his own commentary and on the other hand this sūtra is not known to other grammarians. If these conditions were not existing, we could consider the sūtra VI, 38 as governed by the preceding one, of which it limits the effect *madhye caikācaḥ*) : "(*jja* and) *jjā* are never employed as suffixes of the optative in the third person of the plural, but simply as affixes. One says exclusively *dejjā* (3rd person plural) in face of *hojjasi*, *hojjāsi* and *hojjā* (second person singular)".

1. Cf. Weber, first edition of the *Saptaśataka* (Leipzig, 1870, p. 224).

Mk VI, 39. This future of the passive is known and well confirmed; cf. P i s c h e l *Gramm.* § 549.

Mk VI, 46 : cf. P i s c h e l, *Gramm.* § 553, who gives some examples of the causative suffix even for Māhārāṣṭrī. The example of Mk (*Setubandha* II, 8), on the contrary, is rejected by G o l d s c h m i d t[1].

Mk VI, 48. It is not a case of true addition, but as already remarked above § 472, that of a different arrangement of the subject-matter.

Consequently the study of the conjugation in Eastern grammarians confirms the result obtained from an examination of the phonetics of vowels for Māhārāṣṭrī. These grammarians deliberately follow the teaching of Vararuci : they do not reject any of his doctrines and they try to complete them. So far as it concerns these additions, they are relatively free from one another. The large amount of innovations are on the whole in Mārkaṇḍeya. However, it cannot always be said that these innovations respond to a real necessity; mostly they have in view cases of forms that are foreign to Māhārāṣṭrī lyrics which alone formed the subject-matter of study of Vararuci.

480. *The other bhāṣās*- Next to Māhārāṣṭrī, the Eastern grammarians study Śaurasenī, Prācyā, Āvantī and Māgadhī. Puruṣottama names only some other *bhāṣās*. Mārkaṇḍeya notes also the existence of Bāhlīkī (that he discards on account of its coincidence with Āvantī, excepting the change of *r* into *l*), of Ardhamāgadhī, that is a Māgadhī very close to Śaurasenī and to Dākṣiṇātyā, that he does not know. Rāmaśarman says that Bāhlīkī is simply an Āvantī spoken by some other characters, identifies Ardhamāgadhī with Māgadhī (except in the case of the form of the first person that is *aham* in Ardhamāgadhī as in Sanskrit) and reserves the name Dākṣiṇātyā to a particular literary form that is elsewhere noted by Mārkaṇḍeya too. Dākṣiṇātyā, therefore, is not a true language[2].

1. Cf. note 1 at p. 205 of the translation.

2. Mk. XI, 13 :—*āvantyāmeva bāhlīkī kiṁtu rasyātra lo bhavet* ll
salasiluhasolahaṇibbhalo maludo vahaï ll
dhūrtādibhāṣā tu bāhlīkī iti bharataḥ ll

Mk. XII, 38. *śaurasenyā adūratvādiyamevārdhamāgadhī* ll *spaṣṭam* ll
rākṣasīśreṣṭhiceṭānukarmyāderardhamāgadhī iti bharataḥ ll
yathā "ayja vi ṇo śāmiṇīe hilimbādevīe

481. *Śaurasenī*—The Eastern grammarians accord an important place to Śaurasenī. Mārkaṇḍeya finds himself obliged to subdivide the 158 sūtras that he devotes in 9 *prakaraṇaṣ* by following the order that he has adopted for Māhārāṣṭrī : phonetics of vowels, phonetics of consonants, etc.

482. On the whole the unity of doctrine is very strong in the three Eastern grammarians; Rāmaśarman and Mārkaṇḍeya go absolutely on a par, the column of reference to Mk in the edition of Grierson of this portion of the *Prākṛtakalpataru* has almost no fissure and its figures follow almost always a rigorous order. Puruṣottama is certainly less diffused; however, it is possible that the unique Nepal manuscript is not complete. A particular circumstance in respect of the MS of the *Prākṛtakalpataru* would confirm this hypothesis.

483. As already mentioned above almost all the sūtras of Mk on Śaurasenī are found in RT, excluding some sporadic cases often concerning the *dhātvādeśas*[1]. A single group of important sūtras is wanting in RT, it is that on the personal pronouns (Mk IX, 87-94). It is wanting in Puruṣottama as well, in addition to Mk IX, 88 (=Pu IX, 64 ?).

484. While reading Puruṣottama, one has the impression that there is a lacuna in the text; but it would have been impossible to confirm this impression, in case by accident an analogous lacuna were not evident in the *Prākṛtakalpataru*. In the same way G r i e r s o n has noticed in a note on the text that the kusuma 20 as well as a part of the

puśtaghaḍu kkaaśoe ṇa uvaśamadi" (cf. Veṇīsaṁhāra, III, p. 35).

Mk. XII, 38 comm. *dākṣiṇātyāyāstu na lakṣaṇaṁ nodāharaṇaṁ ca*
kutraciddṛśyate l *kevalam aniruddhabhaṭṭena*
dākṣiṇātyapadālambi saṁskṛtāṅgaṁ vijṛmbhitam l
kāvyaṁ pīyūṣaniḥsyandi dākṣiṇātyānamitīritam ityuktam ll

RT. II, 2, 5 *āvantibhāṣā pratipadyatesau*
bāhlīkibhāṣā ca vibhinnapātrā l

RT. II, 2, 12 *eṣārdhamāgadhyapi kintu tatra*
rahasyametat kavayo vadanti l
hage'hamarthe yadi māgadhī syād
yathārdhamāgadhyaham eva rūpam ll

RT. II, 2, 32 *dākṣiṇ(ātya)-pada-sammilitaṁ yat*
saṁskṛtādibhi(rapi) cchuritaṁ ca l
svādu-sāramamṛtādapi kāvyaṁ
dākṣiṇātyamiti tat kathayanti ll

1. Here is a list of the sūtras of Mārkaṇḍeya that do not have their correspondence in the *Prākrtakalpataru*: Mk. IX, 14, 29, 38, 47, 49, 55, 76, 87-94, 96, 98-100, 103, 105, 117, 120, 124, 127, 135, 140, 143, 147, 151, 152, 153, 158.

kusuma 19 is wanting in the stabaka on Śaurasenī : the question is also regarding the personal pronouns and almost of the same sūtras that are wanting in Puruṣottama.

485. This coincidence may appear miraculous : on the contrary it is quite normal. The personal pronouns are particularly bad-conditioned in the grammatical manuscripts : the repetition at a short distance of the same forms easily results in transcriptional omissions. As a matter of fact the Nepali MS of Puruṣottama has certainly a lacuna in the exposition of the personal pronouns of Apabhraṁśa : Pu XVII, 66 *bhisi tumhehiṁ* (understood the adhikāra *yuṣmadaḥ* of the sūtra 64); Pu XVII, 67 *aṃṭāṅiṣu maī* (it ought to imply here *asmadaḥ* and the text does not allow this).

486. It also appears that the declension of personal pronouns of the principal Prākrit is not complete in the Nepal MS (cf. Pu V, 175, note); but here the role of the adhikāra is respected and the lacunae of this fact is not more evident.

487. Excepting the personal pronouns, that are more complete in the *Prākṛtasarvasva*, Rāmaśarman and Mārkāṇḍeya teach the same facts so far as they relate to Śaurasenī. Puruṣottama has a number of sūtras that are further limited, and among those ones some have no correspondence in other Eastern grammarians.

488. For knowing, in this respect, the doctrine of the Eastern grammarians, it is worthwhile to limit our study to Mārkaṇḍeya whose reading has now become easy due to the fine edition of Bhaṭṭanāthasvāmin and due to the translation of the portion dealing with Śaurasenī of the *Prākṛtasarvasva* by Hultzsch[1].

1. E. Hultzsch, *Neue Beiträge zur Kenntnis der Śaurasenī* : ZDMG 66 (1912), pp. 708-726. This study contains also an index of Śaurasenī words: studied by Mārkaṇḍeya. The excellent translation and the index may render some service : on the contrary it would be proper to guard against the pieces of information contained in the two pages of the introduction. Prācyā is not an "appendage" to Śaurasenī (here Hultzsch may be pardoned for not having understood the classification of the dialects, because he had with him the copy of *Prākṛtasarvasva* that ended with Prācyā : it is true that the introduction should have made him careful). Mārkaṇḍeya did not "invent" a grammar of Śaurasenī; even without the discovery of Puruṣottama, Hultzsch could have arrived at this conclusion, in case he had taken note of the opinion of Lassen on the *Prākṛtakalpataru*. It is not prudent to try to determine the date of Mārkaṇḍeya by reference to the uncertain identification of Vasantarāja, the grammarian with the king of Koṇḍavīdu (Pischel, *Gramm.* § 40).

489. Without entering into a particularly long and fastidious discussion of detail, on account of the bad condition of the manuscripts of the dramas and the enthusiastic discussions inspired by them, it may be affirmed that Śaurasenī of the Eastern grammarians corresponds exactly to the language spoken in classical dramas by female characters.

490. Mārkaṇḍeya has himself made this identification at the end of the Śaurasenīpāda (IX, 158) :

rājapatnyādivaktrendusaṁvāsahṛdayaṁgamā 1
mṛdugambhīrasaṁdarbhā śaurasenī dhinotu vaḥ 11

"Having walked with the faces—these moons !—of the queens and their equals, it comes into our heart; it combines gravity with delicacy,—this Śaurasenī, may it make you happy !"

All the examples of Śaurasenī, that we have been able to locate in the dramas found in Mārkaṇḍeya have been borrowed from the rôles of women.

491. In the classical drama, in which Sanskrit is employed by side of the other dialects, men do not speak Prākrit, unless they are comic characters or when one insists on their provincial nature. Bharata (XVII, 45-46; cf. § 310), it is true, in this second case, leaves to them the choice between Śaurasenī and their natural dialect, in case they are men of distinction, thus emphasising the character of universality of Śaurasenī. But in reality, excepting the *Karpūramañjarī*, that is written entirely in Prākrit, Śaurasenī-speaking men are not frequent in the dramas that have come down to us till now. The vidūṣaka speaks Prācyā; the other male characters are clearly comic in the *Mṛcchakaṭika*, for example, and so on and so forth. Perhaps now it would be useful to take up again here the question of the dialects in classical dramas on the basis of a more historical interpretation of the data provided by the grammarians and by making proper allowance for the process of unification of dialects that should have begun with the authors themselves and has never ceased to continue till the bringing out of the European editions.

492. It is perhaps possible at present to affirm, I believe, that Śaurasenī replaces Sanskrit in case of all characters who do

not have the authority to make use of the language of the gods. The question is not about the native dialect (*deśabhāṣā*) of the characters, but of a language becoming convenient to persons coming from any region of India[1].

493. Prācyā—Prācyā is the dialect of the vidūṣaka and of other comic characters. It is based on Śaurasenī although it employs also the forms of the popular language.

Pischel has treated Prācyā in a concise manner in the beginning of his work (*Grammar* § 22), but in course of the grammatical exposition he constantly identifies it with Śaurasenī. It is true that on this dialect the Eastern grammarians do not teach any important thing and that their teachings have in view particularly the details of vocabulary; but their testimony is in any case explicit. Prācyā is the dialect spoken by certain comic characters. The examples of Mārkaṇḍeya are borrowed from the rôle of the *vidūṣaka* in the *Ratnāvalī*, a thing that shows that he found this dialect even in the literary dramas that have come down to us till the recent times.

494. Moreover, a rule that is common to Puruṣottama, Rāmaśarman and Mārkaṇḍeya appears to indicate an important distinction between Śaurasenī and Prācyā[2]. The question is about the future participle of the verb "to be" for which Pu (X, 9) teaches the form *hokkhamāṇo* in place of Mk. and RT. *okkamāṇo*. Now the theme *hokkha* is well attested in Ardhamāgadhī[3].

495. *Āvantī* is the language of the police, of the officers and of the scoundrels. For the Eastern grammarians Māhārāṣṭrī

1. Mk. X. Intr.—*prācyā vidūṣakaviṭādihāsyapātrabhāṣā* l
prācyā vidūṣakādīnāmiti bharataḥ ll
pūrvāparahataṁ kvāpi kıaciccheko ktisundaram l
grāmyābhyām upamoktibhyām yuktaṁ vakti vidūṣakaḥ ll
iti ca ll

Mk. X, 1 *prācyāsiddhiḥ śaurasenyāḥ.*
RT. II, 2, 1 *prācyāṁ vivicyātha bhaṇāmi bhāṣāṁ*
sā śaurasenīprakṛtiḥ pradiṣṭā ll
RT. II, 2, 4 *bhāṣaiṣā tu vidūṣakaprabhṛti (bhi) rvācyātra nāṭyāgame.*
Pu. X, 13 (understood-*prācyāyāṁ*) *lokoktayo bahulam.*
Pu. X, 14 *śeṣe śaurasenī.*

2. This rule could not be considered by Pischel, who was unable to read the MS of Mārkaṇḍeya on this point (cf. *Gramm.* §22).

3. Pischel, *Gramm.* § 521. Pischel explains it as an error of writing (*hokkha* < *bhoṣya-*) by substituting *kha* for *ṣa* (cf. § 265). This explanation appears to me unacceptable.

of Śaurasenī and Māhārāṣṭrī (Pu, Mk), or of Śaurasenī and Prācyā (RT.)[1]. This mixture should not be homogeneous; according to Mārkaṇḍeya the forms would remain with their different dialectial characteristics, even in the interior of the same sentence. Thus says Mārkaṇḍeya (XI, 1)—in the example *esa kirādo maaṁ anusaranto vedasalaāgahaṇaṁ paīṭṭho*" (this Kirāta, chasing a beast, has entered into the grove made of canes and creepers"), the words *kirādo* and *vedasa* are in Śaurasenī and all the others are in Māhārāṣṭrī.

The same Mārkaṇḍeya (XI, 12) quotes also the opinion according to which the characters who should speak Āvantī are in reality authorised to employ at their option Śaurasenī or Māhārāṣṭrī.

This is the conjugation that provides the particularities in Āvantī of the Eastern grammarians : of the 13 sūtras, that Mārkaṇḍeya devotes to it, 9 are concerned with the verb, 2 define the language itself, and only 2 are devoted to other topics of the grammar[2]. This is almost the ratio that occurs in Pu and RT.

Mārkaṇḍeya localises the country *Āvantī* in the region of the *Cedis*, of the *Mālavas* and of the city of *Ujjayinī* (in the vicinity of actual Bundelkhand and Malwa).

496. Māgadhī offers some phonetical peculiarities that differentiate it from Prākrit. However, Puruṣottama

1. Mk XI, 1 *āvantī syānmahārāṣṭrīśaurasenyostu saṅkarāt* 1
anayoḥ saṅkarād āvantībhāṣā siddhā syāt 11
saṅkaraśca ekasminneva vākye boddhavyaḥ 1
cedimālavojjayinyādir avantīdeśaḥ 1
tadbhavā āvantī dāṇḍikādibhāṣā yadāha bharataḥ 1
dāṇḍikapāṇikapāṇṭikanagarādhipaṇikasadṛkṣeṣu 1
madhyamapātreṣu sadā yojyāvantī tu nāṭyavidhau 11
iti 11 *esa kirādo maamanusaranto vedasalaāgahaṇaṁ paīṭṭho* 11
atra kirādo vedasa iti śaurasenī 1 *anyāni padāni māhārāṣṭrī* 11

Mk XI, 12 *atroktaviśeṣādanyatra māhārāṣṭrīśaurasenyor aicchikaḥ saṅkaraḥ*

RT II, 2, 5 : *āvantibhāṣā pratipadyatesau bāhlīkibhāṣā ca vibhinnapātrā* 1
siddhiḥ samudgacchati śaurasenī-
prācyādvayīsaṅkarato yadīyā 11

RT II, 2, 10 : *eṣā tu bhāṣā nagarādhipasya tathaiva dauḥsādhikadhūrtayośca* 1
saṁyojitā madhyamapātrakāṇāṃ nāṭyāgame dāṇḍikapāṇikānām 11

Pu XI, 1 *athāvantī* 1 *māhārāṣṭrī-śaurasenyoraikyam*

2. Mk XI, 2 *kṣa cchaḥ sadṛkṣe* (ex. *sariccho*); XI, 12 *ccia-ccea ivārthakau* (in place of *eva* for RT. II, 2, 6).

and Mārkaṇḍeya connect it with Śaurasenī and Māhārāṣṭrī. On the whole there are almost no divergences among the three grammarians; we have just to compare directly one with the other to learn the doctrine of the "Easterners" on this peculiar language.

According to Rāmaśarman, it should be spoken by demons and by monks, Buddhists and Jainas. Mārkaṇḍeya adds also the servants, and for this he depends upon the authority of Kohala[1].

497. The *vibhāṣās* of the Eastern grammarians were made a subject of special study by Sir George Grierson.[2] Possibly all of his conclusions merit acceptance and in this connection nothing better can be said than advising the readers to refer to his article that contains also a translation of the passages from Mārkaṇḍeya concerning *vibhāṣās*. *Puruṣottama* adds nothing important, excepting some detail.

The *vibhāṣāḥ*, as noted by Grierson, are employed exclusively on the stage[3]. So it is not astonishing that the name goes so far back as Bharata. Moreover, in case we read again the stanzas of 47-48 of the adhyāya XVII of the *Nāṭyaśāstra* (cf. § 310,), we see that even the order of these *vibhāṣāḥ* is concordant in Bharata and in the Eastern grammarians; and

1. Mk XII, 1. *māgadhī śaurasenītaḥ* ll *siddhyatīti śeṣaḥ* ll
rākṣasabhikṣukṣapaṇakaceṭādyā māgadhīṁ prāhuriti kohalaḥ ll
RT II, 2, 11 *atheha māgadhyanuśiṣyate yā kravyādabhikṣukṣapaṇakānām* l
asyā mahārāṣṭrakaśūrasenabhāṣāpravīṇaiḥ prakṛtī nirukte. ll
Pu XII, 1 *atha māgadhī* l *śaurasenītaḥ prāyaḥ* ll

2. JRAS 1918, pp. 489-517. Cf. also for RT, IA, LVII, 1928.

3. Ibid., p. 516 : "*Vibhāṣās* fall into two classes. One is composed of Śākārī, Cāṇḍālī, Śābarī, Auḍrī and Ābhīrī. These are all degradations-levellings down of Māgadhī or of Śaurasenī or of both. They are spoken by uneducated persons, who are represented as despicable or else as of some despised caste. The other division consists of Ṭakkī (including Drāviḍī). So far from this being a degraded form of speech, it represents a levelling up. Its speakers are semi-educated people, who are trying to "talk fine"; if they occasionally drop into vulgar idioms, it is due to their want of education, not due to their intention...A *Vibhāṣā* is a corrupt form of one or more standard Prākrit dialects, which is used only in stage-plays, and it is there allotted to special characters. The corruption may be either down-grade or up-grade, and may consist in solecisms, or in a mixture of dialects, but in every case it is represented on the stage as a corruption, personal to the speaker, and nothing more."

that for the *vibhāṣāḥ* too, the Eastern grammarians appear to follow the classification of Bharata.

In all events, the examples added by Mārkaṇḍeya and Rāmaśarman to their teaching on the *bhāṣās* and on the *vibhāṣās* are all taken from dramatic works, in addition naturally, to those of the principal Prākrit, Māhārāṣṭrī, that Bharata does not consider to be included among the *bhāṣās* furthermore.

498. Apabhraṁśa of the Eastern grammarians, on the contrary, is a language foreign to the theatre: at least its principal variety, Nāgarāpabhraṁśa, that is the basis of the two others, Vrācaḍāpabhraṁśa and Upanāgarāpabhraṁśa. The norm of this Apabhraṁśa, for Mārkaṇḍeya and Puruṣottama, rests upon the usage of the cultured people, and Rāmaśarman speaks about the usage of the poets[1].

499. The examples of Nāgarāpabhraṁśa cited by Mārkaṇḍeya are almost wholly taken from the *Prākṛtapiṅgalasūtra*, and since Puruṣottama and Rāmaśarman teach the same language, it may be affirmed without risk of committing an error that Nāgarāpabhraṁśa of the Eastern grammarians is identified with the language of which the *Prākṛtapiṅgalasūtra* is a model.

4100. Moreover, of Vrācaḍāpabhraṁśa and of Upanāgarāpabhraṁśa (to which Eastern grammarians hardly devote some sūtras), Rāmaśarman and Mārkaṇḍeya quote about twenty examples from some other minor dialects of Apabhraṁśa. Readers will be able to study them[2] in the two articles of Grierson.

4101. Puruṣottama knows a certain number of these dialects, but lack of a commentary makes his sūtras less instructive[3].

4102. Thus as remarked by Grierson[4], the list quoted by Mārkaṇḍeya includes among the Apabhraṁśa dialects Ṭākkī, that Mārkaṇḍeya himself considers as a *Vibhāṣā*[5].

1. Pu XVII, 91 *śeṣaṁ śiṣṭaprayogāt*. Cf. also Mk XVII, 78 *śeṣaṁ śiṣṭaprayogataḥ*. Cf. RT III, 1, 4 and *passim*.
2. G. A. Grierson, Apabhraṁśa according to Mārkaṇḍeya and "Ḍhakki" Prākrit, JRAS 1913, pp. 875-883; The *Apabhraṁśa Stabakas of Rāmaśarman* (*Tarkavāgīśa*), IA, LII, 1923, pp. 1-8 and 187-191.
3. Pu XVIII, 107-114.
4. JRAS, 1913, p. 883.
5. Mk XVIII. 12 comm. *tākkaṁ ṭakkabhāṣānāgaropanāgarādibhyo-’vadhāraṇīyam*; as against this cf. Mk XVI, 1-13.

It is true that he is careful in explaining Ṭākkī and informs us about the view of Hariścandra that it should be ranked among the Apabhraṁśa-dialects :

Mk XVI, 2 :—

hariścandrastvimāṁ bhāṣāmapabhraṁśa itīcchati l
apabhraṁśo hi vidvadbhirnāṭakādau prayujyate ll
drāviḍīmapyatraiṣa manyate tathā coktam l
ṭakkadeśīyabhāṣāyāṁ dṛśyate drāviḍī tathā l
tatra cāyaṁ viśeṣosti drāviḍairāhṛtā param ll *iti*[1] ll

"However, Hariścandra, desires that this language should be classed among the Apabhraṁśa-dialects, because he says : "scholars authorise the use of Apabhraṁśa in theatral compositions." Drāviḍī too should be included (in the denomination of Ṭākkī). In fact it is said—"Drāviḍī is illustrated in the speech of the country of Ṭakka; the only difference consists in the fact that it is spoken by the people (considered to be originaire) of the Dravidian country."

This very important passage expresses its complete meaning in case one compares it with the last stanza of the stabaka on Apabhraṁśa of Rāmaśarman.

RT. II, 3, 31 :—

śakārakauḍra-draviḍādivācopabhraṁśatāṁ yadyapi saṁśrayanti l
syānnāṭakādau yadi saṁprayogo naitāsvapabhraṁśatayā tatheṣṭiḥ ll

"Although the languages Śakāraka, Auḍra, Draviḍa and others of the same type have the characteristics of Apabhraṁśa, in case they are employed on the stage, etc., they should not be considered to be Apabhraṁśa."

We see here how the classification of the languages is made by the Prākrit grammarians according to the literary usage and not according to the nature of speech. A dialect, whatever it be, used on the stage was a *bhāṣā* or a *vibhāṣā* according to the degree of respectability of the characters to whom it was assigned.

A dialect, not employed in non-theatral literature, was an Apabhraṁśa. So there is nothing extraordinary that Ṭākkī should sometimes be considered as a *Vibhāṣā* and sometimes as an Apabhraṁśa: this depends upon the texts in which it figures.

1. Cf. also Pu XVI, 10 *hariścandratvimāṁ ṭakkabhāṣāmapabhraṁśam icchati na prākṛtam.*

In case Mārkaṇḍeya did not know examples of Ṭākkī other than those provided by the dramas, he was obliged, according to his system to call it a *Vibhāṣa*. Hariścandra, who was not a grammarian, struck by the characteristics of the language, could consider it as an Apabhraṁśa, inasmuch as in his view this exclusion of Apabhraṁśa from the scene had not been generally accepted. However, Pṛthvīdhara, who is not a grammarian, calls Śākārī an Apabhraṁśa[1].

4103. *Paiśācī*. On the contrary it is difficult, for want of examples and texts, to know about the works that were considered by Eastern grammarians as having been written in Paiśācī. Moreover, Mārkaṇḍeya and Puruṣottama knew only the three varieties of Paiśācī (K e k a y a p a i ś ā c i k a Ś a u r a s e n a p a i ś ā c i k a and P ā ñ c ā l a p a i ś ā c i k a). Rāmaśarman adds at least three other pure Paiśācīs (*gauḍapaiśācika*, *māgadhapaiśācika* and *vrācaḍapaiśācika*[2]) and four mixed *Paiśācīs* (*saṁkīrṇapaiśācika*). These mixed dialects are well known in Indian literature, and the S a r a s v a t ī k a ṇ ṭ h ā b h a r a ṇ a (II, 17) gives a list of these that corresponds—in essence, but not in respect of the names—to that of Rāmaśarman. There are several passages where verses are written in two different languages alternately (= Sarasvat. *miśra* RT *padaśuddha*, some others in which two dialects are mechanically mixed up together, like rice and sesamum or rice in a ball (= Sarasvat. *saṁkīrṇa*, RT *aśuddha*) or others in which the same passage has the same meaning in two different languages (= Sarasvat. RT *saṁkīrṇa*).

4104. Rāmaśarman cites as an example of this last category a stanza from the drama Mālatīmādhava recited by Mādhava when he desires to be taken for Lavaṅgikā; as the

1. Cf. Introduction to the commentary on the *Mṛcchakaṭika* (p. 1 of the edition Nirṇayasāgar Press, Bombay, 1926); *apabhraṁśapāṭhakeṣu śākārībhāṣāpāṭhako rāṣṭriyaḥ*: " among the characters speaking Apabhraṁśa, the brother-in-law of the king speaks Śākārī."

2. G r i e r s o n, *Eastern Schools*, etc; p. 137 adds also *sūkṣmabhedapaiśācika*. The text, however, does not appear to warrant this use of the word *sūkṣmabheda* :

RT III, 3, 13 :

jajñe śabhedādaparaṁca paiśācikaṁ bhavet tatkila sūkṣmabhedam I
gūḍekṣumādhuryāvadasya tāvanna vidyate nirvarcanāya śaktiḥ II

same Rāmaśarman recognises, here we have the case of a passage that may be read in Sanskrit as well as in Śaurasenī[1]. Not a single word presents a characteristic Paiśācī.

4105. This problem would be difficult to solve in case Rāmaśarman was something different from a clumsy arranger of verses. Everything becomes clear after we consult any treatise on the dramatic art or rhetorics that describes the different languages allotted to the different literary types. After the languages are examined, the possible admixtures are always enumerated, whether the question is, as for Daṇḍin, to authorise the use of diverse dialects in the drama or whether one desires really to allude to these hybrid creations that were meant to offer literary pastime in India[2].

4106. Rāmaśarman should have one of these treatises before him; on the other hand, Paiśācī often terminates the enumeration of the pure languages: with his habitual carelessness he did not comprehend that the group of mixed languages was opposed to that of the pure languages in the classification and on the contrary he only believed that they were bare continuation of Paiśācī, that he was going to explain; without a blinking he considered the mixed languages as sub-divisions of Paiśācī.

Consequently it is not necessary to get perplexed at the "mixed Paiśācīs", an invention of Rāmaśarman.

4107. Among the three varieties of Paiśācī studied also by the other Eastern grammarians, the most important, that is the one which serves as a basis for others, is K e k a y a - P a i ś ā c ī. Mārkaṇḍeya cites a short passage in this language and says that he has taken it from the *Bṛhatkathā*. As pointed out by G r i e r s o n, at least one of the two cited words would be wrong in Paiśācī as taught by Hemacandra[3]. We know that

1. This is the verse that with the corrections of G r i e r s o n (*Eastern Schools* etc., p. 130) reads :

sarale sāhasa-rāgaṁ parihara rambhoru muñca saṁrambham l
virasaṁ virahāyāsaṁ soḍhuṁ tava cittamasahaṁ me ll

2. Daṇḍin, Kāv. I, 32 (ed. B ö h t l i n g k) ;

tadetadvāṅmayaṁ bhūyaḥ saṁskṛtaṁ prākṛtaṁ tathā
apabhraṁśaśca miśraṁ cetyāhurāryāścaturvidham ll

Cf. on the other hand, the *Sarasvatīkaṇṭhābharaṇa* (ed. K. M., 95), II, 17 and ss.

3. JRAS, 1913, p. 391 : *The Eastern School*, etc., p. 121, Mk XIX, 9, 10 : *kupaci kvacit* ll ......*bṛhatkathāyām kupaci pisālam*.

Pischel (*Gramm.* § 27) had sought to see in the examples of Hemacandra the remnants of the extinct *Bṛhatkathā*. Without entering into this question, that would take us far from the track of the subject, we may refer in any case, to the fidelity of Mārkaṇḍeya in respect of citations (cf. § 456). His testimony in respect of the language of the Bṛhatkathā is consequently not devoid of worth.

4108. It may here be noted that the striking coincidences and the certain divergences of detail do not require here a very lengthy discussion: of course it is something different that the position would become clear in case we would have a synoptic edition of the three Eastern grammarians.

4109. The work of Rāmaśarman is known to us in a single later-day incorrect manuscript : it has resisted at several points the penetrating analysis of a Grierson; but it is now read and edited in full; the obscure task will be further reduced in case some others come forward to examine it. The grammar of Puruṣottama too has the lamentable distinction of being preserved in a single manuscript, that too without a commentary. This work too would be profitable only after its repeated comparisons by other scholars. Mārkaṇḍeya, who leaves to us his work the most complete, we may add also the most learned, is nicely edited; but it is not convenient to consult it as it is not provided with an index. Moreover, some other manuscripts have to be utilized to make the edition worthy of being dependable. Sir George Abraham Grierson announced in 1918 that he had at his disposition 5 manuscripts from different sources and written in different characters[1] and at the same time he promised a critical edition of Mārkaṇḍeya.

4110. It is very regrettable that some other engagements should have upto the present day prevented him from keeping his promise; but on the other hand, possibly he too would be partisan to a synoptic edition of the Eastern grammarians. Grammatical forms sieved first from a comparison of manuscripts and then from that of books would thereby attain a certain firmness and would be in a position to contribute better to a linguistic analysis. One would be less exposed to

1 The Prākrit Vibhāṣās, JRAS, 1918, notes at pp 503 and 504

the danger, still so much prevalent today in the field of Middle Indian study, of propounding fashionable theories on the basis of wavering data that are reduced to the ground by a simple careful reading of a manuscript.

4111. The brief summary of the doctrine of Eastern grammarians that we have drawn up in our opinion leads us to the following conclusions :—

(a) The school of Eastern grammarians exhibits a great unity of teaching : the three actually known representatives do not differ except at certain points of detail.

(b) The date of the Nepal manuscript of Puruṣottama allows attribution to this school a much more ancient epoch than the 17th century A. D. It flourished in the same condition at least in the 13th century and there is nothing that may indicate that Puruṣottama was its founder. We are even in a position to assume that he had predecessors from the fact that his name is never mentioned by Mārkaṇḍeya or by Rāmaśarman. Śākalya, about whom we know nothing, should have been one of these predecessors, since he is cited by all the three.

(c) The condition in which we actually find it, the school of Eastern grammarians is very eclectical : we may easily recognise several of the sources from which it has drawn its materials.

(d) First of all the grammar of the Māhārāṣṭrī lyrics was made rigid and codified and for this the undisputed authority is V a r a r u c i : this was followed by the rules regarding the use of dialects on the stage. We have seen after examining the chapter XVII of Bharata that there were rules written in Prākrit. Such a literature, made for the actors, was destined to disappear; so it is not astonishing that we have not found its some other traces. But it could go over and enter into the grammatical works on Prākrit. The correspondences between the *Nāṭyaśāstra* and the Eastern grammarians, so far as they concern the *bhāṣās* (other than Māhārāṣṭrī) and the *vibhāṣās*, show that grammars and treatises on the dramatic art were closely connected to one another. The *bhāṣās* and the *vibhāṣās* are merely dialects spoken by actors on the stage, whence their evident character of artifice or at least of convention.

(e) But the theatre was not the unique domain of the

Indian dialects; several of them possessed an already rich literature.

(f) Since the moment they came to be employed in the lyrics, they became *Apabhraṁśa* ; it is probable that these lyrics had been particularly flourishing in *Nāgarāpabhraṁśa*; it is possible that there existed grammars of this Apabhraṁśa and that these grammars had been utilized by the Eastern grammarians.

(g) Are we attracted by our fascination for symmetry or are we permitted to imagine that Paiśācī had been the language of stories ? This type—the tradition of the Bṛhatkathā makes this authentic—employed might have in the beginning a particular language, which—without entering into the question of relationship that it might have with this or that real tongue of India—had remained the model for all the posterior works. It was necessary to draw its rules and to add them, as was done by the Eastern grammarians, to the grammars of the dialects employed on the scene and in lyric poetry.

(h) Let us admit for a moment that the stories of Marseilles in France—that a Parisian would never dare narrate without putting the *assent* in it—or in Germany the Jew-stories, become a type of widely circulating and very popular literature; will it be so astonishing to think that one may be tempted to write rules of pronunciation and of grammar necessary for the narrator, in order that the desired effect may be attained ? In this case we would not have a veritable grammar of the Marseilles-dialect or of Yiddish—far from this—but something that would approach very much the sūtras of the Prākrit grammarians on Kekayapaiśācī.

(i) The Eastern grammars, in our opinion, are also collections, as much complete as possible, of the rules that regulated the execution of different literary types. An author might possibly have felt the necessity of discussing the principles of writing gāthās in Māhārāṣṭrī, following the example of Hāla, of the rôles of dialects in a drama like the Mṛcchakaṭika or the Śakuntalā, of verses or poems in Apabhraṁśa, as in the *Prākṛtapiṅgalasūtra* or in the *Bhavisattakaha* and stories on the model of the *Bṛhatkathā*.

4112. The pieces of information that we have, therefore, have the value only for the particular texts that the Eastern grammarians had in view while they were writing their grammars. It has been seen in the chapter on Vararuci that the rules of Māhārāṣṭrī-lyrics are perfectly in accord with the language of the anthology of Hāla. Should we then accuse the grammars in case they do not adapt themselves now to Śaurasenī of the dramas for which they were not written ?

4113. And should the fault be considered to lie with the grammarians, in case majority of the Indian and European scholars took pains to correct and normalise all the manuscripts of classical dramas to the extent of levelling all the dialectical differences, when even authors like Kālidāsa had to take so much pains to honour them ?

4114. Lastly are we justified in taking a decision about the grammar of the language of the Bṛhatkathā, when the work itself has disappeared?

4115. The task of the Eastern grammarians had not been easy in the course of this production, so extended in time and space, on account of this continual confusion of languages and literary types.

4116. I cannot dare say that their performance had been fine; but an equitable judgment, with all the attenuating circumstances, may be pronounced in their favour.

4117. M ā r k a ṇ ḍ e y a, particularly—a bad linguist, but a fine philologist—would merit to be taken out of his clumsy edition in Devanāgarī, devoid of notes and index for the purpose of being introduced honourably into the European Indianism.

CHAPTER IV

5. KRAMADĪŚVARA

51. The grammar of K r a m a d ī ś v a r a, the S a ṁ k ṣ i p t a s ā r a, has enjoyed great popularity in the eastern regions of India. A large number of commentaries and appendices have sprung up about it. In 1738 Father P o n s, a Jesuit missionary, had made its abridgement and sent the same to Paris : it was also due to him that in 1733 a copy of the eighth book, that deals with Prakrit, was acquired in the Bibliothèque du Roy[1].

52. Nearly a century later M o n t g o m e r y M a r t i n tells us that at Dinajpur (Dinadjpour) students spend ten years in studying the S a ṁ k ṣ i p t a s ā r a of Kramadīśvara[2].

1. *Lettres édifiantes et curieuses écrites des Missions étrangères,* nouvelle édition, *Mémoires des Indes*, t. VIII. A Lyon, Vernarel, Cabin 1819, p. 39 (of Father Pons, missionary of the society of Jesus, to Father du Halde, of the same society) : "A Careical, sur la côte de Tanjaour aux Indes Orientales, November 23, 1740... *Anubhūti* (*Anoubhout*) was the first scholar who formed a structure of grammar : this is the *Sārasvata* (*Sarasvat*), a work worthy of Sarasvatī, according to the Indians, the goddess of speech and speech itself. Although it is the briefest of all the grammars, on account of its antiquity it has been very popular in Indian schools. P a n i a, along with S ā r a s v a t a (*Sarasvat*) formed a great work on the rules of Sanskrit (*Samskeret*). King J u m a r a n a n d i n (J a m o u r) got it abridged through K r a m a d ī ś v r a (*Kramadisvar*); and this grammar that I have abridged and I sent two years ago and which was undoubtedly handed over to you. K a l ā p a (*Kalap*) composed from it a (work), that is more appropriate to the sciences. There are its three other authors, but the glory of its invention mainly goes to A n o u b h o u t"

M. J e a n F i l l i o z a t had found in the Bibliothèque Nationale and he took the trouble of showing me the grammar written by Father Pons, who follows the sūtras of Kramadīśvara. It is included in the catalogued collection Fonds Sanskrit 551. Mr. Filliozat thinks that the letter of Father Pons has been corrected too. It is communicated in the masculine. It is likely that he had wanted to give an idea of Sanskrit to Father de Halde by placing before him his French adaptation of the Saṁkṣiptasāra at the time when a manuscript of a grammatical work written in the Bengali characters did not have much chance to be of interest for him.

2. M o n t o g o m e r y M a r t i n, *History of Eastern India,* 1838,

53. This notability may very well be accommodated in India with outright ignorance of the date of the work and of the historical personality of its author; after we have exhausted all our efforts to remove this lacunae, we can simply resign ourselves to other European scholars. Montgomery Martin had already tried to obtain information from Pandits, but they were not in a position to satisfy his curiosity. All that we know—and there is almost nothing precise—had been put together and examined by Zachariae[1].

After him nothing important has been found.

54. Kramadīśvara was probably an inhabitant of (West) Bengal, that is the province bounded on the north by the Gaṅgā, and on the east by the Hugli, because it is there that Rājendralāl Mitra tells us that the *Saṁkṣiptasāra* is mostly studied. This single argument appears insufficient to me, but perhaps it finds a confirmation in the stanza that concludes the 8th pāda and consequently the whole grammar of Kramadīśvara :—

vidyātaporthī vādīndraḥ pūrvagrāmī dvijaḥ kaviḥ ।
cakrapāṇisuto jyāyānnaptāsau śrīpateḥ kṛtī ॥

The ancestral house of Pūrvagrāmin or Pūrvagrāma is situated in Rāḍhā according to N. Dasgupta. Subsequently a branch of the family migrated to Chittagong[2].

55. As regards the date of composition of the *Saṁkṣiptasāra*, we know nothing at all. We have taken up the habit of placing *Kramadīśvara* between Hemacandra (1088-1172) and Vopadeva (13th century). This may be provisionally admitted, subject to the condition that these dates are not consi-

vol. II, p. 713; "The course of study in a Hindu academy begins with vyakorno or Sangskrit grammar and literature. For the first 10 years some study a grammar called Songkhyeptosar, said to have been composed by a Brahman Komodiswor, concerning whose history the Pandits could give me no information. The history of grammar is sometimes facilitated by the commentary of Goyichondro".

1. Th. Zachariae, *Citate in Kramadīśvara's Saṁkṣiptasāra* : Bezz. Beitr. V, 1880, pp. 22-63. We have borrowed all the pieces of information from him of which the sources have not been expressly stated.

2. *The Bengali commentators on the Amarakoṣa* : *Indian Culture*, Calcutta, October 1935, p. 265, with reference to Nārāyaṇa Vidyāvinoda (cf. p. 134).

dered to be like insurmountable frontiers and that one is always inclined to change these with the least amount of suspicion.

56. The first seven books of the *Saṁkṣiptasāra* form an abridgement of the grammar of Pāṇini and its eighth chapter is devoted to Prākrit. The entire work has been provided with a commentary Rasavatī (*vṛtti*) by Jūmarananadin: we have not found a single manuscript of the *Saṁkṣiptasāra* that in the colophon does not mention Jūmaranandin and his commentary. On this account this school of grammar is called also Jaumara. Its adversaries rejoice greatly with the name Jūmaranandin, since that would be the name of a weaver[1]. In the colophon on the contrary, Jūmaranandin is honoured with the epithet Maharājādhirāja Śrīmajjūmaranandin, a thing that is attested by Father Pons (cf. § 51).

57. This *Saṁkṣiptasāra*, with the commentary of Jūmaranandin, has been commented upon several times. The commentary (*ṭīkā*), that is most famous, is that of Goyīcandra (Autthāsani (or-li l)*kamahāpaṇḍitaśrīgoyīcandra*, who stops at the end of the chapter VII. It has been edited in full by Śyāmācaraṇa Kaviratna[2]. There are commentaries upon this commentary (the *Vyākaraṇadīpikā* of Nyāyapañcānana, (cf. footnotes, § 512), the *vyākaraṇādarśa* of Vaṁśivādanakavicandra and the Ṭippanī of Abhirāma Sarvavidyālaṁkārabhaṭṭācārya[3]), who naturally do not comment upon this pāda, that is devoted to Prākrits.

On this very account perhaps Belvalkar has declared that this eighth pāda had been added posteriorly[4]. However, there is nothing in the text that may authorise us to make this exclusion.

58. All the manuscripts of the Saṁkṣiptasāra, that I have been able to know, begins with the stanza :

1. S. K. Belvalkar : *Systems of Sanskrit Grammar*, Poona 1915, p. 108.

2. Calcutta, Medical Hall Library, 1911. The edition contains also the 8th book of the *Saṁkṣiptasāra*. The commentary of Goyīcandra is very voluminous and very rarely we find whole of it in a MS.

3. Cf. Zachariae, 1, 1, p. 23 and the *Catalogues* of the *India Office Library*.

4. Systems of Sanskrit Grammar, p. 109.

śivaṁ praṇamya sarveśaṁ sarvabhāṣāsu lakṣaṇam I
saṁkṣiptasāramācaṣṭe paṇḍitaḥ kramadīśvaraḥ II

In his commentary Goyīcandra[1] explains these words as follows: *śivaṁ praṇamya sarvabhāṣāsu saṁskṛta-prākṛta-paiśacyādiṣu saṁkṣiptalakṣaṇaṁ kramadīśvaranāmā paṇḍita ācaṣṭe bravītīti ślokārthaḥ* : and he adds further below : *saṁskṛtabhāṣālakṣaṇāni samāpyāṣṭamena pādena* (*prākṛtabhāṣā*) *lakṣaṇāni viracitāni.*

This proves that when Goyīcandra wrote his commentary the *Saṁkṣiptasāra* was divided, as at present, into eight pādas, of which the last one was devoted to Prākrits. We do not have any external ground to suspect the authenticity of this last section of the *Saṁkṣiptasāra.*

In addition to the rules on Prākrits, the eighth pāda contains a brief treatise on prosody and rhetorics too.

59. The manuscripts of this eighth pāda are very rare. In Europe I know of a single Bengali MS in Paris, Fonds Sanskrit 569, acquired for the Bibliothèque Nationale in 1733 through the efforts of Father Pons. This manuscript does not bear its date, but probably it was transcribed in the 17th century. It contains also a fragment of the *Prākṛtadīpikā*-commentary (*ṭīkā*) of Caṇḍīdeva Śarman, transcribed in the same hand: this fragment terminates at the sūtra 84 of Kī (=41 of the *halkārya* of the printed editions and contains the whole of the phonetics of vowels and a portion of the phonetics of consonants[2].

It is this Bengali manuscript that was utilized by Lassen in his *Institutions* through a copy made for him by Jacquet[3].

1. This was consulted by me in the MS of the Bibliothèque Nationale, Fonds Sanskrit 590.

2. He begins thus :—

oṁ namaḥ śivāya
praṇamya gurumānandaṁ sāndrakāruṇyavāridhim I
śrīkṛṣṇākhyaṁ parātmānaṁ tadīyaprītihetave II
śobhākarakulodbhūtaśrīcaṇḍīdevaśarmaṇā
kriyateṣṭamapādasya ṭīkā prākṛtadīpikā II

tatra "sarvabhāṣāsu lakṣaṇaṁ saṁkṣiptasāramācaṣṭe" (=Kī 1, *maṅgala*) *ityayena prathamaṁ pratijñātaṁ sampūrṇasarvabhāṣāsu saṁskṛtaprākṛtādirūpāsu yallakṣaṇaṁ tadeva spaṣṭaṁ vaktavyamiti* I *tatredānīṁ sampūrṇasaṁskṛtabhāṣālakṣaṇaṁ lakṣaṇāntaram ārabhate: samṛddhyetyādi,* etc.

3. This transcription, made so carefully that it can veritably replace the original, is preserved in the Bibliothèque Nationale (Fonds Sanskrit 578).

This eighth pāda with the commentary of Jūmaranandin had been edited by Śyāmācaraṇa Kaviratna in his complete edition of the *Saṁkṣiptasāra*, already referred to above. Besides Grierson (JRAS 1925, p. 25) and Pischel (Gramm. § 37) had utilized an edition brought out in Calcutta in 1889 that I do not know. On the contrary I have made use of an Indian edition in the Devanāgarī script; my copy has its first folio missing, and the end contains the signature of the printer[1]. Moreover, M. Helmer Smith had lent to me the rotographic copy belonging to Sir George Abraham Grierson of the edition prepared by Rājendra Lāl Mitra for the Bibliotheca Indica that was never published.

510. The text of the printed editions is sensibly in agreement with that of the Bengali MS of the Bibliothèque Nationale, excepting some divergences of reading that are imputable to the form of the Bengali character.

511. Another work, the *Prākṛtapāda* of Nārāyaṇa Vidyāvinoda, too was considered by Rājendralāl Mitra to be a commentary on the Prākrit grammar of Kramadīśvara[2]. But as noted by Pischel[3] the Prākṛtapāda is a wholly independent of the Saṁkṣiptasāra. A copy of this work is preserved in the library of Oxford and I was able to consult its transcription made by Helmer Smith[4].

512. The manuscript of the Oxford Library consists only of six *paricchedas* corresponding to the first seven sections of the grammar of Vararuci (ed. Bhāmaha—Cowell). The two books on the declension of nouns and pronouns form only a single whole (cf. above § 2212).

The introductory stanzas are the same as in the *Notices* of Rājendralāl Mitra; consequently there is no doubt that both of them relate to the same work.

Moreover, the beginning, cited by R. Mitra too, is sufficient to explain his mistake. The first two sūtras of Vararuci are connected together as in Kramadīśvara : *samṛddhyādiṣu at ādvā*.

1. Printed by Pitambar Bandyopadhyaya at the Anglo-Sanskrit Press, N. 2 Narbadi Nostgar's Lane.

2. Rājendralāl Mitra; *Notices*, IV, p. 162, No. 1594.

3. Gramm. § 37.

4. Aufrecht, Cat. Bibl. Bodl. p. 181; cf. also C. Bendall, *Cat. of Skt. mss. in the British Museum*, London, 1902, No. 377.

In the introduction the author declares that he has abridged an earlier work[1] : *saṁkṣepeṇa*: this would refer to *Saṁkṣiptasāra* of Kramadīśvara; the first sūtra confirms this

1. The introductory-verses of the *Prākṛtapāda* studied by Pischel in his Gramm. § 37 are quoted below :—

oṁ namo gaṇeśāya
prāksargād eka etasmin bahudhā yovabhāsate 1
taṁ vande nityanānandaṁ nandanandanamīśvaram 11
pūrvagrāmikule kalānidhinibhacchatrī sumerusthito 1
bhrātā tasya jaṭādharo dvijavaro bāṇeśvarastatsutaḥ 11
tatputraḥ prathitobhavatkavivaro nārāyaṇo nāmataḥ 1
tenedaṁ kriyate sukhāya viduṣāṁ yat prākṛtaṁ lakṣaṇaṁ 11
kṛtinā yat kṛtaṁ pūrvaṁ tan nirastaṁ durātmanā 1
idānīṁ tat samuddhṛtya saṁṣepeṇocyate mayā 11

In spite of so much details about the family, we have here no information about the age of Nārāyaṇa Vidyāvinoda (since this is the complete name of the author of the Prākṛtapāda. Another work that should certainly be ascribed to him is the commentary on the *Amarakośa*, the *Śabdārthadīpikā*, in the beginning of which Nārāyaṇa repeats almost word for word the stanzas devoted to his genealogy (cf. *Catalogue, India Office*, II, p. 273, No. 964). According to N. N. Dasgupta (*Indian Culture*, October, 1935, p. 265) Nārāyaṇa could be placed towards the end of 15th century A. D. or the beginning of the 16th century; but this hypothetical dating is uniquely based on the identification of Jaṭādhara, grandfather of Nārāyaṇa with the author of the lexicon Abhidhānatantra, Now this identification is too far from being sure, and Aufrecht, *Cat. Cat.* does not accept it.

Ordinarily Nārāyaṇa is considered to be the author of two grammatical works of the school of Kramadīśvara, and it is one of the reasons for considering the *Prākṛtapāda* a commentary on the 8th pāda of the *Saṁkṣiptasāra* (cf. for example, *Cat., Ind. Office* II, p. 221, No. 830 and references). The two works are the *Gaṇaprakāśa* (ibid No. 838, p. 224), commentary on the *gaṇas* of the Saṁkṣiptasāra and the Vyākāraṇdīpikā, commentary on the commentary written by Goyīcandra for the *Saṁkṣiptasāra* (ibid p. 221, No. 830). I believe, on the contrary that the author of these two works is the son of the former. In fact his name is Nyāyapañcānana, and he himself gives the name of his father as Vidyāvinoda, and he belongs to the same *kula* of the Pūrvagrāmins (cf. § 54), whence descended Kramadīśvara as well. Cf. Introduction to the Gaṇaprakāśa :

natvā kṛṣṇapadadvandvam arcitaikāntasādhanam 1
gaṇaprakāśaḥ kriyate nyāyapañcānanena ca 11

Colophon :— *iti pūrvagrāmilokulakalānidhimahāmahopādhyāyavidyāvinodātmaja-śrīmadācārya-pañcānanakṛto gaṇaprakāśaśca sampūrṇaḥ* 1

hypothesis and no further investigation has been made by anybody. It would suffice, however, to glance at the second sūtra for setting aside the view considering the Prākṛtapāda to be a commentary on the *Saṁkṣiptasāra*. Kī says *it pakvādeḥ* and the Prākṛtapāda *id īṣatpakvasvapnavetasavyajanakamṛdaṅgāreṣu ca* like Vararuci.

513. This view is supported by the sequence as well. The *Prākṛtapāda* of Nārāyaṇa Vidyāvinoda is simply a different edition of Vararuci, wholly analogous to that of Vasantarāja (cf. § 244). The sūtras are the same, except that there are certain differences in respect of the detail : thus for example, the natural habit of Nārāyaṇa Vidyāvinoda to amalgamate the adhikāra in the sūtras that follow. This is already attested in the beginning of the work where *āderataḥ* of Vararuci is included in the sūtra on the optional lengthening of the *a* of *samṛddhi* etc. One could think that Nārāyaṇa Vidyāvinoda had wanted here to begin his work with a word of *maṅgala*; but this reason is not valid for the sūtras of Vararuci III, 10-11; *yuktasya* and *ṣṭhasya ṭhaḥ* are mixed up together in Nārāyaṇa Vidyāvinoda (Oxford MS, end of the fol. 8 recto); *yujaṣṭasya ṭhaḥ* or for Vr. III, 59-60; *viprakarṣaḥ* and *kliṣṭa-śliṣṭa-ratna-kriyā-śārṅgeṣu' tatsvaravat pūrvasya.* Nārāyaṇa Vidyāvinoda (fol. 12 verso) *kliṣṭaśliṣṭaratnakriyāśārṅgeṣu vikārastatsvaravat svaraśca pūrvasya.*

It is rather a case of refinement of the grammarian, happy at his ability to reduce the number of sūtras through an artifice.

On the contrary, at one place a *kārikā* of Vasantarāja has entered into the text : Vas. I, 25 under the sūtra *udūto madhūkādiṣu* (cf. Vr. I, 24) adds :—*mūlatāmbūlayostu ottvam ūkārasyeṣyate budhaiḥ* l *mollaṁ* l .. *tambolaṁ* l. This treatment of *mūlya* and *tāmbūla* forms, in addition, the subject-matter of a sūtra in Nārāyaṇa Vidyāvinoda (MS Oxford, fol. 3 R).

514. But in case we leave aside these minute differences, the accord between the Prākṛtasañjīvanī of Vasantarāja and the Prākṛtapāda of Vidyāvinoda is striking[1]. Every time the form of a sūtra of

1. Cf. for example in regard to the irregular words the verses of Vasantarāja (IV, 35) that occur ad verbatim in Vidyāvinoda.

Vasantarāja differs from that of Bhāmaha, it is the former who is followed by Nārāyaṇa Vidyāvinoda.

The citations of Vasantarāja occur very often in Vidyāvinoda as well. Moreover, Vidyāvinoda had desired to identify them and he had added the names of their ostensible authors.

We shall learn further about the *kārikās* from the following list. According to Vidyāvinoda, these ślokas would be going back to famous grammatical treatises.

Vararuci :—

Vas. II, 7 *tasya ḍatvaṁ harītakyāṁ prābhṛte mṛtake tathā* I

Nār. Vidyā. harītakyāṁ (ḍa)kāraḥ syāt prākṛte mṛtake tathā II
iti vararuciḥ.

Vas. II, 30 *mlecchavācye lacādeśau na hare kāmarūpiṇi* I

Nār. Vidyā. mlecchavācikirāte co na hare kāmarūpiṇi II
iti vararuciḥ.

Vas. IV, 16 *saṁskāre saṁskṛtāyaṁ tu nityaṁ bindur vilupyate* I

Nār. Vidyā. saṁskārasaṁskṛtādau tu nityaṁ bindurvilupyate iti vararuciḥ II

Vas. V, 51 *savvesiṁ āmi savvāṇaṁ sarvaliṅgeṣu tatsamam* I

Nār. Vidyā. savvesiṁ† vātha savvāsiṁ† sarvaliṅgeṣu tatsamam I
iti vararuciḥ.

Vas. V, 55 *ādeśaḥ sarvaśabdasya kāle ṅerāi iṣyate* I

Nār. Vidyā. pakṣe ca ṅer iādeśaḥ kāle syāt sarvaśabdataḥ II
iti vararuciḥ.

Vas. VI, 5 *akārāntān niyamyete ntamāṇau kvāpi paṇḍitaiḥ* I

Nār. Vidyā. akārāntān† niyasyante† māṇau kutracid bhavaiḥ II
iti vararuciḥ.

Kātyāyana := (Vararuci ?)

Vas. V, 11 *sarvādiṣvidamo dīrgho na tvanyeṣāṁ ṅasau bhavet* I

Nār. Vidyā. sarvādiṣvidamo dīrgho na tvanyeṣāṁ ṅasau bhavet II
iti kātyāyanaḥ.

Vas. V, 42 *bhisbhyasorāṁsuporitvaṁ rājñokārasya ceṣyate* I

Nār. Vidyā. bhisbhyasor āṁsuporpitvaṁ rājñokārasya ce bhasyāt † iti kātyāyanaḥ.

Vas. V, 55 *kāle ṅeretad asyāhe ekaśabdād iā tu vā* I

Nār. Vidyā. iṣṭo ṅeretadastvāha ekaśabdād iā tathā I
iti kātyaḥ.

Vas. V, 60 *ādeśāvidamaścānyau sau puṁsyamiaṁ striyām* 1
Nār. Vidyā. *ādeśāvidamaścānyau sau puṁsi amiyaṁ striyām* 1
iti kātyaḥ.

Śākaṭāyana

Vas. IV, 18 *nāntaṁ napuṁsake viddhi puṁlliṅgepi praśasyate* 1
Nār. Vidyā. *nāntaṁ napuṁsakaṁ viddhi puṁliṇgepi pracakṣate* 11
iti śākaṭāyanaḥ.
Vas. IV, 23 *prāyahśabdaḥ kagacādīnāṁ lopātivyāptibādhaka ityeteṣu udāharaṇeṣu kagacādinā lopo yādṛcchikaḥ* 1
Nār. Vidyā. *prāyaḥśabdakādināṁ lopotivyāptibādhaka iti śākaṭāyanavacanāt.*
Vas. V, 42 *ṅasiṅyor jasśasorājña irvādeśenajādike* 1
Nār. Vidyā. *ṅasiṅyor jasśaso rājñaḥ pūrvadeśena*† *jādvitekif*
iti śākaṭāyanaḥ.

Vas. V, 55 *ālā ityapi yattadbhyāṁ kāle vācye vadanti te* 1
Nār. Vidyā. *alā ityapi yattadbhyāṁ kāle vācye vadanti ṅeḥ* 11
iti śākaṭāyaṇaḥ.

Mahābhāṣya

Vas. V, 59 *napuṁṣake svamoḥ katvaṁ na kimaḥ syād aluptayoḥ* 1
Nār. Vidyā. *napuṁsake svamo ka(tva)ṁ na kimaḥ syācca luptayoḥ* 11 *iti bhāṣyam.*

Kāśikā

Vas. IV, 25 *bhavetāṁ matupontyasya ākārastu tathā kvacit* 1
Nār. Vidyā. *bhavetāṁ matupontyasya*<*ā*>*kāro tathā kvacit* 11
iti vāmanaḥ.
Vas. V, 41. *ṇo ṅaserṇatvadvitvaṁ syāt rājño lopaśca jasya vā* 1
Nār. Vidyā. *ṇo ṅaservā bhaved dvitaṁ rājño lopaśca jasya* 1
iti vāmanaḥ.
Vas. V, 61 *syāt pratyayāntarepyatvaṁ striyāmanyatra cedamaḥ* 1
Nār. Vidyā. *syāt pratyayāntarepyevaṁ striyāmanyatra vedama*
iti kāśikāvṛttiḥ.
Vas. V, 80 *āhuḥ e di tu ityanyānādeśānāni yuṣmadaḥ.*
Nār. Vidyā. *tathā ca kāśikāvṛttiḥ* 11
āhe vedi tu† *ismān*† *ādeśān yuṣmadaṣṭayā* 11
Vas. VI, 4 *ire ityapi vādeśaśtipo jherjhasya ca smṛtaḥ* 1

Nār. Vidyā. ire ityapi ādeśaḥ<*pratha*>*masya smṛto budhaiḥ* ll
iti vāmanaḥ.

J i n e n d r a

Vas. V, 58 *striyāmapi sahaivāmā syācca siṁ idamopi vā* l
Nār. Vidyā. striyāmapi† *saivāmā syāt itīdamo*† *vā* ll
iti jinendraḥ.

K ā t a n t r a

Vas. VI, 12 *kātantrepyuktaṁ bhaviṣyati bhavisyantyāśiśca tisra iti* l
Nār. Vidyā. tathā ca kātantram l *bhaviṣyantyāśīḥ śvastana iti.*

This last quotation—the only one of which Vasantarāja mentions his source—is eventually found in the *Kātantra* (cf. ed. L i e b i c h III, 1, 15 *bhaviṣyati bhaviṣyantyāśīḥśvastanyaḥ* and the variants)

It is also the single citation that corresponds to a general fact of grammar and so it might be found in Sanskrit grammatical treatises.

515. As regards others it is evident that the attributions of Nārāyaṇa are wrong. So how these kārikās meant to complete the sūtras of Vararuci on Prākrit grammar could occur in the *Mahābhāṣya* of Patañjali or in the *Kāśikā* ? But why did Nārāyaṇa add these names ? This is a sort of perversity in the variety of attributions: why was the name of even Jinendra dragged in for attributing to him a rule on the genitive plural of the pronoun *idam* in Prākrit ?

516. I express my inability to solve this problem : the list of citations—which without this would not merit to be printed—will suggest perhaps some other explanation that I could not find on account of these fantastical attributions.

517. L a s s e n at once saw that Kramādīśvara knew and reproduced a large portion of the sūtras of Vararuci on the principal Prākrit[1].

518. Since his view has been generally accepted, it is of no use to revert to this question. However, as admitted by

1. Cf. particularly, Inst., p. 39-49 of the Excursus V.

Lassen himself, the sūtras of Vararuci are presented in the Saṁkṣiptasāra at times under different aspects and in a different order. Moreover, Kramadīśvara added a certain number of new sūtras and on the other hand he ignored many of those that occurred in the Prākṛtaprakāśa.

519. A comparison with the different commentaries on Vararuci has not been instructive. On the whole Kramadīśvara appears to have known a redaction of the sūtras that was closer to that of Bhāmaha than to that of Vasantarāja. On the other hand in certain cases it is the reading of Vasantarājā[1] that he has adopted.

520. In most of the cases Kramadīśvara, stands in opposition to all the commentators on Vararuci and Vararuci himself. Thus for example he knew the phenomenon of *yaśruti* (Kī II, 6, 7, cf. Hc. 1, 180) that appears to be unknown among the sūtras of Vararuci. The number of sūtras of Vararuci that do not have their correspondences in the *Saṁkṣiptasāra* is quite considerable : Vr. II, 18, 19, 37; III, 4, 13, 19, 25, 34, 49, 51, 54, 56 (attested in Bhāmaha alone); IV, 3, 4, 8, 11, 12, 17, 21, 26, 27, 29, 30, 31; V, 2, 3, 5, 10, 13, 17, 24, 25, 27, 28, 29, 41, 44, 46, 47; VI, 1, 12, 13, 16, 17, 21, 22, 33, 38, 42, 47, 60, 61, 62; VII, 5, 11, 17, 21, 27, 29; VIII, 5 (attested only in Bhāmaha) 9, 20 (attested only in Bhāmaha), 42, 44, 58, 59, 61, 65, 71; IX, 11, 17 (attested only in Bhāmaha.

521. It may here be mentioned that these may be interpolations and marginal notes, having been got included into the body of the text. and that Kramadīśvara helps us in reconstructing the original Vararuci. Unfortunately the list of innovations of Kramadīśvara is almost equally long : Kī I, 12, 14, 20, 31; II, 6, 7, 15, 33, 37, 60, 73, 75, 84, 97, 107, 110, 113, 114, 116, 124, 125, 130, 143-148; III, 10, 22, 46, 53, 54, 88; IV, 21, 27, 32, 33, 34, 35, 36, 46, 17, 27, 30, 32, 34, 35, 37, 38, 47; 50, 69, 81, 82, 83 comm. (*prākṛtaṁ gāthādau, taraṁ hārye*)[2].

1. Ex. Kī I, 4 *śayyāder et*=Bhāmaha I, 5 *e śayyādiṣu* vis-a-vis Vas. I, 5 *e ca śayyādiṣu*; Kī I, 8 *lavaṇabadarayor nityaṁ* = Bhāmaha I, 6 *o badare dena*; 7 *lavaṇanavamallikayorvena*, vis-a-vis Vas. I, 6 *o badare dena* without anything further (but a kārikā of Vas. I, 6 adds *otvaṁ saha vakāreṇa lavaṇepyasya cesyate*). However Kī I, 13, 28, 32, 33; II, 16, 26, 34, 76, 101, 109; III, 29, 49, 50, 62, 78 etc. On the other hand Kī I, 10 *sadāśabdasyed vā* = Vas I, 10 *it sadā* vis-a-vis Bhām. I, 11 *it sadādiṣu*. However, Kī II, 47, 135; III, 48 (=Vas. VI, 11) etc.

2. Some errors possibly may have crept into my lists in the sense

522. Perhaps it will be astonishing to note that I speak of Kramadīśvara without ever indicating if I do this on the basis of the Bengali manuscript of the Bibliothèque Nationale or on that of the edition printed at the Anglo-Sanskrit Press or on that of the rotograph of the edition prepared by Rājendralāl Mitra. I do it because the text almost does not differ in this regard: moreover, the quotations given by Pischel in his grammar and taken, as stated by him, from the Calcutta edition of 1889, too point to a text identical with the one known to me through my three sources.

523. This accord is hopeless, since we have to admit that the sūtras of Kramadīśvara do not have a perfect form and so they do not merit such a religious respect.

524. For example a sūtra such as Kī I, 27 *ṛt* is certainly laconical, because it does not have a single more letter in any of the copies of the *Saṁkṣiptasāra*, pāda VIII. In all the copies, the commentary interprets this monosyllabic sūtra only as *ṛkārod bhavati* and that it teaches change of *ṛ* into *a*, a thing that is very frequent in Prākrit. The preceding sūtras do not authorise elision of an *a*. Since the corresponding sūtra of Vararuci (I, 27) has the form *ṛtot*, it would be possible to imagine that a copyist has left a portion of it while writing—a copyist, perhaps three copyists, perhaps more, not to mention a Paṇḍit like Rājendralāl Mitra.

525. It appears exactly as if all the editors of the eighth pāda had taken the trouble of coming over to Paris to copy the Bengal manuscript of the Bibliothèque Nationale or if all of them had the possibility of copying it before the MS was carried to France from India.

526. Now this eighth pāda, in regard to the sūtras of Vararuci on the principal Prākrit, is at the same time incomplete and elaborated. In brief it is *Saṁkṣipta*, if one so likes, to call it so, but not of only Vararuci. And the choice of Kramadīśvara cannot in all cases be defended.

that I was not able to know always in a corrupt or difficult sūtra of Kramadīśvara the original text that for him might have correspondence among the sūtras of Vararuci. Thus for example Kī II, 74 that presents itself in all the texts in the form *lobhārthe vāṣme* and should evidently be corrected as *loṭārthe vāṣpe* (=Vr. III, 38); Kī II, 126 had been deplaced and had been rendered incomprehensible; probably even the sūtra that preceded it has dropped, but in any event there is no doubt that Kī II, 126 corresponds to Vr. IV, 13.

527. Kramadīśvara had wanted at all costs to be concise, and to attain this end he did not hesitate to sacrifice even the essential sūtras of Vararuci. On the contrary, while he was doing this, he brought in some sūtras of a different origin of which the importance had been secondary.

528. For example, he has always tried to diminish the number of sūtras by incorporating the adhikāras in the sūtras that follow. We have already seen that Nārāyaṇa, the commentator on Vararuci, too has done the same thing (cf. § 513). Moreover, in the book on declension, he has repeated in respect of each of the endings the modifications of the thematic vowel; whilst Vararuci had said only once for all that the *-a-* of the theme could become *-e-*, etc.

529. Lastly he has always thoughtlessly shortened the list of examples given by Vararuci. Let us take for example the beginning of the word : —

Kī I, 2. *it pakvādeḥ.*

Vr 3. *id īṣat-pakva-svapna-vetasa-vyajana-mṛdaṅgāṅgāreṣu.*

Kī I, 15. *nīḍāderet.*

Vr I, 19. *ennīḍāpiḍakīdṛgīdṛśeṣu.*

Kī I, 18. *at pathyādeḥ.*

Vr I, 13 *at pathiharidrāpṛthivīṣu*, etc.

530. At the first sight one could approve of this reform of Kramadīśvara and we could even hold the view that this is not all, and that on the contrary the sūtras of Vararuci were enlarged by later commentators; but this favourable mental disposition does not resist a more careful observation: firstly in the commentary of Kramadīśvara we find the words that were enumerated by Vararuci, there is nothing more, nothing less. Then Vararuci too applies often °*ādi-* or °*sama-* or °*rūpa-* for indicating the categories of words. In case he has not done this in these other cases, therein he has a motive behind it. When Vararuci, for example, says *ā samṛddhyādiṣu vā* (I, 2), it was a case of an *ākṛtigaṇa*; a large number of Māhārāṣṭrī words undergo this lengthening of *a*. In the same manner, the sūtra *ita et piṇḍasameṣu* (Vr I, 12) is meant to indicate the homogeneity of words in which *i* becomes *e* before a consonant-group.

531. Thus we see that when Vararuci has, for example, enumerated the words that have the treatment *a*>*i*, there he

has in view a treatment that holds good for a group of well-defined words only. It is true that he could have enumerated these words without wasting much space and without loss of too much time, since he was writing the rules about a type of clearly delimited texts. Sometimes we have the impression that he worked upon some indexes of words of the Māhārāṣṭrī lyrics.

532. It is this adherence to a group of texts in which lies the value of the effort of Vararuci, a thing that is partly missing in the grammar of Kramadīśvara.

533. This too should be noted that Kramadīśvara had written an appendix to his grammar of Sanskrit : so he was accustomed to refer to a Gaṇapāṭha : he continued the same habit for Prākrit as well, where probably the Gaṇapāṭha did not exist.

534. So I believe that for the principal Prākrit Kramadīśvara does not convey the interest that was lent to him by Cowell, who perhaps knew nothing about him excepting the extracts cited by Lassen[1].

535. Kramadīśvara is capable of rendering the only service of guaranteeing the sūtras of Vararuci, when there is an agreement between the two. In cases where there is no agreement, his testimony is not of great value. In addition to Vararuci, he had certainly utilized some other sources (the list of the innovations attests this, unless he himself was not its author, a thing that *a priori* is difficult to be admitted).

536. Among these sources, Pischel had sought to include Hemacandra[2], but in 1886 in the face of insistence of Zachariae, he loyally admitted that there was nothing to prove that Kramadīśvara knew Hemacandra[3]. However, he was convinced that Kramadīśvara had been posterior to Hemacandra, because "he knew a larger number of dialects"[4]. We now know that this is not the single proof.

537. Besides the dialects studied by Kramadīśvara are not very numerous. In addition to the principal Prākrit, he studies Apabhraṁśa, Śaurasenī, Māgadhī, Paiśācī; incidentally

1. Cf. Preface to the edition of Vararuci, p. XII.
2. De Gramm. Prācṛ, p. 16.
3. BB V, p. 27 note.
4. Gramm. § 37.

he mentions Ardhamāgadhī and relieves himself in a few words of all the dialects of the theatre. This is perhaps the last list that made Pischel disquiet; the names of these dialects, however, are found in the *Nāṭyaśāstra,* that is certainly anterior to the *Siddhahzmacandra*

538. We have seen that Mārkaṇḍeya (cf. § 4100) subdivides Apabhraṁśa into three dialects: Nāgara, Vrācaḍa and Upanāgara. Kramadīśvara, I believe, adopts the same subdivision.

539. Jacobi[1], who knew merely the extract from Kramadīśvara—from the fragment very correctly edited by Lassen—(Inst. p. 449 ss.), made confusion in these names and he imagined that Vrācaḍa was the principal Apabhraṁśa studied by Kramadīśvara all along in the sūtras 1-68 of the 4th section of the *aṣṭama pāda*. This confusion influenced his entire theory about the Apabhraṁśas: fortunately Jacobi knew the texts fully well and was able to take advantage of the wrong interpretations of the sūtras of the grammarians. Notwithstanding this confusion, a reader would be benefitted by studying his introduction to the *Bhavisattakha*, by simply removing this confusion in substituting Vrācaḍāpabhraṁśa by Nāgarāpabhraṁśa every time when the matter relates to the principal Apabhraṁśa of Kramadīśvara (p. 72*). Naturally Vrācaḍa is no more the "most ancient Apabhraṁśa".

540. Just a glance at the passage of Kramadīśvara edited by Lassen will easily explain the confusion of Jacobi. Kramadīśvara explained in the first 66 sūtras the rules of an Apabhraṁśa-dialect without naming it. This is followed by a treatment of phonetics, declension and conjugation. In the sūtra 67 we pass on to another dialect.

agrādirvrācaṭāḍau. The sūtra in this form has no sense, it is rather *yugrādir* that should be read, as indicated by the commentary—a thing that Jacobi did not know :

vrācaṭāḍirapabhraṁśabhedaḥ l *tatra vrācaṭādau dohādau yuktarephasamuccāraṇam* l *sarpiḥ sarpi* l *jrudruprabhṛtiprayoktavyam* l *ktvā eppi eppiṇu*[2].

"In (the Apabhraṁśa-dialects of the type of) Vrācaṭa,

1. Introduction to the Bhavisattakaha, pp. 71* and ss.

2. Cf. Kī IV, 2 *adho ro lug* vā. Ex. *putra, putto* (Skt. *putra*).

etc. the consonant *ra* in group is preserved even when it precedes. The example in the commentary is *sarpi*; whilst *ra* is sometime preserved in the principal Apabhraṁśa in case it is the second member of the group[1].

541. The commentary adds that in these dialects too *jrum* and *drum*[2] are employed in the place of *yad* and *tad* in the accusative singular and in the absolutive the affixes *-eppi* and *-eppiṇu*[3].

542. In case one is a little familiar with the practice of the Prākrit grammarians, he at once knows that this sūtra with its commentary serves to indicate the peculiarities that distinguish *Vrācaṭāpabhraṁśa* from the dialect, so to say, the "normal one." that has been treated.

The commentary in fact says :—*vrācaṭādirapabhraṁśabhedaḥ* : "the dialects Vṛācaṭa, etc. are subdivisions of Apabhraṁśa". And it adds that this type of dialect is the dialect of the *dohās* (*dohādau*, *aḍilā*, etc.), that is to say, of the rhyming poetry ?).

This dialect, Kramadīśvara adds, behaves in all other respects like Nāgara, that is to be studied in the *rāsakas* etc : Kī IV, 70 *śeṣo nāgare rāsakādau.*

Since the expression "all other respects" comprehends almost the whole of grammar, and taking into consideration the convention of the gramarians, it follows that the dialect explained previously is the Nāgarāpabhraṁśa, employed particularly for compositions in the *rāsaka* metre.

543. An admixture of this dialect—Vrācaḷa—and of Prākrit is the Upanāgara employed in the gāthās :

saprākṛtamiśra upanāgare gāthādau.

For Mārkaṇḍeya on the contrary Upanāgara is an admixture of Nāgara and Vrācaṭa.

Jacobi should not have erred in succession to Lassen, in case the Indians had followed the practice of keeping their sub-divisions distinct by leaving a little space by the sides of the words indicating the titles. But this is a practice unknown in their manuscripts that are generally covered by compact

1. As Jacobi knew it and says according to the rotograph of Grierson in his edition of the Sanatkumāracaritam, p. xx of the introduction.

2. Cf. Kī IV, 49 *jruṁ druṁ yattadayor amā* (=Hc IV, 360).

3. Cf. Kī IV, 50 *ktva evyādiḥ* (Hc IV, 439).

rectangles of writing traversed only by the inexorable parallels for the *mātrās*.

544. As regards the literary dialect that corresponds to the principal Apabhraṁśa of Kramadīśvara, it is almost the same as treated by Hemacandra : after having compared the respective sūtras, I have acquired even the conviction that Hemacandra and Kramadīśvara had certainly utilized a common source, the source that Kramadīśvara did not disturb through foreign elements, whilst it is mixed up with others in Hemacandra. In Kramadīśvara there occur several forms that Hemacandra did not know of, but these are cases of minute differences, sometimes imputable to the uncertainty of the text of the *Saṁkṣiptasāra*[1].

545. The group of the sūtras on the declension of nouns in Apabhraṁśa will suffice, I hope, to demonstrate the analogies that exist between Kramadīśvara and Hemacandra:

Kī	Hc
IV, 17 *dīrghādiḥ saṁbuddhau*	cf. Comm. Hc. IV, 330.
IV, 18 *kvaciddhrasvaḥ*	cf. Comm. Hc. IV, 330.
IV, 19 *kvacidetvam*	
IV, 20 *jaso ho*	IV, 346 *āmantrye joho hoḥ*
IV, 21 *lukprathamādvitīyayoḥ*	IV, 344 *syamjasśasāṁ luk*
IV, 22 *atā svamorudvā*	IV, 331, *syamorasyot*
IV, 23 *puṁsyocca*	IV, 332 *sau puṁsyod vā*
IV, 24 *eṁ ṭā*	IV, 383 *eṭ ṭi*
IV, 25 *anusvāraśceṇaḥ*	IV, 342 *āṭ ṭo ṇānusvārau*
IV, 26 *puṁsi ṇā vā*	
IV. 27 *hiṁ saptamyāḥ*	(cf. IV, 341 ?)
IV. 28 *ṅeridetau cātā*	IV, 334 *ṅinecca*
IV. 29 *bhyasoto huṁ*	IV, 337 *bhyaso huṁ*
IV. 30 *ṅaserhe adū*	IV, 336 *ṅaser hehū*
IV. 31 *hosussā ṅasaḥ*	IV, 338 *ṅasaḥ suhossavaḥ*

1. Jacobi, Introduction to the Bhavisattakaha, p. 71* appears to contradict me on this point. "In any case his presentation is not dependent upon that of Hemacandra, and he teaches many deviating forms"; but we should not forget that Jacobi started with the hypothesis of Pischel, i. e. Hemacandra had been utilized by Kramadīśvara, a statement that cannot be proved.

IV. 32 *āmo haṁ*	IV, 339 *āmo haṁ*
IV. 33 *heṁ cedudbhyām*	IV, 340 *huṁ cadudbhyām*
IV. 34 *bhyaso haṁ*	cf. IV, 341 *ṅasibhyasṅīnāṁ hehuṁhayaḥ*
IV. 35 *hohaṁ ṅasiṅasoḥ*	cf. prec.
IV. 36 *hes striyām*	IV, 350 *ṅasṅasyor he*
IV. 37 *puṁsklibayoı idudbhyām*	
IV. 38 *jasśasorudotau*	IV, 348 *stiiyāṁ jasśor ud ot*
IV. 39 *ṭā e*	IV, 349 *ṭā e*

546. The concluding portion of the aṣṭamapāda of the *Saṁkṣiptasāra* is almost inutilizable. What arguments would it provide to the requisition of Th. Bloch ! No new information and such an inextricable confusion of the known facts that one would be goaded to doubt the whole, but no effort to introduce an order into this bush on the part of any of the Indian editors.

547. Such a resignation is impossible for the people of the West. Lassen[1] was the first scholar to remark that in case Kramadīśvara is to be studied literally, one ought to arrive at some amazing conclusions : the principal Prākrit would not be Māhārāṣṭrī; Śauraseni would present only some lexical peculiarities. But Lassen reacted prudently: *certum itaque est corrigendum esse locum utrumque ope testimoniorum ceterorum* = in order that we may make best use of the testimonies, we have to correct them consequently", an advice that was followed by Grierson : on the rotograph of the edition of Rājendralāl Mitra he made the pencil correction, in the sūtra IV, 70, of *mahārāṣtryāṁ* as *śaurasenyāṁ* and thus he resolved the problem brought to light by Lassen : in this way Māhārāṣṭrī again becomes the principal Prākrit and Śaurasenī gets possession of the sūtras to which it is entitled.

548. And certainly Grierson was right. Certain sūtras further below (Kī IV, 97) are relevant to Paiśācī. Apparently it has claim to only one sūtra[2], since immediately thereafter are defined Ardhamāgadhi and the dialects of the theatre. But it is evident that the treatment of Paiśācī is taken up again after

1. Inst. Excursus, p. 51.
2. *hak: hage cāhamarthe.* And this sūtra really does not come here by right, since it still belongs to Māgadhī that precedes (cf. Vr XI, 9; Hc IV, 301; Mk XII, 32).

this interruption, because the sūtras Kī IV, 101 *vargādyau tricaturthayoḥ* (=Vr X, 3; Mk XIX, 2) or 110 *hṛdayasya hitaakaṁ* (=Vr X, 4; Hc IV, 310; Mk XIX, 11) can belong only to this last dialect.

549. All this may be explained as accidents to which the manuscripts might have been subjected, such as an interversion of folios etc. Without doubt, it would be possible even to reconstruct the original text. However, it would be a fruitless effort, because, I may repeat again, that the *Saṁkṣiptasāra* adds nothing new in respect of these dialects.

550. In the track of hypotheses one would suppose also that this portion contains interpolations; it is very probable, but difficult to prove. In reality we have a single manuscript, the Fond Sanskrit 569 of the Bibliothèque Nationale, since the Indian editions, some details excepted, are its faithful reproduction. This manuscript may not be anterior to the seventeenth century. How were the manuscripts of the aṣṭamapāda of the *Saṁkṣiptasāra* presented before this date? Did they too contain the same number of dialects and the same errors in respect of their subject-matter? It is possible that they were not so; but it would not attain certainty till the time when chance will provide us with a manuscript of the aṣṭamapāda reduced to its real proportions. And in the domain of conjectural reconstructions, one may exert his mind more fruitfully than to find again with so much of trouble what Hemacandra, Mārkaṇḍeya and the pseudo-Vararuci have already taught us.

CHAPTER V

6. HEMACANDRA

61. The chance, that permitted Hemacandra to attain in the climate of India the extraordinary age of 84 years, has continued to be favourable to him even after his death.

62. This chance has been favourable in preserving his souvenir among the Jainas as a community that has been full of religious zeal and talent for publicity. Then it was chance that did him the honour of early publication of his work under the editorship of Richard Pischel.

63. In the second half of the last century the interest for Prākrit studies had been very great. Cowell's edition of the grammar of Vararuci had a second edition only a few years after its publication. By the side of the adhyāya VIII of the Siddhahema candra, it looked very small and this enhanced the fame of Hemacandra. It shone out like the midday sun after the early dawn. Vararuci, Hemacandra and posterior grammarians, about whom people had some sufficiently vague knowledge, were following a harmonious curve, the inevitable curve of all that lives on the earth, and he even appears in all the human activities : the primitive, the renaissance and the baroque.

64. No grammar, according to Pischel[1], has the importance of the *Siddhahemacandra* : he does not even dare discuss the subject for fear of being carrid too far away : "*nescirem mehercle unde initium faciendum, ubi finis ponendus esset*[2]- from the first appearance we do not know where the last boundary lies". This fear survived after the edition of the *Siddhahemacandra* and after the publication of the *Grammatik der Prākrit Sprachen,* since he had not made any important further advancement beyond what he had said in his dissertation[3].

1. De. Gr. Prācr., p. 27.
2. De Gr. Prācr., p. 26.
3. Cf. Preface to the edition, p. VI and Gramm. § 36.

65. In case Pischel had been less modest, he would have recognised that the *"magni moment*-great moment" was even not the adhyāya VIII of the *Siddhahemacandra*, but the edition thereof executed by him so carefully with a clear typographical presentation, based on so solid a doctrine and provided with such a detailed index that it appeared to foresee and satisfy all the curiosities. We have thus acquired the habit of becoming content with it for all researches on Prākrit grammar, so much so that the eclecticism of Hemacandra had almost never been wanting.

66. As regards the intrinsic value of Hemacandra, in relation to other Prākrit grammarians, it has been exaggerated by Indians and Europeans under the influence of Jaina propaganda and Pischel's authority.

67. One may pronounce a severe judgment on the Prākrit grammarians as a whole. Th Bloch did this and I would not feel inclined to defend them on the same ground: an absolute judgment based on a kind Platonic idea of grammar is not the subject under discussion.

68. But I ought to say that in my opinion, among the Prākrit grammarians, in no way does Hemacandra exhibit any particular brilliance, and above all he does not represent the perfection and the maturity of Prākrit grammar between Vararuci and decline of posterior Prākrit grammarians. As remarked by Pischel, he certainly has had several predecessors, whose works had been utilized by him. I have also the impression that he was outright lacking in originality and that it would suffice to know his sources of information for the purpose of making each current of his grammar easily separated and restored. It is nevertheless what has been transmitted by Indian tradition, a thing that is recognised by Hemacandra himself.

69. Hemacandra was born in the year 1145 of the Vikrama-era on the full-moon night of the month of Kārttika (November—December 1088 or 1089 A. D.) in the city of Dhandūka, situated near Ahmedabad, where begins the Gujarat peninsula. His parents belonged to the caste of traders, and both of them were Jainas[1]. He wrote his grammar for satis-

1. For all the biographical pieces of informations about Hema-

faction of King Jayasiṁha. In a very flattering style he has composed a *praśasti* of thirty five-verses in honour of the Caulukya princes, beginning from Mūlarāja down upto his patron Jayasiṁha, whom he exalts as :—

samyaṅniṣevya caturaścaturopyupāyāñ-
jitvopabhujya ca bhuvaṁ caturabdhikāñcīm I
vidyācatuṣṭayavinītamatirjitātmā
kāṣṭhāmavāpya puruṣārthacatuṣṭaye yaḥ II 34 II
tenātivistṛtadurāgamaviprakīrṇa-
śabdānuśāsanasamūhakadarthitena I
abhyarthito niravamaṁ vidhivadvyadhatta
śabdānuśāsanamidaṁ munihemacandraḥ II 35 II

"He has properly employed in turn the four means; he conquered and quietly possessed the earth surrounded by the four oceans; he has formed his understanding by his study of four sciences; he has subdued his soul, by thus attaining the highest goal of the four human activities[1]."

"At the demand of such a personality, repelled by the multitude of lengthy, difficult disorderly grammars, Monk Hemacandra composed according to the rules this most recent grammar."

610. According to the *Prabhāvakacaritra*, a collection of biographies of twenty-two Jaina sages, composed in the 13th century by *Prabhācandra* and *Pradyumnasurī*, *Hemacandra* asked King Jayasiṁha to procure for him a copy of the most ancient eight grammars; they were all available only in the library of the temple of Sarasvatī in Kashmir. Hemacandra had his desired satisfaction : so his grammar is a compilation from anterior works. The reading of the *Siddhahemacandra* confirms the tradition on this point : however, the efforts made for

candra, cf. G. Būhler, *Über das Leben des Jaina Mönches Hemacandra*, Wien 1889 (Denkschriften der Kais. Akad. der Wiss. Wien, Bd. XXXVII.)

1. On the four means to be employed against the enemies, cf. Manu VII, 107-109; on the four sciences necessary to a king, cf. Manu VII, 43, on the four ends of human activity, cf. Amarakośa II, 7, 57. The conquest of the earth encircled by four oceans is a common hyperbole in the praśasti-style. The number 4, that figures in all the pādas, is probably in relation with the 8 adhyāyas and the 32 pādas of the grammar of Hemacandra. Cf. p. 18.

identifying the sources of Hemacandra had not been very happy.

611. First of all from the author himself we obtain very feeble help: in his grammar he does not mention by name any of his predecessors, except in respect of an isolated word, *Hugga*, a strange as well as unknown name, in the context of the change of *k* into *h* in certain words like Skt. *cikura*>Pkt. *cihura* (Hc I, 186, Vr IX, 4). The commentary of Hemacandra notes that *cihura* occurs in Sanskrit too: *cihuraśabdaḥ saṁskṛtepīti huggaḥ*. Pischel translates—Hugga says that the word *cihura* occurs in Sanskrit too; but he is not able to advance any other proof of the existence of this Hugga. The manuscripts of Hemacandra have different spellings :—*hugjaḥ, durgaḥ*; Trivikrama (I, 3, 17) has *huṁgācāryaḥ* that in another manuscripts becomes *āhurācāryāḥ*; Lakṣmīdhara (p. 74 of the printed text *bhṛṅgācāryaḥ*/ (MS *bhṛṅgyācāryaḥ*). These variations prove that Hugga was even unknown to the copyists and to the disciples of Hemacandra.

612. In the Hugga-problem there has been no progress since the age of Pischel, I have the impression it will never advance, because *huggaḥ* is apparently an error for *siddhaḥ*. This error followed by the intrusion of *iti* could have occurred in one of the first manuscripts of Hemacandra, unless it goes back to Hemacandra personally : *cihuraśabdaḥ saṁskṛtepi siddhaḥ*, the word *cihura* is authorised in Sanskrit too." Cf. a little above in an analogous case (Hc. I, 171) *moro maūro iti tu moramayūraśabdābhyāṁ siddham*, translated by Pischel as : "however, the words *moro* and *maūro* are explained by the words *mora*- and *mayūra*-[1]".

613. In case even *hugga* originated from a false reading, we have nothing more to guide us excepting the anonymous quotations : *ityanye, iti kecit, iti kaścit*, etc. This is the argument adduced by Pischel, Th. Bloch and Jacobi, and these citations have been studied with attention and discussed vigorouly. Here is their complete list :—*kaścit* (II, 80; III, 81); *kecit* (I, 67, 209; II, 80, 128, 138, 145, 159, 188; III 19, 25, 103 153); *keṣāṁcit* (I, 1); *anyaḥ* (III, 103, 117); *anye* (I,

1. Note on Hc. I, 171. "The forms *moro* and *maūro*. are explained from the words *mora* and *mayūra*. Accordingly Hc appears to consider *mora* as a Sanskrit word; upto this day the word has not been attested in Sanskrit.

30, 35, 88; II, 168, 174, 207; III, 177); *anyaiḥ* (IV, 2); *anyeṣām* (IV, 327); *eke* (I, 35).

As remarked above under note to § 238. only one of these citations (IV, 327) concerns a dialect other than the principal Prākrit. So it has been supposed that *iti kaścit* or *ityanye* could refer to one of our grammarians, namely, Vararuci in the first place and Caṇḍa in the second. It is this relation of Vararuci with Hemacandra that attracted firstly the attention of the European scholars, but everybody all along has been basing his argument on these anonymous citations for supporting or refuting this hypothesis. Pischel does not dare express his view clearly; according to him "the polemic of I, 209 and I, 145 is not sufficient to prove a direct allusion to Vararuci". But the word "possibly" is repeated by Pischel 23 years later in his Grammatik der Prākrit Sprachen[2]. Hemacandra had utilized Vararuci. Th. Bloch does accept the "possibility" of a direct connection between Hemacandra and Vararuci[3].

614. Even the two passages selected by Pischel do not suffice to convince him. In this regard Th. Bloch was right. In case we had only these two passages—the most characteristic of the citations of Hemacandra—it would be impossible to demonstrate that Hemacandra had ever utilized the sūtras of Vararuci.

615. Hc I, 219 besides betrays so well a lack of critical faculty of Hemacandra that it deserves to be studied in particular :—*rudite dinā ṇṇaḥ* ll *rudite dinā saha tasya da ityārabdhavantaḥ* l *sa tu śaurasenī-māgadhī-viṣaya eva dṛśyata iti nocyate* l *prākṛte hi ṛtuḥ riū uū rajatam rayayaṁ ...ityādayaḥ prayogā bhavanti* l *na punarudū rayadaṁ ityādi* l *kvacid bhāvepi vyatyayaścetyeva siddham.* ll

"In the (verbal from) *rudita*, *-ta* with the syllable *-di* becomes *ṇṇa* : example : *ruṇṇaṁ*. Here some (scholars) have preferred to deviate from the rule: in the words like *ṛtu-* etc. in place of *ta* there is *da*. But this *da* is attested only in the domains of Śaurasenī and Māgadhī, hence it is not read here. It is so, because one says in Prākrit *riū* and *uū* in place of *ṛtu-*, *rayayaṁ*

1. Preface to the edition of Hemacandra, p. VI.
2. Gramm. § 36.
3. KZ. 1895, pp. 339-345.

in place of *rajatam*. Such is the usage for all the words of this type. And we do not have *udū*, *rayadaṁ*, etc. In case sometimes they be met with, we have to explain them just as due to a confusion (of dialects; cf. Hc IV, 447)."

616. The rule on sonorisation of intervocalic *t* in fact is found in Vararuci (II, 7). According to Pischel, it is based on a bad reading, and Hemacandra has rightly refuted it : in Prākrit *t* always drops and never becomes *d*[1]. Th. Bloch affirms that Hemacandra does not allude to the rule of Vararuci. Firstly he says : the examples of Hemacandra are different from those of Vararuci, next the sūtra of Vararuci is placed elsewhere. These two arguments are equally bad. The examples belong to the commentary of Bhāmaha and not to the sūtras of Vararuci; so they prove nothing; and the fact, that Hemacandra introduced an allusion to a sūtra of Vararuci in a circumstance other than the one for which the sūtra had been written, does not make any modification in the matter of dependence of Hemacandra vis-a-vis on Vararuci.

617. A point that has not been clearly indicated either by Th. Bloch or by Pischel is that this sūtra on the sonorisation of intervocalic *t* has no relationship with the case of the verbal *ruṇṇa-* < Skt. *rudita-*. Even an Indian grammarian would be incapable of deriving *ruṇṇa-* from *rudita-*, on account of the change of *t* into *d*.

618. There exists no lien, because Hemacandra according to his habit has just copied without reflexion.

619. The sūtra of Trivikrama (I, 3, 49) on the verbal form *ruṇṇa* is in fact as follows :—*rṇo dinā rudite*. In the list of technical terms Trivikrama has explained that the reduplica tion of a consonant is indicated by the symbol *-r* : Tr. I, 4, 12 (=Siṁharāja IV, 19=Lakṣmīdhara p. 12) *rito dvitvam*.

620. The commentary added by Lakṣmīdhara, for example, to the sūtra Tr. I, 3, 49 (p. 78 of the Ṣaḍbhāṣācandrikā) explains the circumstance in which Hemacandra had committed this error : *rṇo dinā rudite* l *atra dinādityavayavena saha ṇatvaṁ rid bhavati* l *ritvāddvitvam* l *ruditakaraḥ* l *ruṇṇaaro*-ll "In the word *rudita* reduplicated *na* (=with *r*)

4. I rather believe that Hemacandra is responsible for normalization of the treatment of intervocalic *-t-* in posterior MSS.

replaces *ta* and the element *-di*. The reduplication (is caused) on account of the *rit*. Example : *ruditakaraḥ, ruṇṇaaro*."

621. Hemacandra, who, probably had before him an analogous text, read something like *ṛtvādi* "the gaṇa *ṛtu-* etc." in place of *rittvāt*, "on account of *rit*". It is why the sūtra of Vararuci (II, 7) on the sonorisation of certain intervocalic *-t-* is quoted for explaining *ruṇṇa*< *rudita-*.

622. From verifiction of this material error committed by Hemacandra, we deduce several important conclusions .

623. (1) Firstly one is obliged to remark that Hemacandra did not always understand what he was copying and that consequently all his affirmations should be subjected to criticism and be accepted only to the extent they are in accord with some other grammarians or some the known texts.

(2) Since we do not have at our command all the sources from which Hemacandra derived his materials for his grammar, we run the risk of unearthing the errors and their mechanism.

(3) Then this sūtra on the verbal form *ruṇṇa* offers a new topic for the already old discussion on the originality of the sūtras of Vālmīki. As demonstrated by Pischel, Trivikrama depends entirely on Hemacandra, but it appears to us that Hc I, 209 irrefutably proves that Hemacandra knew the sūtras of Vālmiki and their technical terms. So the sūtras in themselves were anterior to Trivikrama (cf. §§ 73-74 and 732).

(4) Lastly the polemic of Hemacandra against the sūtra that requires an intervocalic *-d-* in certain words of the principal Prākrit warrants us to disbelieve our actual texts in respect of the treatment of the intervocalics. Vararuci and all of his commentators, Kramadīśvara and the Eastern grammarians knew all these words with intervocalic *-d-* in Māhārāṣṭrī. When one thinks that dropping or sonorisation of intervocalic *-t-* remains for European scholars the criterion for separation of Śaurasenī and Māhārāṣṭrī, we immediately realise that our knowledge of Prākrit and of its dialects rests on a very weak foundation.

624. However, the very fact that vocalisation of the intervocalic *-t-* is admitted in Māhārāṣṭrī by almost all the grammarians forbids us to consider Hc I, 209 as alluding to

Vararuci directly. Hemacandra was able to find this rule in a somewhatsoever different grammatical work. Consequently we would be inclined with Pischel and Th. Bloch to throw into doubt that Hemacandra had possibly utilized directly the ten sūtras cf Vararuci. But the reading of the Siddhahemacandra itself leads us to strong conviction that this suspicion is not justified: Jacobi[1] too had the impression that the sūtras of Hemacandra, when they were not integrally found in Vararuci, they should be considered as *vārttikas*. This idea contains a good amount of truth; one cannot expect to find its demonstration in the short review by Jacobi of Pischel's edition of the grammar of Hemacandra; but it should suffice to warn Th. Bloch and Pischel.

625. But Th. Bloch would have believed to have betrayed his mission in case he had admitted, even for an instant, a continuity of teaching of the Prākrit grammaians; this would have led the reader to consider a little more seriously of their teachings, and Th. Bloch tried to prove at all cost that their all efforts were monologues of mad persons, without any connection with the language of the texts. As regards Pischel, his rigorous spirit did not allow him to be content with such an impression, and on the other hand, after he had badly selected the means of demonstration, he could not get out of the impasse. Since the dissertation on the Prākrit grammarians he made no progress at this point : "probably" Hemacandra had utilized Vararuci.

626. It is not a paradox, but I believe the honesty of Pischel that led him unto error : probably he could not even imagine that one could utilize the work of another person without mentioning him. In case Hemacandra would have made use of Vararuci, he should have told this : utmost it may be admitted that he does name him directly. So in case references by Hemacandra to his anonymous predecessors do not refer to Vararuci, it is useless to search elsewherfe for a proof of the indebtedness of Hemacandra to Vararuci.

627. Now in case we leave aside for a moment the citations of Hemacandra, it is easy to demonstrate that Hemacandra knew all the sūtras of Vararuci in their actual form.

1. Jenaer Literaturzeitung, 1876, p. 797.

628. There is a common means to prove this, so common that it has not struck the mind of scholars. We may investigate into the measure in which the sūtras of Vararuci are found in the grammar of Hemacandra. The following are the results of this verification :—

Vararuci, ed. Bhāmaha-Cowell.

1st *pariccheda* (phonetics of vowels).

All the sūtras of Vararuci occur in Hemacandra; the order is sometimes different.

2nd *pariccheda* (phonetics of single consonants). The same result. A single sūtra is wanting. It is Vr II, 7, that is known to Hemacandra, but he has omitted it intentionally (cf. § 616).

3rd *pariccheda* (phonetics of conjunct consonants). The same result.

4th *pariceheda* (*sandhi*, etc.). The same result.

5th *pariccheda* (declension of nouns). The same result, except Vr V, 10, 25, 44 (For these sūtras cf. §§ 2515, 2528.

6th *pariccheda* (declension of pronouns).

The same result, in case my correction is admitted (cf. § 2529) of Vr VI, 62 which would then correspond to Hc. III, 129.

7th *Pariccheda* (conjugation).

The same result, except Vr. VII, 9, 22, 29.

8th *pariccheda* (*dhātvādeśa*). Same result, excepting Vr. VIII, 9 (for which, however, cf. Hc. I, 198), 10, 20, 26, 61, 62, 65.

9th *Pariccheda* (particles). The same result, except Vr. IX, 17.

10th *pariccheda* (Paiśācī).

Out of the 14 sūtras, 3 are wanting (Vr. X, 4, 10, 11) and 1 concerns in Hc. a different dialect (Vr. X, 3 Hc. IV, 325).

11th *pariccheda* (Māgadhī).

Of the 17 sūtras , 8 are wanting (Vr. XI, 5, 6, 10, 11, 13, 15, 16, 17).

12th *pariccheda* (Śaurasenī).

Of the 32 sūtras, 26 are wanting (Vr. XII, 2, 3-8) 11, 13-22, 24-31).

629. In case what I have said in the chapter on Vararuci

appears convincing, we shall not be astonished to find that the proportion of the sūtras of Vararuci that do not have their correspondences in Hemacandra is so low for the principal Prākrit (15/424), goes up in the section on the dialects (3/14 for Paiśācī, 8/17 for Māgadhī, 26/32 for Śaurasenī). Vararuci is not the author of the books on dialects, and the 12th paricheda was probably added at a very recent date. Hemacandra could very well ignore it.

630. 15 sūtras out of 424 is a figure that speaks for itself. And this may further be reduced[1].

631. So in case more than 96% of the sūtras of Vararuci are found in Hemacandra, it is no more necessary to search elsewhere for proof that Hemacandra had utilized Vararuci.

632. However, these results may be checked by proceeding to a similar verification of the groups of sūtras.

633. Let us take for example the sūtras IV, 6-20 of Vararuci. It is a very characteristic group on account of being very heterogenous; here we have a talk about the variations of the themes, the changes in the gender, certain rules of sandhi, etc.

Vararuci	Hemacandra
Vr IV, 6, *antyasya halaḥ* (understood *lopaḥ*)	Hc 1, 11 *antyavyañjanasya* (understood *lug*)
	Hc I, 12 *na śradudoḥ*
	Hc I, 13 *nirdurorvā*
	Hc I, 14 *svarentaraśca*
Vr IV, 7, *striyāmāt*	Hc I, 15 *striyāmādavidyutaḥ*
Vr IV, 8 *ro rā*	Hc I, 16 *ro rā*
Vr IV, 9 *na vidyuti*	cf. Hc. I, 15
	Hc I, 17, *kṣudho hā*

1. Should one, for example retain Vr. VIII, 20 *jighrateḥ pāpāau*, that is wanting in the best manuscripts of the edition of Bhāmaha, who is unknown to other commentators of Vararuci, to the Eastern grammarians, and to Kramadīśvara, who introduces a verbal theme *pā-*, *pāa-* having the meaning of *ghrā*, "to smell", that is not found in the text ? It is evident that the *sūtra* of Vararuci is to be corrected thus :—Vr. VIII, 20 *jāgarteḥ pāpāau*, "for *jāgṛ-* "to wake" are substituted *pā* and *pāa-*; *pāa-*, *pā-* (Skt. *pā-* "to protect") are attested (in the *Piṅgalasūtra* for example, cf. s. v. *pā* in the *Prākrit dictionary* of Hargovind Das T. Sheth). However, they are not employed in Māhārāṣṭrī lyrics and the sūtra was certainly interpolated later in the *Prākṛtaprakāśa*.

Vr IV, 10 *śarado daḥ*	Hc I, 18 *śaradāderat*
Vr IV, 11 *dikprāvṛṣoḥ saḥ*	Hc I, 19 *dikprāvṛṣoḥ saḥ*
	Hc I, 20 *āyurapsarasorvā*
	Hc I, 21 *kakubho haḥ*
	Hc I, 22 *dhanuṣo vā*
Vr IV, 12 *mo binduḥ*	Hc I, 23 *monusvāraḥ*
Vr IV, 13 *aci maśca*	Hc I, 24 *vā svare maśca*
Vr IV, 14 *nañor habli*	Hc I, 25 *ṅañaṇano vyañjane*
Vr IV, 15 *vakrādiṣu*	Hc I, 26 *vakrādāvantaḥ*
	Hc I, 27 *ktvāsyāder ṇasvor vā*
	Hc I, 28 *viṁśatyāderluk*
IV 16 *māṁsādiṣu vā*	Hc I, 29 *māṁsādervā*
IV 17 *yayi tadvagāntaḥ*	Hc I, 39 *vargentyo vā*
IV 18 *nasāntaprāvṛṭśaradaḥ puṁsi*	Hc I, 31 *prāvṛṭśarattaraṇayaḥ puṁsi*
IV 18 & 19 *na śironabhasī*	Hc I, 32 *snam adāmaśironabhaḥ*
	Hc I, 33 *vākṣyarthacavanādyaḥ*
	Hc I, 34 *guṇādyāḥ klībe vā*
IV 20 *pṛṣṭhākṣipraśnāḥ striyāṁ vā*	Hc I, 35 *vemañjalādyāḥ striyām*

634. As we see, within this group, the order of the sūtras of Vararuci has been respected. Hc I, 12-14 clearly present the appearance of a later addition. It is a sign of mental disorderliness of Hemacandra that the cases of the interior sandhi have been placed under the adhikāra of final consonants. Hc I, 15 appears to combine in one single sūtra the sūtras Vr. 7 and 9, but here the text of Vararuci was not well established and it is possible that Hemacandra was not the author of this alteration. Vr IV, 9 precedes the 8 in the *Prākṛtasañjīvanī*. The forms taught in Hc I, 20-22 do not occur in Māhārāṣṭrī lyrics. The sūtras on the anusvāra already presented difficulties to Bhāmaha and to the other commentators of Vararuci (cf. for example the extension made by Bhāmaha of the rule Vr IV, 16). On the whole the edition of Hemacandra is better. Even the sūtras Hc I, 33-34 are not devoid of utility.

635. This example alone should suffice for us to close the discussion on the correspondences between Hemacandra and Vararuci, but there would be no difficulty in finding a few others. Cf. for example in the chapter on conjugation, Hc III, 139-146 that follow the order of Vr VII, 1-7 and which

like him breaks up the numeration of the verbal terminations for describing the forms of the root *as* "to be".

636. Moreover, is it so necessary to place the separation of consonant-groups by a vowel (*viprakarṣa*) after reduplication of consonants? (Hc II, 89-115 and Vr III, 50-66) ? And can this be explained otherwise than by the imitation of the fact that *iti* (becoming *ia*) occurs in Hemacandra in the same way as in Vararuci in the section on the phonetics of vowels (Hc I, 91 and Vr I, 14) whilst on the contrary the modifications of *iva* find their place in the section of particles (Hc II, 182 and Vr IX, 16) ?.

637. The fact that almost all the sūtras of Vararuci occur in Hemacandra appears to me an irrefutable proof of a direct relation between Hemacandra and Vararuci. But the analogy in the grouping of the sūtras brings in the certitude. There would be a single means of denying this correspondence; it would be attributing to the sūtras of Vararuci a character of absolute necessity, as they would appear identical to the minds of all the grammarians busy with describing Prākrit.

* * *

638. The direct relationship between Hemacandra and Vararuci cannot be proved except in the case of the principal Prākrit. The other dialects have been certainly treated by utilization of other sources.

639. Simultaneously with Māhārāṣṭrī Hemacandra has studied the dialect of the ancient *ṛṣis* — Ārṣa.

640. The certain pieces of information furnished by him on this subject are contained in the commentary.

641. Then he deals in succession with Śaurasenī (IV, 260-286), Māgadhī (IV, 287-302), Paiśācī (IV, 303-324) with its subdivision Cūlikāpaiśācika (IV, 325-328) and Apabhraṁśa (IV, 329-448).

642. Leaving aside Ārṣa, to which Hemacandra does not devote any special section, we have five languages in all. As pointed out by Jacobi[1], during a long period of time in India these five languages with Sanskrit alone were considered in the country to be literary languages. The earliest mention of the ṣaḍbhāṣās is found in the 9th century in the *Kāvyālaṁkāra*

1. Introduction to the Bhavisattakaha, p. 81*.

of Rudraṭa[1], but this classification may be going back to an earlier period.

Rudraṭa (II, 11-12) says :—

vākyaṁ bhavati dvedhā gadyaṁ chandogataṁ ca bhūyopi ||
bhāṣābhedanimittaḥ ṣoḍhā bhedosya saṁbhavati ||
prākṛtasaṁskṛtamāgadhapiśācabhāṣāśca śūrasenī ca ||
ṣaṣṭhotra bhūribhedo deśaviśeṣād apabhraṁśaḥ || 12 ||

Two things are remarkable in these verses : firstly the opposition between Apabhraṁśa, of which the number of dialects gets multiplied on account of the differences in the local tongues and the unique languages regulated according to a fixed norm, and next the place of honour accorded to Prākrit. These two points have been treated in detail by Namisādhu, one of the commentators of *Kāvyālaṁkāra.*

I reproduce here the text of this commentary as it is given in the edition of Kāvyamālā; I have only corrected some evident mistakes of reading.

vākyalakṣaṇam abhidhāya tasya bhedapradarśanārthamāha—
—vākyaṁ bhavati dvedhā gadyaṁ chandogataṁ ca bhūyopi ||
bhāṣābhedanimittaḥ ṣoḍhā bhedosya saṁbhavati ||
vākyamiti l *vākyaṁ ca dvividhaṁ bhavati* l *katham* l *ekaṁ gadyam utkalam* l *anyacchandogataṁ chandonibaddham* l *bhūyas tathāpi bhāṣābhedāt ṣoḍhā bhedo vākyasya saṁbhavatīti* l *ṣoḍhetyanena yad uktaṁ kaiścid yathā—prākṛtaṁ saṁskṛtaṁ caitad apabhraṁśa iti tridhā ityetannirastaṁ bhavati* ll *kās tā bhāṣā ityāha—*

prākṛtasaṁskṛtamāgadhapiśācabhāṣāśca sūrasenī ca |
ṣaṣṭhotra bhūribhedo deśaviśeṣād apabhraṁśaḥ ||
prākṛteti l *sakalajagajjantūnāṁ vyākaraṇādibhiranāhitasaṁskāraḥ sahajo vacanavyāpāraḥ prakṛtiḥ* l *tatra bhavaṁ saiva vā prākṛtam* ll *"ārisavayaṇe siddhaṁ devāṇāṁ aḍḍhamāgahā bāṇī" ityādivacanād vā prāk pūrvam kṛtaṁ prāk kṛtam bālamahilādisubodhaṁ sakalabhāṣānibandhanabhūtaṁ vacanam ucyate* ll *meghanirmuktajalamivaikasvarūpaṁ tadeva ca deśaviśeṣāt saṁskārakaraṇācca samāsāditaviśeṣaṁ sat saṁskṛtādyuttara-*

1. The Kāvyālaṁkāra (a treatise on Rhetorics), with the commentary of Namisādhu, edited by Pandit Durgāprasāda and Kāshīnātha Pāṇḍuraṅga Parab (Kāvyamālā No. 2).

vibhedān āpnoti l *ata eva śāstrakṛtā prākṛtam ādau nirdiṣṭam* l *tadanu saṁskṛtādīni* l *pāṇinyādivyākaraṇoditaśabdalakṣaṇena saṁskaraṇāt saṁskṛtam ucyate* l *tathā prākṛtabhāṣaiva kiñcidviśeṣalakṣaṇānmāgadhikā bhaṇyate* l *taccedaṁ yathā— rasayor laśau māgadhikāyām* l *rephasya lakāro dantyasakārasya tālavyaśakāraḥ* l *yathā—surā śulā* l *sarasī śalasī ityādi* l *tathā etvam akārasya sau puṁsi* l *yatha—eso puriso eśe puliśe ityādi* l *puṁsyevaitvam* l *tena taṁ śalilam* l *tathā ahaṁ-vayamor hage ādeśaḥ* l *yathā—hage saṁpatte hage saṁpattā* l *tathā jadya-yor*[1] *yakāro bhavati yathā—yyāṇadi yyāṇāvādī jāṇaī jaṇāvedi* l *yasya ca* l *avayyaṁ mayyaṁ viyyāhale* l *avadyam madyaṁ vidyādharaḥ* l *tathā kṣasya ·konādau* l *yathā—yaśke laśkase yakṣo rākṣasa iti* l *anādāvityeva* l *kṣayajaladharaḥ śkayayalahale*[2] *iti na syāt* l *skaḥ prekṣācakṣyoḥ* l *prekṣācakṣyor dhātvoḥ kṣasya skādeśaḥ* l *yathā—peskadi ācaskadi* ll *tathā chasya śco bhavati* l *yathā—piścile āvaṇṇavaścale* l *tathā saṣoḥ*[3] *saṁyogasthayostālavyaśakāraḥ yathā—viśnū*[4] *vihaśpadī kāśyagālaṁ* l *arthasthayoḥ thasya stādeśaḥ* l *yathā—ese aste esorthaḥ* l *samupastide samupasthitaḥ* l *tathāñjaṇyanyavrajīnāṃ*[5] *ño bhavati* l *yathā—ñja* l *añalī añjaliḥ* l *ṇya—puñakamme puṇyukarmā puñāhaṃ puṇyāham* l *nyasya ca ahimañuḥ abhimanyuḥ* l *kañakā kanyakā* l *vrajeḥ kṛtādeśasya vavvaī vañaī* l *tathā tasya dakāronte* l *yathā māledi hodi ryāṇadi ityādi* l *anyallakṣaṇaṁ granthāntarāllakṣyācca jñeyamiti* l *tathā prākṛtameva kiṁcidaviśeṣāt paiśācikam* l *yathā ṇanor nakāraḥ paiśācikyām* l *yathā—†āgaṁnūnayanamatītyādi* l *tathā dasya vā takāraḥ* l *yathā—vatanaṁ vadanam* l *prākṛtalakṣaṇāpavādaśca cātra* l *yathā—tasya na dakāraḥ* l *yathā—pāṭaliputram tathā pasya na bakāraḥ* l *yathā—padīpo anekapo* l *tathā kagacajatadapayavānām anādau yathāprayogaṁ lopaḥ svaraśeṣatā ca na kartavyā* l *yathā krameṇa—ākāśaṁ migaṁko vacanaṁ rajataṁ vitānaṁ madano supuriso dayālū lāvaṇṇaṁ* l *evaṁ suko subhago sūcī gajo bhavati* l *nadītyādi ca* l *tathā khaghathadhaphabhāmāṁ ho na bhavati* l *yathā—mukhaṁ megho ratho vidyādharo viphalaṁ sabhā ityādi* l *tathā thaṭhayor ḍhopi na bhavati* l *yathā—pathamaṁ puthuvī maṭho kamaṭho* l *tathā jñasya ño*

1. Text *jayyaror.*
2. Dolci and the printed text have *khayayalahale.*
3. Text *ṣaśoḥ.*
4. Dolci—*viśnuḥ.*
5. Text *ovvīnāṁ.*

bhavati l *yathā—yañakosalaṁ rāñā lapitaṁ* l *tathā hṛdaye yasya paḥ* l *hitapakaṁ* l *tathā sarvatra takāro na vikriyate* l *eti bimbam ityādiṣu* l *ityādayonyepi prākṛtavihitā vyañjanādeśā na kriyante* l *te ca bṛhatkathādilakṣyadarśanajjñeyā iti* l *śūrasenyapi prākṛtabhāṣaiva* l *kevalamayaṁ viśeṣaḥ* l *yathā śūrasenyām asvasaṁyogasyānādau tasya do bhavati tathā tado dīsadi hodi antaridam ityādiṣu* l *asvasaṁyogasyeti kim* l *matto pasutto* l *svagrahaṇāt niccindo andeuraṁ iti syādeva* l *anādāvityeva* l *tena tadetyādau na bhavati* l *tathā ryasya yyo bhavati yathālakṣyam* l *ayyaütta payyākulīkadahmi* l *yathālakṣyamityeva* l *tena kayyaparavaso vajjakajja ityādau na bhavati* l *iha thadhvamāṁ dho vā bhavati* l *idha hodha parittāyadha* l *pakṣe itha hoha parittāyaha* l *tathā pūrvasya puravo vā* l *yathā—na kovi apuravo* l*pakṣe apuvvaṁ padaṁ* l *tathā kaduya kariya gaduya*[1] *gacchiya iti ktvāntasyādeśaḥ* l *tathā edu bhavaṁ jayadu bhavaṁ tathā āmantraṇe bhayavaṁ kusumāuha ityādi* l *tathā inaḥ ā vā* l *yathā—bho kaṁcuiyā* l *ataśca bho vayassā bho vayassa* l *tathā ilopa idānīmi* l *yathā—kiṁ dāṇiṁ karaīssaṁ* l *nilajjo dāṇiṁ so jaṇo* l *tathā antyaniyamād idetor*[2] *ṇo bhavati* l *yathā—jutaṇṇimaṁ kiṇṇimaṁ evaṇṇedaṁ* l *yathāprayogamityeva* l *tena kim* l *etthaṁ karaīssaṁ* l *tadastā bhavati* l *yathā tā jāva pavisāmi* l *tathā evārthe yyeva* l *yathā—mama yyeva ekassa* l *haṁje ceṭyāhvāne* l *haṁje caturie* l *hīmāṇahe nirvedavismayayor nipātaḥ* l *yathā—hīmāṇahe palissaṁtā hage ediṇā niyavihiṇo duvvilasideṇa* l *hīmāṇahe jīvaṁtavacchā me jaṇaṇī* l *ṇaṁ nipāto nanvarthe* l *yathā—ṇaṁ bhaṇāmi* l *ammahe harṣe nipātaḥ* l *hīhībho vidūṣakāṇāṁ harṣe* l *śeṣaṁ prākṛtasamaṁ draṣṭavyamiti* l *tathā prākṛtamevāpabhraṁśaḥ* l *sa cānyairupanāgarābhīragrāmyatvabhedena tridhoktas tannirāsārtham uktaṁ bhūribheda iti* l *kuto deśaviśeṣāt karaṇāt* l *tasya ca lakṣaṇaṁ lokād eva samyagavaseyam* l *sāmānyaṁ tu kiṁcid idam* l *yathā nalopopabhraṁśedho rephasya* l *yathā—†prakhura bhrāyara vaghrena† ityādi* l *tadvadabhūtopi kvāpyadho rephaḥ kriyate* l *yathā—vrācāḷa uvraca uvracaü krākha krūkhityādi* l *tathādantasya ukāro bhavati* l *yathā—gotru gajiṁdru malidu cāritu ityādi* l *tathā ṛtaḥ sthāne ṛkāro vā bhavati* l *yathā tṛna-samu gaṇijai* l *pakṣe taṇaṁ ityādi* l *lakṣyādavaseyam* l *vyatyayo bahulam bhāṣā lakṣaṇasya* l *yathā—thakārahakārayoḥ śūrasenyām*

1. Text *kaḍḍyaya.........gaḍḍaya.*
2. Text *ihetor.*

dhatvamuktaṁ māgadhyāmapi bhavati l *ābhīrībhāṣā apabhraṁśasthā kathitā kvacinmāgadhyāmapi dṛśyate* l *śūrasenyāṁ idānīṁśabde ilopa uktaḥ śuddhaprākṛtepi bhavati* l *tathā kagacajatadapayādīnāṁ paiśācikyāṁ svaraśeṣatvābhāvobhihitaḥ* l *khaghadhaphabhādīnāṁ hatvādyabhāvaśca śūrasenayāmapi bhavati* l *ityādyandapi sāṁkaryaṁ mahākavilakṣyād avaseyamiti* l *viśeṣatastu bhāṣālakṣaṇaṁ granthāntarādavaseyam iti* ll

TRANSLATION

Having explained the characteristics of the language, he proposes to describe its subdivisions:—

"Language, it is of two kinds: prosaic and metrical; besides it is multiple too: it has six sub-divisions on account of the subdivisions of the languages."

"Language" etc. "Language is of two types". How ? One type is prosaic, that is free. The other is poetic, that is bound by the metre. Still on account of dialectical differences language may be divided into six types. By stating that it has six subdivisions, the opinion of certain authors that this is of three kinds: Prākrit, Sanskrit and Apabhraṁśa[1] is refuted. What are those (six) languages? He says:

Prākrit, Sanskrit, Māgadha, Piśācabhāṣā and Śūrasenī, here the sixth language is Apabhraṁśa, that has several divisions according to the difference in locality.

Prakṛti etc.: not embellished by grammar etc., the natural function of language, that is common to all the living-beings of the whole world[2]. This is *prākṛta*, the base. What has originated there, (from this *prakṛti*) or this (*prakṛti*) itself is *prākṛt* : On the authority of the statement: "the Jaina canon affirms that Ardhamāgadhī is the language of the gods[3]", the word *prākṛta* would be derived from *prāk*, formerly, plus *kṛta*, made, i.e. made formerly, is Prākṛta; it is easily learnt by children and women. Prākrit is the connecting link between different

1. Bhāmaha, Al, I, 16.

[2. The French original has: the natural function of speech, common to all living men and lacking in all the decorations brought by grammatical rules, etc. this is the base.]

3. First half of a hemistich in Āryā of which I do not know the original.

languages.[1] Like water discharged by the clouds, it is always of a single form and that very one, on account of embellishments, gets modified, develops different peculiarities and obtains forms that are distinct from those of Sanskrit[2] etc. It is on this account that the author has placed Prākrit at the top, followed by names of the other languages. The word Sanskrit is derived from *saṁskṛ-*, on account of the words being governed according to the rules of grammars of Pāṇini and others.

Similarly it is this very Prākrit language that on account of its particular characteristics is called Māgadhikā. Thus for example—'‘In Māgadhikā in place of *ra* and *sa* (we have) *la* and *śa*, i.e. *la* for *repha* and palatal *śa* for dental *sa*: examples—*surā* = *śulā*; *sarasī* = *śalaśī*, etc. In place of *o* one says *e* in the masculine nominative singular: e.g. *eso puriso* = *eśe puliśe*, etc., "in the masculine" because one says *taṁ śalilam*. *aham* and *vayam* are substituted by *hage*." Ex. *hage śaṁpatte*, *hage śampattā*[3]. In place of *ja* and *dya* one says [4]*ya*". Examples, *yāṇadi*, *yāṇavade*, *jāṇai jāṇavade*[5]; *avayyaṁ*, *mayyaṁ*, *viyyāhale*; *avadyam*, *madyam*, *vidyādharaḥ*. "In place of non-initial *kṣa* one has *śka*". Examples—*yaśke laśkase* = *yakṣo rākṣasaḥ*, etc. ‘‘Non-initial", because *kṣayajaladharaḥ* becomes *khayayalahale*. We have said *śka* in *prekṣ-* and *ācakṣ-*, that is to say in the verbs *prekṣ* and *ācakṣ* there takes place the substitution of *ska* for *kṣa*: Examples *peskadi*, (*prekṣate*), *acasākadi* (*ācaṣṭe*). In place of *cha* we say *śca*: for example *piścile āvaṇṇavaścale*. "In place of *ṣa* and *sa* in a

[1. The French original has : Prākrit is the base of all the languages.]

2. An analogous picture is found also in the Gaüḍavaho (92-94). The whole of this passage, with its scholastic brilliance reminds us of the *de vulgari eloquena* of Dante. The definition of Prākrit corresponds to that of the "*vulgaire*; de. *vulg. el.* I, 1. *vulgarem locutionem asserimus, quam sine omni regula, nutricem imitantes, accipimus.*" We call the common language of the people vulgar that does not observe any rule and that we accept by imitation. Like Prākrit, the "vulgaire" is distinguished and takes diverse forms in different countries: *de vulg. eie* I, 16 *in qualibet redolet civitate, nec cubat in ulla.*"

[3. Dolci has *saṁpatte* for *śaṁpatte* and *samapttā* for *śaṁpattā*.]

[4. In the text Dolci has *jadyayro*; in the footnote she says "texte *jayyayor*". But while trying to correct the error of the printed text she too erred. The correct reading is *yadyayoḥ*.]

[5. The translator is unable to understand how Dolci has *yyāṇadi yyāṇavādī jāṇai jāṇavede* in the text.]

group we say palatal *śa*." Example: *viśnu* (Skt. *viṣṇu*), *vihaśpadī* (Skt. *bṛhaspati*), *kāsyagālaṁ*[1]. "In the words *artha* and *stha* in place of *tha* we have *sta*." Example *eśe aste = eṣorthah, samupastide = samupasthitaḥ*. In place of *ñja*, *nya* and *ṇya* and in the root *vraj*- one says *ña*". Examples—*ñja*: *añalī = añjaliḥ*; *ṇya*: *puñakamme = puṇyakarmā, puñāhaṁ = puṇyāham*. "In place of *nya* too: *abhimañū*[2] = *abhimanyuḥ*; *kañakā = kañyakā*'. In place of *vraj*-, when one makes a substitution one says *vavvaī, vaññaī*[3]". "In place of *ta* one says *da* in the interior of a word: examples *māledi, hodi, yyāṇadi*, etc". The other rules should be learnt from other works and usage in literature.

Paiśācika is a Prākrit language, but it has its own certain peculiarities etc. In Paiśācika one says *na* in place of *ṇa* and *na*. Example:—*agaṁnū naya namati*. In place of *da* one may say *ta*. Example—*vatanaṁ = vadanam*, There are certain limitations (exceptions) to the rules of Prākrit. "In place of *ta* one does not say *da*". Example: *pāṭaliputram*. In place of "*pa* one does not say *va*". Examples *padīpo, anekapo*. "*ka, ga ca, ja, ta, da, pa, ya, va*", in non-initial syllables, do not undergo any dropping, leaving as residue a vowel. Examples are:—*ākāśaṁ, migaṁko, vacanaṁ, rajataṁ, vitānaṁ, madano, supuriso, dayālū, lāvaṇṇaṁ*; *suko, subhago, sūcī, gajo, bhavadi, nadī* etc. "One does not have *ha* for *kha, gha, tha, dha, bha*". Examples:—*mukhaṁ, megho, ratho, vidyādharo, vīphalaṁ, sabhā*, etc. "In place of *tha* and *ṭha* one does not have *ḍha*". Examples:—*pathamaṁ, puthuvī, maṭho, kamaṭho*. "In place of *jña* one has *ña*", Examples:—*yañakosalaṁ, rāñā lapitaṁ*. "In the word *hṛdaya*, in place of *ya* one has *pa*: *hitapakaṁ*". Everywhere *ta* remains unchanged : ex. *eti biṁbaṁ*, etc.

Some other substitutions of consonants taught for Prākrit do not take place and relevant cases should be deduced from examples attested in the Bṛhatkathā, etc.

Śūrasenī too is a Prākrit language. It has only the following particularities:—

In Śūrasenī, for *ta*, not combined by its own self and non-initial, there is *da*. Examples:—*tado, dīsadi, hodi, antaridaṁ* etc. Why not combined by its ownself? *matto, pasutto*. On

[1. The translator is unable to follow Dolci, who has *tālavyaśakāraḥ* in the text and dental *s* in the translation, when the examples *visṇu*, etc. are given with dental *s*, obviously against Namisādhu.]

[2. Dolci *abhimañuḥ*, that is wrong.] [3. Dolci *vanai*.]

account of the use of the words "not combined by its own self" one says *niccindo andeuram*. On account of "non-initial", one should say *tadā* without a change in the initial (consonant). "In place of *rya* one has *yya*." According to the examples *ayyaütta payyākulīkadahmi*. "According to the examples, because in *kajjaparavaso vajja kajja*, etc. this change has not taken place. "In *iha* and in the verbal terminations *-tha* and *dhvam* (in lieu of *ha*) there may be *dha*: *idha, hodha, parittāyadha*". Besides *itha, hoha, parittāyaha*. "In place of *pūrva* one may say *purava*". Example : *na kovi apuravo*. Besides *apuvvaṁ padaṁ*: *kaduya, kariya, gaduya, gacchiya* are substitutes of the absolutives (of the roots *kṛ* and *dā*): *edu bhavaṁ jayadu bhavaṁ*, while one says *bhayavaṁ kusumāuha* etc. "In place of the suffix *in* one may have *ā*." Example. *bho kaṁcuiyā*. "In place *a* too:" *bho vayassā, bho vayassa*." In the word *idānīm* there is fall out of *i*. Examples:—*kiṁ dāṇiṁ karaīssaṁ, nilajjo dāṇiṁ so jaṇo*. When there is *i* or *e* following a final-*m* we may add one *na*". Example—*jutaṇṇimaṁ kiṇṇamaṁṇevaṇṇedaṁ*. According to the usage, therefore, *kiṁ etthaṁ karaīssaṁ*. "In place of *tad* one has *tā*." Example—*tā jāva pavisāmi*. In the sense of *eva* one says *yyeva*. Example—*mama yyeva ekassa*. "*hañje* is used in calling a maid-servant." Example—*hañje caturie*. "*hīmāṇahe* is a particle expressing disgust or astonishment." Example—*hīmāṇahe palissaṁtā hage ediṇā niyavihiṇo duvvilasideṇa, hīmāṇahe jīvaṁtavacchā me jaṇaṇī*." *ṇaṁ* is a particle that is used in the meaning of *nanu*." Example—*ṇaṁ bhaṇāmi*." *ammahe* is a particle expressing joy." *hihībho* is used to express the joy of buffoons". "In other respects there is no difference from Prākrit.

Apabhraṁśa too is a Prākrit language. Some others say that it has three divisions: Upanāgara, Ābhīra and Grāmya. Rudraṭa has used the word (*bhūyaḥ*) "multiple" with the intention of rejecting this classification. Why ? On account of diversity of the regions. Because its rules should be deduced in consonance with the usage alone. However, there is a general characteristic common to all Apabhraṁśas. "In Apabhraṁśa there is no dropping of *ra* placed after (a different consonant)." Examples—*prakhura, bhrāyara, vaghreṇa* etc. At times one adds a non-existing *ra* even after another consonant. Example—*vrācaḷa uvraca uvracau krākha krukhi* etc. "In place of the final *a* of the theme one has *u*." Examples—*gotru, gajiṁdru mālidu cāritu*, etc.— *ṛ* may be retained. Example—*tṛṇasamu gaṇijjaï*: optionally *taṇam* etc. are to be deduced from examples.

Often there is exchange of rules for each language. Thus the substitution of *dha* for *tha* and *ha*, that takes place in Śūrasenī, occurs in Māgadhī too. The language of the Ābhīras, that has been defined as Apabhraṁśa, is sometimes (taught) in Māgadhī. The dropping of *i* of the word *idānīm* of Śūrasenī is found in pure Prākrit too. One teaches that in Paiśācikī too *ka*, *ga*, *ca*, *ja*, *ta*, *da*, *pa*, *ya*, etc. do not drop. In Śūrasenī too there may be the absence of *ha* in place of *kha*, *gha*, *dha*, *pha* and *bha*, etc. These confusions and others of the same kind are to be ascertained from examples quoted from great poets; but for the details the rules of languages are to be derived from a different work.

643. The interest for this commentary had already been shown by Jacobi, who had made use of it to a large extent in his introduction to the *Bhavisattakaha*. For us it has, moreover, a particular value: it reveals one of the sources of the grammar of Hemacandra in the portion concerning the dialects.

644. Namisādhu, who too was a Jaina, wrote his commentary in the Saṁvat 1125 = 1069 A.D.[1], some years before the birth of Hemacandra.

645. Namisādhu did not write a book on grammar. At the end of his discourse he refers the reader to a treatise of a specialist. But he has intercalated in his text some sūtras for describing the characteristics of the dialects. The resemblances between these sūtras and the corresponding ones of Hemacandra, excepting naturally the technical terms characteristic of Siddhahemacandra, are striking.

646. I cannot do better than by quoting them here side by side and pointing also to the coincidences between Hemacandra and Vararuci.

Māgadhī

Namisādhu	Hemacandra
rasayorlaśau māgadhikāyām	IV, 288 *rasor laśau* (Vr. XI, 3)
etvamakārasya sau puṁsi	IV, 287 *ata et sau puṁsi māgadhyām*

1. Cf. Among others S.K. De, Sanskrit Poetics, Vol. I, p. 98.

Ex. *eso puriso=eśe puliśe puṁsyevaitvam/tena taṁ śalilam*	*..eśe puliśe.../puṁsīti kiṁ/jalaṁ*
ahaṁvayamor hage ādeśaḥ	IV, 301 *ahaṁvayamor hage*
Ex. *hage saṁpatte, hage saṁpattā*	(cf. Vr. XI)*...hage śaṁpattā.*
yadyayor yakāro bhavati	IV, 292 *jadyayāṁ yaḥ*
Ex. *yāṇādi, yāṇavadi*	(cf. Vr. XI, 4, 7)...
mayyaṁ viyyāhale	*yāṇādi, yāṇavade... mayyaṁ viyyāhale*
kṣasya śkonādau	IV, 296 *kṣasya+kaḥ* (*anādau* understood)
Ex. *yaśke, laśkase*; *kayayyalahale*	(cf. Var XI, 8) *..ya† ke, la† kase*; *khayayalahalā*
skaḥ prekṣācakṣyoḥ	IV, 297 *skaḥ prekṣācakṣyoḥ......*
Examples—*peskadi, ācaskadi*	*peskadi, ācaskadi*
chasya śco bhavati	IV, 295 *chasya śco bhavati*
Examples—*piścile, āvaṇṇavaścale*	*..piścile..āvannavaścale*
ṣaśoḥ saṁyogasthayoḥ tālavyaśakāraḥ	IV. 289 *śaṣoḥ saṁyoge sogrīṣme*[1]
Ex. *viśnuḥ vihaspadī*	*..buhaspadī,..visṇuṁ*
arthasthayoḥ thasya stādeśaḥ[2]	IV, 291 *stharthayoḥ staḥ*
Ex. *eśe aste, samuvastide*	*uvastide, astavadī, śastavāhe* (compound of *artha*)
ñjaṇyanya<vraj> iṇāṁ ño bhavati	IV, 293 *nyaṇyajñañjāṁ ññaḥ*
Ex. *aññalī,...puññāhaṁ*; *ahimaññu, kaññakā*; *vaññadi*	*ahimaññu°*; *kaññakā°*; *puññāhaṁ*; *aññalī.*
tasya dakāratā	IV, 302 comm. *todonādau sūrasenyāmayuktasya*

Paiśācī

ṇanor nakāraḥ paiśācikyāṁ	IV, 306 *ṇo naḥ* (Vr. X, 5)
dasya vā takāraḥ	IV, 307 *tadostaḥ...*
Ex. *vatanaṁ*	*vatanakaṁ*
tasya na dakāraḥ pasya na vakāraḥ	Cf. IV, 325 (Vr. X, 3) for Cūlikāpaiśācī.

1. The reading of Namisādhu alone appears to be acceptable; cf. Pischel, Gramm. §302-3.

2. The example *kāsygālaṁ* shows that Namisādhu should have the correspondant of Hc. IV, 290.

kagacajatadapayavānām anadau yathāprayogaṁ lopaḥ svaraśeṣatā ca na kartavyā	IV, 324 *na kagacajādiṣaṭ sūtroktam......śamyanta*
khaghathadhaphabhānāṁ ho na bhavati	
thaṭhayorḍhopi na bhavati	
iñasya ño bhavati	IV, 303 *jño ññaḥ paiśācyām*
Ex. *raññā lapitaṁ*	(Vr. X. 9)
	IV, 304 *rājño vā ciñ...raññā lapitaṁ* (Vr. X, 12)
hṛdaye yasya paḥ	IV, 310 *hṛdaye yasya paḥ*
Ex. *hitapakaṁ*	*hitapakaṁ* (Vr. X, 14)
sarvatra takāro na vikriyate	cf. above Hc. IV 307

Śaurasenī

śūrasenyāmasvasaṁyogasyānādau tasya do bhavati	IV, 260 *to donādau śaurasenyāmayuktasya* (Vr. XII, 3)
Ex. *tado... matto...*	*tado... matto*
svagrahaṇāt niccindo, andeuramiti syādeva	IV, 261 *adhaḥ kvacit..niccindo, andeuraṁ*
ryasya yyo bhavati yathālakṣyam	IV, 266 *na vā ryoyyaḥ*
Ex. *ayyaütta payyākulīkadahmi ...kajjaparavaso*	*ayyaütta payyākulīkadahmi kajjaparavaso*
iha thadhvamāṁ dho vā bhavati	IV, 268 *ihahacorhasya*
Ex. *idha, hodha, parittāyadha; iha, hoha, parittāyaha*	*...idha, hodha, parittāyadho//pakṣe iha, hoha, parittāyaha*
pūrvasya puravo vā	IV, 270 *purvasya puravaḥ*
Ex. *...apuvvaṁ padaṁ kariya*	*...apuvvaṁ padaṁ*
kaduya gaduya gacchiya iti kvāntasyādeśāḥ	IV, 272 *kṛgamoḍaduaḥ* (Vr. XII, 10)
	...kadua gadua..karia gacchia...
(...) *edu bhavaṁ jayadu*	Cf. Hc. IV, 264-265 *edu bhavaṁ* (265)..
bhayavamāmantraṇe l *bhayavaṁ kusumāuha ityādi*	*bhayavaṁ kusmāuha* (264)
tmaḥ ā vā	IV, 263 *ā āmantrye sau veno naḥ..*
Ex. *bho kaṁcuiyā ataśca*	*bho kañcuiā*
Ex. *bho vayassā, bho vayassa*	
ilopa idānīmi	IV, 277 *idānīmo dāṇiṁ*
antyān † *mādihator* † *ṇo bhavati*	IV, 279 *montyaṇṇovedetoḥ*

Ex. *juttaṇṇimaṁ...evaṇṇedaṁ*	*juttaṁ ṇimaṁ...evaṁ nedaṁ*
tadastā bhavati[1]	IV, 278 *tasmāt tāḥ..*
Ex. *tā jāva pavisāmi*	*tā jāva pavisāmi*
evārthe yyeva	IV, 280 *evārthe yyeva* Vr. XII, 23.
hañje ceṭyāhvāne	IV 281 *hañje ceṭyāhvāne*
Ex. *hañje caturie*	...*hañje cadurike*
hīmāṇahe nirvedavismayayor nipātaḥ	IV, 182 *hīmāṇahe vismayanirvede*
Ex. *hīmāṇahe palissaṁtā hage ediṇā niyavihiṇo*	*hīmāṇahe palissaṁtā hage edeṇa niavidhiṇo*
duvvilasideṇa / hīmāṇahe jīvaṁtavaacchā me jaṇaṇī	*duvvilasiteṇa hīmāṇahe jīvaṁtavaścā me jaṇaṇī*
ṇaṁ nipāto nanvarthe	IV, 283 *ṇaṁ nanvarthe*
ammahe harṣe nipātaḥ	IV, 284 *ammahe harṣe*
hīhībho vīdūṣakāṇām harṣe	IV, 285 *hī hī vidūṣakasya* (Ex. *hī hī bho*, etc.)
śeṣaṃ prākṛtasamaṁ draṣṭavyamiti	IV, 286 *śeṣaṁ prākṛtavat*

Apabhraṁśa

na lopopabhraṁśedhorephasya	IV, 398 *vādho ro luk*
tadvadabhūtopi kvāpi	IV, 399 *abhūtopi kvacit*
adhorephaḥ kriyate	IV, 331 *syaamorasyot*
adantasya ukāro bhavati	cf. IV, 329 *svarāṇām svarāḥ prāyopabhraṁśe*
ṛtaḥ sthāne vā bhavati	
Ex. *tṛna°*	..*tṛṇu*
vyatyayo bahulaṁ bhāṣālakṣaṇasya	IV, 447 *vyatyayaśca*

647. From this comparison it results that Hemacandra and Namisādhu have much of common points in respect of simple coincidences. Namisādhu is a commentator and not a grammarian: it is very probable that he had borrowed these sūtras from a grammar that was in use in his age.

648. The comparison is not instructive for Apabhraṁśa that received in the *Siddahemacandra* a grand development (118 sūtras), but for the three other dialects it is full of information. First of all from the references that have been added by me, it is clear that these sūtras are mostly wanting in the

1. This is the etymology of Lassen (Institut. p. 222, 3); cf. also Pischel, Gramm, §425.

corresponding portions of the Prākṛtaprakāśa, ed. Bhāmaha-Cowell. Then the number of sūtras common to Namisādhu and Hemacandra is considerable in itself : 12/16 for Māgadhī, 7/26 for Paiśācī (that Namisādhu does not distinguish from Cūlikāpaiśācī), 19/27 for Śaurasenī. So the common source had been amply utilized by Hemacandra; the materials taken from this common source form the most considerable parts of the sections on Māgadhī and Śaurasenī, if not almost the whole. Since up to this moment we have been arguing as if Namisādhu has cited all the sūtras from this unknown grammar, whilst it is more probable that a commentator of a work on rhetorics has just made out a selection from the sūtras. That he did not have the intention to write a treatise on grammar finds its proof in the fact that he does not give a single rule for the principal Prākrit, the language that was too common and too familiar and very much used, and could have its characteristics described in some lines.

649. In addition to this quantitative correspondence, the relationship between Namisādhu and Hemacandra is demonstrated by the close concordances resulting from a simple reading. I would, however, like to invite attention to the examples given under the sūtras that are often the same in Hemacandra and Namisādhu, and among which the one cited in respect of the interjection *hīmāṇahe* in Śaursenī (Hc. IV, 282) is particularly interesting. The sentences are not in Śaurasenī, but in Māgadhī. Pischel had seen this already (cf. note on Hc. IV, 282) and Hemacandra himself does not ignore it, since he rejects one of the two sentences in the section on Māgadhī (Hc. IV, 302).

650. One may try to explain this common "mistake" with the help of a hypothesis that seems to answer simultaneously to several other questions arising from a reading of Hemacandra.

651. The sections on Śaurasenī and Māgadhī of the Siddhahemacandra are not first hand works and this is so not only in the sense that they were composed after more ancient grammatical works, but probably they were composed after certain indications found in a treatise on dra-

matic art or in a treatise on rhetorics of the type commented upon by Namisādhu.

652. Śaurasenī and Māgadhī, being dialects exclusively used on the scene, it is probable that people had taken up the habit of briefly stating their characteristics in treatises on dramatic art. In these very treatises one should teach the interjections employed by different characters. These interjections were mechanically incorporated in the sections on Śaurasenī by an unscrupulous commentator (Namisādhu himself) followed by Hemacandra. We do not at all find any other way to explain the example in Māgadhī (IV, 282) in the section on Śaurasenī and nor do we know, why for example, the interjections are repeated in connection with Māgadhī (commentary on Hc. IV, 302).

653. For Bharata, for the eastern grammarians, the vidūṣaka speaks Prācyā: now his habitual interjection *hī hī* is taught by Hemacandra in the section on Māgadhī (IV, 302) or in the section on Śaurasenī (IV, 285).

654. In case we attribute any value whatsoever to the teaching of Hemacandra on these theatrical dialects, one would conclude from this that the vidūṣaka could, in accord with the condition, speak either Śaurasenī or Māgadhī, a thing that is contradicted by all that we know about the Indian drama.

655. This too should be noted that the circumstances that corroborate our hypothesis—that Hemacandra speaks for example about *ceṭīs* (IV, 281), without having forewarned us that the matter related to the characters playing on the scene. In case we had no information from sources other than from his own grammar, we would deduce from it that the interjection *hañje* is reserved for maid-servants in the dialects spoken about Mathurā and we would have perhaps tried to trace in this detail the souvenir of an ancient language of caste.

656. The main objective of Hemacandra, a Jaina monk, was to lay down the rules for the language of the texts of his religion; for the exclusively scenic dialects like Śaurasenī and Māgadhī, he, therefore, confined himself to the task of copying certain sūtras that he found in a work of dramatic art or of rhetorics.

657. In a peculiar circumstance, the first European scholars, who studied Hemacandra, were chiefly interested in the theatre, in a theatre that Hemacandra had hardly made blossom in his grammar. From this fact originated the discussion between P i s c h e l and Th. B l o c h on the value that should be attributed to grammarians in general and to Hemacandra in particular. The problem posed in this manner could not, however, he solved.

658. The value of the grammarians is variable; it depends upon their knowledge of the texts in respect of which we direct our inquiry to them. Vararuci is a very sure guide for the Sattasaī of Hāla and in general for the gāthās in Māhārāṣṭrī; the eastern grammarians know well Śaurasenī and in general the dialects employed on the scene. Hemacandra may be consulted with profit in respect of Apabhraṁśa of the dohās and so on. But on the contrary we should not refer to Hemacandra for information on Śaurasenī and Māgadhī that are very much sacrificed in his grammar.

659. In addition to Vararuci and this common source of Hemacandra and Namisādhu, the grammar of Hemacandra has undergone still very important influence that was brought to light the moment when Hemacandra came to be known in Europe; this is that of the religious texts of the Jainas.

660. Hemacandra has himself, in his commentary on the principal Prākrit, pointed out to some of the specialities of Ārṣa, the language of the Jaina-canons, that has been called Ardhamāgadhī by P i s c h e l and Jaina Prākrit[1] by J a c o b i and M ü l l e r.

661. The name Ardhamāgadhī is known to Hemacandra as well, who prefers it to Ārṣa for (the purpose of avoiding confusion with Māgadhī (cf. Hc. IV, 287 and notes of P i s c h e l).

662. Hemacandra was well conversant with the texts of his religion; his teachings with regard to Ārṣa are almost always correct. With the aid of the index of W i k r e m-

1. Cf. P i s c h e l, Gramm. §16-17: J a c o b i, The Kalpasūtra of *Bhadrabāhu*, edited with an introduction, etc. Abhandlungen der DMG VII, Bd. Leipzig, 1881; E. M ü l l e r, Beiträge zur Grammatik des Jaina Prākrit; Berlin, Harrwitz, and G r o s s m a n n, 1876.

singhe one finds in the grammar of Pischel almost all the words cited by Hemacandra and attested in the words of the Jaina canons[1].

663. But even if Hemacandra had believed to have distinguished Ārṣa, he did not have even the sample of the much more recent language of non-canonical Jaina works, that is ordinarily called Jaina Māhārāṣṭrī[2].

664. It is evident that Hemacandra knew well this Prākrit. Jacobi had even thought in the beginning that Māhārāṣṭrī taught by Hemacandra could justly be Jaina Māhārāṣṭrī and not that of the Sattasaī of Hāla and of the epical poems[3]. Later he modified his opinion by admitting with Pischel that Hemacandra owed much to his predecessors and that the citations in his grammar identified up till now had been taken from Hāla, from Rāvaṇavaho, from the Gaüdavaho etc[4].

665. Probably Hemacandra did not know so well the lyric—Māhārāṣṭrī; probably even when he mentioned Māhārāṣṭrī or even Prākrit he had in mind the language employed by the Śvetāmbaras in their all non-canonical writings. And in case he had been anything but a compilator, he would have given to us a systematically complete account of this Jaina Māhārāṣṭrī that we could put most profitably in opposition to lyric Māhārāṣṭrī studied by Vararuci.

666. Unfortunately Hemacandra preferred to follow the current tradition and to compose one more grammar of Gāthā Māhārāṣṭrī. Now and then he found the means, in regard to a word or an isolated form to furnish some rules on Jaina Māharāṣṭrī[5].

667. This much is certain and this has been universally

1. For the purpose of verification of this affirmation I give here a list of passages where Hemacandra cites particularities of Ārṣa. Hc. I, 3, 26, 46, 57, 79, 118, 119, 151, 177, 181, 206, 228, 245, 254; II, 17, 21, 86, 98, 101, 104, 113, 120, 138, 143, 146, 174, III, 162; IV, 238, 283, 287.

2. Cf. Pischel, Gramm. §16 and 20.

3. Edition of the *Kalpasūtra*, p. 19.

4. Introduction to the edition of the Bhavisattakaha.

5. Ausgewählte Erzählungen in Mahārāṣṭrī zur Einführung in das Studium des Prākṛit Grammatik. Text, Wörterbuch. Published by H. acobi, Leipzig, S. Hirzel, 1886.

recognised : it is, however, easier to describe precisely the parts of this Māhārāṣṭrī. The parts of the Uttarādhyayana-sūtra—Ṭīkā of Devendra published by Jacobi have caused a deception on this point. A simple comparison of the index of these passages with the index of the grammar of Hemacandra will convince at once that we need not try to find in this type of texts the model of the "Jaina" parts of the grammar of Hemacandra. But as remarked by Leumann here we have before us later-day texts written by an author who was more familiar with Sanskrit than with Prākrit[1].

668. M. L. Alsdorf has recently examined a text in Jaina Māhārāṣṭrī of the greatest importance, that is the language of Vasudevahiṇḍī of Saṅghadāsagaṇin, published by Munimahārāja Caturavijaya and Puṇyavijaya in the Ātmānanda Jaina Grantha Ratnamālā[2].

669. Having been given the small space that was accorded to him, M. L. Alsdorf could give only a resumé of this text which for him was probably much anterior to the 6th century A. D. Since he promises us a complete study, it would be better to take up again the question of the influence of the texts in Jaina Māhārāṣṭrī in the teaching of Hemacandra of the principal Prākrit, when M. Alsdorf would have delineated the characteristics of the language of Vasudevahiṇḍī.

However, some of the data supplied by M. Alsdorf already permit us to hope that this time we have in hand a text that is really instructive so far as Hemacandra is concerned.

670. In the Vasudevahiṇḍī for example (Alsdorf, p. 321) the first person of the present indicative in *-aṁ* instead of in *-ām* is frequently attested. Pischel does not speak about it in his grammar, although Hemacandra explicitly

1. *Die Āvaśyaka Erzählungen*, published by E. Leumann, Part 1, Leipzig 1897. This text, the most important in the opinion of Pischel (Gramm. § 20) has not been published in full. On account of there being no commentary or an index, it helps little in respect of comparison and at times the reading is very difficult.

2. M.L. Alsdorf, *A specimen of archaic Jaina—Māhārāṣṭrī*; Indian and Iranian Studies, presented to G.A. Grierson onhis eighty-fifth birthday 7th January 1936, (BSOS, London Vol. VIII, parts 2 and 3, pages 319-333.

teaches this[1]; in the Vasudevahiṇḍī we often find in place of *diṇṇa* the verbal *datta* (p. 327) taught by Hc. (I, 46), a form that according to Pischel (Gramm. § 566) is found only in the Pallava inscription and in some proper names. Lastly the form *mai* of the locative singular of the pronoun of the first person (p. 331), taught by Hemacandra for the principal Prākrit and attested by Pischel (§418) only in Ś., occurs twice in the Vh.

671. So we are able to affirm that the principal Prākrit of Hemacandra consists not only of Māhārāṣṭrī of the gāthās and of the epic poems, but also that of the language of Jaina canonical and non-canonical works. In case Hemacandra had broken through the fence of the traditional Prākrit grammar, he would have been able to separate these dialects and would have made his work more scientific. He preferred to mix up all, and since he does not indicate the sources of his examples, the confusion is irremediable.

672. Let us assume for a moment that Pischel had got printed his Grammatik der Prākrit Sprachen without indicating the dialects from which the forms had been borrowed. It would not be an exaggeration to say that it would become unutilizable. The resumé of the grammar of the Sattasaī given in the first edition of Hāla by Weber or the one that Jacobi has placed in the beginning of his edition of the Jaina stories would render us best service.

673. In this sense it may be said that the grammar of Hemacandra has rather caused harm to our knowledge of different Prākrits. However, now we have begun to know more of the texts and Hemacandra becomes by this fact less dangerous, because we are able to prefix mentally to the forms taught by him the abbreviations to which we have become accustomed through the grammar of Pischel: JM, Mg., AMg.

674. Lastly let us examine the two last dialects studied by Hemacandra : Paiśācī and Apabhraṁśa.

675. It is difficult to take up the question of

1. Hc. III, 141 *tṛtīyasya miḥ—bahulādhikārāt mipsthānīyasya merikāralopaśca.*

Paiśācī of Hemacandra without venturing into the rich literature that has sprung about this dialect[1].

676. As the texts have disappeared, the teachings of the grammarians have been carefully studied. At this actual hour it is almost impossible to take a firm opinion. In the absence of the corresponding texts the sūtras of the Prākrit grammarians are very little instructive.

677. I would, however, like to hazard a hypothesis in respect of the differences that the Paiśācī of Hemacandra presents in relationship with the Paiśācī of the eastern grammarians.

678. The examples of Paiśācī and of Cūlikāpaiśācika given by Hemacandra had been considered by Pischel as extracts from the famous Bṛhatkathā. On the other hand the only quotation from the Bṛhatkathā given by Mārkaṇḍeya (XIX, 9) *bṛhatkathāyāṁ kupaci pisālaṁ* is in a dialect that does not obey the rules Hemacandra[2].

679. The genuineness of all the citations of Mārkaṇḍeya (cf. § 458) would persuade us to accord to him the highest credit; on the other hand Hemacandra cites sufficiently big passages that appear well to have been taken from a story.

680. Lacôte, however, in his essay on the Bṛhatkathā, independently arrived at the conclusion that the passages cited by Hemacandra might have been borrowed not from the Bṛhatkathā of Guṇāḍhya, but from the Bṛhatkathāsaritsāgara in Paiśācī that was the original of Kṣemendra and Somadeva[3].

681. This more recent Kashmirian Bṛhatkathāsaritsāgara might have been the source of the citations of

1. For the purpose of reorientation a bibliography will be found in the new edition of the Kathāsaritsāgara (Tawney—Panzer) in 10 volumes: vol. 1, pp. 92-93, to which should be added the work of F. Lacôte on the Bṛhatkathā cited below (§. 680), the article of P. V. Rāmānujaswāmi, Hemacandra and Paiśācī Prākṛta (IA LI, 1922, pp. 51-54) and that of Prabodhacandra Bagchi, Śulika Cūlika and Cūlikā Paiśācī in the Journal of the Department of Letters, Calcutta University Press, 1931, p. 1-10.

2. Cf. for the details Grierson, The Eastern School. etc. p. 121.

3. Contributions àl 'histoire des contes indiens. Essai sur Guṇāḍhya et la Bṛhatkathā : Paris, Leroux, 1908, p. 206.

Hemacandra, whilst Mārkaṇḍeya laid down the rules for the language in which was written the Bṛhatkathā of Guṇāḍhya.

682. It is not neecssary to consider with Grierson[1] that in the 17th century Mārkaṇḍeya was still able to read the book in question: Puruṣottama (XIX, 20), amongst others, teaches the same change of *kvacit* into *kupaci.*

683. The short passage from the Bṛhatkathā cited by Mārkaṇḍeya for illustrating this rule could then be found in one of the older eastern grammarians, if not in a commentary on Puruṣottama himself that Mārkaṇḍeya probably knew.

684. As regards the Apabhraṁśa of Hemacandra the preliminary remark is that this dialect has for him a unity and a stability that are unknown to other grammarians[2].

685. For Hemacandra it was a question of a well defined language without dialectical subdivisions; the examples of some dohā-types create through their contents the impression of an anthology of the type of Hāla.

686. Two of the stanzas cited by Hemacandra, as noted by Pischel, occur in the Sarasvatīkaṇṭhābharaṇa. The same Pischel has critically edited and translated them[3] along with the other dohās that are found in other rhetorical treatises.

687. In respect of form and style they remind us of the gāthās of the Sattasaī and they are almost always the expression of a feeling of a fugitive sensation of a girl, of a woman in love. But a new theme appears in these dohās and this is that of admiration for the valour of a warrior, a theme unknown to the Sattasaī:—

IV, 351.

1. JRAS, 1913, p. 391.

2. In reality the examples cited by him present among themselves dialectical differences; cf. Jacobi, Introduction to the Bhavisattakaha, p. 72. [PC. expressly says : *apabhraṁśastu yo bhedaḥ ṣāṣṭhaḥ sotra na lakṣyate deśabhāṣāditulyatvānnāṭakādāvadarśanāt* ll *anatyantopayogāccātiprasaṅgabhayādapi* l *nehoktāḥ.*]

3. Gramm. § 29 and Materialen zur Kenntnis des Apabhraṁśa, ein Nachtrag zur Grammatik der Prākrit-Sprachen. Berlin Weidmann : 1902 (Abhandlüngen der königlichen Gesellschaft der Wissenschaften zu Göttingen, Philosophisch-historische Klasse, Neue Folge, Bd. V, No. 4.)

bhallā huā ju māriā bahiṇi mahārā kantu l
lajjejjaṁ tu vaaṁsiahu jaï bhaggā gharu entu ll

"It is good that my husband has been killed; O sister, I would have felt ashamed before my friends in case he had run away and returned back home[1]."

688. In between the ages of the Sattasaī and these Apabhraṁśa dohās the Mussulman—invasion had drenched India in blood.

689. I wonder if some of these dohās were not written by the invaders: One of them appears to me particularly revealing: Hc. IV. 386.

khaggavisāhiu jahiṁ lahahuṁ pia tahiṁ desahiṁ jāhuṁ l
raṇadubhhikkheṁ bhaggāiṁ viṇu jujjhaṁ ṇa valāhū ll

"Let us go, my darling, into the country where we may obtain (whatever we desire) with the force of the sword; since broken by battle and famine, we cannot rejoice without fighting."

690. Booty of combat, joy of conquest, exhaltation of military virtues, all this is sung in the *dohās* : one would in vain search for their traces in the gāthās of the Māhārāṣṭrī lyrics.

691. Without concluding that the *dohās* possessed by us are of the age of the Mussulman-invasion, they may be a continuation of a literary type hatched in an epoch of plunder and war.

1. Cf. also on Hc. IV, 354, 357[1], 379[1], 387[3], 395[5], etc.

Chapter VI

TRIVIKRAMA AND THE SŪTRAS OF VĀLMĪKI, ETC.

71. Sir George Abraham Grierson has postulated a "Western School" as against the "Eastern School." The former should really be designated the "Southern School," because all the grammarians who belong to it lived in the south of the peninsula and the most ancient manuscripts of their works are written in the Grantha characters or in the Malayālam or Telugu script.

72. The chief of this school is generally considered to have been Trivikrama: the sūtras commented upon by him were also utilized either wholly or partly by Siṁharāja, Lakṣmīdhara and Appaya Dīkṣita.

73. From the very beginning, and particularly since the edition of Siṁharāja by Hultzsch, the question has been raised leading to the inquiry if Trivikrama himself was the author of the sūtras of his grammar and if, therefore, the other works are directly derived from it or if on the contrary Trivikrama was just a commentator and had merely reproduced more ancient sūtras.

74. The question is still being discussed in India.

75. The grammar of Trivikrama[1], the Prākṛtavyākaraṇa, or the Prākṛtavyākaraṇavṛtti— the two names alternating in the colophons of one and the same manuscript—is a very imposing work on account of its volume. It has not been published in full[2]; but it is easy to arrive at a conclusion regarding its contents, because, Pischel, who had copied in his own hand a manuscript of Trivikrama,

1. Cf. Pischel, *de gramm Prācr.*, pp. 27-39; *Gramm.* §88; Tukaram Laddu, Prolegomena zu Trivikramas Prākrit Grammatik, Inaugural Dissertation... Halle, 1912 (translated into English by P.V. Ramanujaswami: And Bhandarkar, X, 177-218); Bhattanatha Svamin, *Trivikrama and his followers*: Indian Antiquary XL, 1911, pp. 219-223. Cf. also the Introduction of Hultzsch, to the edition of Siṁharāja. [An edition of the work has been published by P.L. Vaidya in the Jaina Saṁskrti Śaṁrakṣaka Saṁgha, Sholapur, 1954.]

2. The first adhyāya appeared in the Granthapradarśanī in 1895 some extracts and also the plan of the work are given by T. Laddu.

preserved at Tanjore,[1] had utilized it amply in his notes on the grammar of Hemacandra. He had also published two of the lists of deśī and provincial words given by Trivikrama in his grammar[2].

76. Moreover, the sūtras are reproduced in their primitive order at the end of the edition of the Ṣaḍbhāṣācandrikā of Lakṣmīdhara, in the Bombay Sanskrit Series.

77. The sūtras are in the āryā-verses and more rarely in ślokas; there are more than a thousand (1085) sūtras that are divided into 12 pādas grouped in three adhyāyas.

78. The name of Trivikrama is not probably unknown to this subdivision.

79. As regards the contents of this grammar, it is easy to describe it: it is a metrical reproduction of the grammar of Hemacandra. The technical terms are different, because Trivikrama adopted certain symbols of the Pāṇinian type, that he presents in the beginning of his grammar; they are selected for the purpose of rendering his treatment more concise[3]. Sometimes the original order of Hemacandra is slightly changed, but this has always been done for metrical reasons.

710. The examples too, in most cases are common to Trivikrama and Hemacandra: Trivikrama generally adds the Sanskrit translation; it also appears that his text ordinarily represents an advancement upon that of Hemacandra. Pischel has often preferred it in his edition of the examples in Apabhraṁśa.

711. Although Trivikrama gives an abundant amount of information concerning his family, it has not been possible to fix his date with certainty.

712. From the introductory stanza (see below 732) we learn that he was a Jaina and that his teacher's name was Arhanandi Traividyamuni. He cites Hemacandra who is the youngest of the scholars studied by him, as a consequence

1. Cf. T. L a d d u, Prolegomena. p. 16.

2. *Die deśīśabdas bei Trivikrama*; BB III, 1879, 235-265; VI, 1881, 84-105 and XIII, 1888, 1-21;=T. I, 3, 105 (or 106 according to the MSS); I, 4, 121, Trivikrama calls them *nipātas*=indeclinable words. Other lists are found in T, II, 1, 30; III, 1, 132 and III, 4, 71 (where the words are called *deśya*.

3. A list thereof will be found in T. L a d d u, Prolegomena, p.46.

of his plagiarism that he has indulged in, one would expect something better than this dry mention.

713. So Trivikrama is posterior to Hemacandra (born in 1088).

714. In his turn he has been utilized and cited by Lakṣmīdhara and Appaya Dīkṣit. Since the latter quotes the former, it is Lakṣmīdhara who gives the *terminus post quem*. However, Upadhye tries to date Trivikrama, on the basis of an inscription of Halebiḍa[1], that announces in 1236 A.D. the death of Śakalacandra, a disciple of Arhanandi Traividyadeva. In case the latter is the same person as the teacher of Trivikrama, it follows that Trivikrama composed his grammar in the beginning of the 13th century A.D.

715. The Ṣaḍbhāṣācandrikā of Lakṣmīdhara, for the grammar of Trivikrama, is what the Siddhāntakaumudī is for the Aṣṭādhyāyī of Pāṇini. It is easily accessible in the edition of Kamalāśaṅkara Prāṇaśaṅkara Trivedī[2]. The editor has spared no pain: introduction, notes, paradigms of forms, index of Prākrit words, nothing is wanting in this big volume of more than six hundred pages.

However, sometimes the critical spirit is wanting[3]. It is further curious to find in a later-day work that Lakṣmīdhara has omitted a number of examples of Trivikrama. The date of Lakṣmīdhara is fixed with a strong probability towards the middle of the 14th century A. D.

From the introductory stanzas in the Ṣaḍbhāṣācandrikā we learn that Lakṣmīdhara[4] belonged to the Carakūri family that lived on the bank of the Kṛṣṇā in the country of the

1. A.N. Upadhye, A Note on Trivikrama's date : Ann. Bhandarkar O. R. I. XIII, p. 171-172; the inscription was published in the Annual Report of Archeological Survey of Mysore of the year 1929, inscription No. 14, p. 74-75.

2. The Ṣaḍbhāṣācandrikā of Lakṣmīdhara...by Rao Bahadur Kamalāśaṅkara Prāṇaśaṅkara Trivedi, Bombay 1936, Bombay Sanskrit and Prakrit Series, No. 71.

3. Cf. for example the note at p. 4, where the editor conjectures that bhāṣā, vibhāṣā, etc. are subdivisions of *tadbhava*.

4. A commentary on the Gītagovinda, the Śrutirañjanī, preserved in the Tanjore Library, is the work of one Lakṣmaṇasūri. But the introductory stanza being almost the same as in the Ṣaḍbhāṣācandrikā, it follows that Lakṣmīdhara is another name of Lakṣmaṇasūri. Lakṣmaṇasūri was a

Āndhras and has been famous in the Kāśyapa gotra. The name of the father of Lakṣmīdhara was Yajñeśvara, his mother was Sarvāmbhikā and Koṇḍabhaṭṭa[1], his elder brother.

717. Lakṣmīdhara was a very pious Brāhmaṇa. He was a Sannyāsī, disciple of Kṛṣṇāśrama; in his religious life he assumed the name Rāmānandāśrama and under this name composed a commentary on the Anargharāghava[2].

Sometime before hence P. K. Gode had discovered another work of Lakṣmīdhara, the Bharataśāstragrantha[3]. This discovery confirms the impression that the beginning verses of the Ṣaḍbhāṣācandrikā had created in me : Lakṣmīdhara belonged to the Southern School by accidence of birth, but his culture was very much different from that of Trivikrama. I hope to have shown by examples the little importance that Hemacandra accorded to the theatre. Trivikrama does not adopt some other attitude: he was himself a Jaina, his culture should not have been different: for the Jainas Prākrit is the language of religious propaganda. Lakṣmīdhara, on the contrary, probably considered the Prākrits as dialects used on the scene. In fact at the end of his introductory stanzas, Lakṣmīdhara quotes a classification of all the languages, including Sanskrit, taken from a work on dramatic art, the Rūpakaparibhāṣā (vv. 23-32)[4].

718. Evidently it is to be regretted that the grammar of Trivikrama does not give sufficient place to the dialects spoken on the scene; he did not choose to reproduce the text, but he tried to fill the lacunae by copying in the introduction a passage on the allocation of dialects to the different characters.

protege of King Tirumalarāja of the Aravidu dynasty of Vijayanagar who reigned from 1561-68 A.D. till 1574-1577 A.D. according to the inscription. Cf. Bhattanathasvamin, IA. 40 (1911), p. 223; the introduction to the edition of the Ṣaḍbāṣācandrikā, p. 16 and in the last place ABORI, XV, p. 240-242.

1. Cf. Introductory stanzas (6-13) of the Ṣaḍbhāṣācandrikā.

2. Cf. Introduction to the Ṣaḍbhāṣācandrikā, p. 16 and *Ann. Bhandarkar* XV, p. 242.

3. Ann. Bhandarkar XV, 240-242.

4. One Rūpakaparibhāṣā has been cited by Aufrecht, *Cat. Cat.* p. 533; for Bhattanathasamin (IA 1911, p. 222), it is a chapter of the Rasārṇavasudhākara of Siṁhabhūpāla.

719. Besides, contrary to the habit of Hemacandra and that of Trivikrama, he cites Bhāmaha. Grierson has attempted to find an explanation of this fact in the circumstance that Bhāmaha was an inhabitant of Kashmir, so an originaire of a country that is midway between the East and West. But Trivikrama and his commentators are rather southerners than westerners, and Kashmir for him was as far away as Bengal.

720. In the stanza No. 22 of the introduction Lakṣmīdhara says:—

traivikramaṁ haimacandraṁ guror jñātvā ca bhāmahaṁ ।
kavisaukhyāya tat sarvamatra saṁkṣipyate mayā ॥

"Having learnt from (my) teacher the works of Trivikrama, Hemacandra and Bhāmaha (the commentator of Vararuci?), for the convenience of the poets, I have abridged them all."

721. I am not sufficiently conversant with Jaina literature to state that this is the general usage; but so far as grammatical works are concerned, I am in a position to affirm that the Jainas do not quote the names of the authors belonging to a different creed. Trivikrama mentions Hemacandra alone (cf. the introductory stanza No. 11 of his grammar, p. 187), because among the authors known to him Hemacandra also was a Jaina.

722. Lakṣmīdhara, who was a Brāhmaṇa, did not have the same hesitation; so he could name Bhāmaha. In Lakṣmīdhara we find mention of a Prākrit grammar too: the Ṣaḍbhāṣārūpamālikā of Durgāṇācārya[1]. It has not been possible for me to find any trace of this work even in catalogues of manuscripts or elsewhere.

1. P. 22 of the printed edition in vol. II, 2, 9. It relates to the vocative of the themes in *a*. One may say *he rāma* beside *he rāmo*. In place of the sūtra *sor luk*, at times the reading *soḥ śluk*, that is to say lengthening of a vowel after dropping, in lieu of simple elision : so one should say *he rāmā*. This is an exceptional treatment (cf. Hc. III, 38 comm.) and for the purpose of normal treatment we should extend the force of the *adhikāra bahulam* as has been done by Durgāṇācārya *soḥ slukam aṅgīkṛtya śiti dīrghaḥ iti dīrghe prāpte bahulādhikārānna bhavatīti ṣaḍbhāṣarūpamālikākāreṇa durgāṇācāryeṇoktaṁ cintyam.*

723. For Lakṣmīdhara, Trivikrama is not the author of the sūtras, but exclusively of the commentary:—
stanzas 14—16

tena lakṣmīdharāryeṇa ṣaḍbhāṣācandrikānaghā l
vidvatkavicakorāṇāṁ prītaye kriyatedhunā ll

vāgdevī jananī yeṣāṁ vālmīkir mūlasūtrakṛt l
bhāṣāprayogā jñeyāste ṣaḍbhāṣācandrikādhunā ll

vṛttiṁ traivikramīṁ gūḍhāṁ vyacikhyāsanti ye budhāḥ l
ṣaḍbhāṣācandrikā taistadvyākhyārūpā vilokyatām ll

"This Lakṣmīdhara now composes the irreproachable Ṣaḍbhāṣācandrikā so that it may make scholars and poets happy, like the moonlight, the *cakora*[1]. The practice in the languages, of which the mother is the goddess of learning and for which Vālmīki composed the original sūtras, is attained by following the path of Ṣaḍbhāṣācandrikā. The scholars who desire an explanation of the subtle commentary of Trivikrama, should study the Ṣaḍbhāṣācandrikā which is its interpretation".

724. A new adaptation of Trivikrama that is more recent than the aḍbhāṣācandrikā, on account of the latter being cited in it, is P r ā k ṛ t a m a ṇ i d ī p a of A p p a y a Dīkṣita. I know this work only from the notices of the catalogues of manuscripts and from what has been said about it by Bhattanatha Svamin[2]. A part of this work was published in the Granthapradarśanī, (Nos. 3, 5, 6, 8-10, 13).

725. The author was born in 1554 A.D. and he was alive in 1626. In the introductory stanzas he attributes his work to Chinabommabhūpa, and later, considering this too big a sacrifice, he found means for inserting his name

1. Cf. E. H u l t z s c h, Reports on Sanskrit Manuscripts in Southern India I (Madras 1895), p. VIII and 23; S. Kuppuswami Sastri, A Triennial Catalogue of MSS collected during the triennium 1916-17 to 1918-19 (Madras 1922), p. 3231 and *id. ibid*...during the triennium 1922-23 to 1924 25 (Madras 1923) p. 6302; IA., 1911, p. 221.

2. Cf. P i s c h e l, Gramm. §41.

in the colophon. This is at least the explanation given by Bhattanatha Svamin[1].

726. Appaya Dīkṣīta was a Brāhmaṇa and like Lakṣmīdhara he accorded a preferential status to the theatral Prākrits. And an important point is that he names among his sources Vararuci:—

sūkṣmārthaṁ grāhayatāṃ mandānapi nāṭakaṁ mṛdūpāyaḥ ǀ
tasyāpi jīvitamidaṁ prākṛtamaprākṛtena yanmiśram ǁ1ǁ

ye trivikramadevena hemacandreṇa ceritāḥ ǀ
lakṣmīdhareṇa ye granthāḥ bhojena ca mahīkṣitā ǁ2ǁ

ye puṣpavananāthena ye vā vārarucā api ǀ
vārttikārṇavabhāṣyādyā appayajvakṛtāśca ye ǁ3ǁ

te vistṛtatvāt prāyeṇa saṁkṣeparucibhirjanaiḥ ǀ
agṛhītā vilambyante sandhyārkakiraṇā iva ǁ4ǁ[2]

"The agreeable means for learning fineness even by persons who have a feeble mind is the theatre, because the essence of the theatre is the mixture of Prākrit with what is not Prākrit.

"The works of Trivikrama and Hemacandra and those of Lakṣmīdhara and of King Bhoja, those of Puṣpavananātha or even those of Vararuci, the ocean of Vārttika, the bhāṣyas, etc. (the critical notes and commentary) of Appayajva, the public, that generally likes brevity, does not comprehend them on account of their being voluminous in the manner that they decline like the rays of the setting sun."

727. So Appaya Dīkṣita contradicts Sir George Abraham Grierson who is of the opinion that Western grammarians do not cite Vararuci. I may repeat it is the Jainas,

1. For other details on the personality and works of Appaya Dīkṣita, cf. S.K. De, *Studies in the history of Sanskrit Poetics*, Luzac and Co. 1923, vol. I, pp. 265-274.

2. S. Kuppuswami Sastri, A Triennial Catalogue 1922—23 to 1924-25, p. 6302.

like Hemacandra and Trivikrama, who do not like to name the infidels.

728. The third work, probably the oldest of all those that comment on the same sūtras as were commented upon by Trivikrama, is the Prākṛtarūpāvatāra of Siṁharāja. It has been perfectly edited by H u l t z s c h[1]: one cannot but regret one thing, that such a zeal and such a competence should have been exercised on a text so little interesting.

729. The P r ā k ṛ t a r ū p ā v a t ā r a consists of a little more than half of the sūtras of Trivikrama (575/1085) but the commentary is very poor; it does not give examples taken from literary texts and in most cases they are limited to a dry catalogue of forms. In his introduction Hultzsch, following Pischel, says that all of these forms are found in Hemacandra and Trivikrama; they alone would justify the edition of the Prākṛtarūpāvatāra; but Pischel had noticed that, at least a portion of these forms that are particular to Siṁharāja were all theoretically derived from the sūtras and were not found in the texts. Therefore, they are of almost negligible interest.

730. Siṁharāja does not cite Prākrit grammarians; his commentary is absolutely independent of that of Trivikrama.

731. The date of S i ṁ h a r ā j a cannot be fixed on the basis of very rare citations given by him[2]; but the name of his father Samudrabandhayajvan in the colophon and in the S i n d h u b a n d h a in the stanza No. 3 of the introduction[3] permitted T. Gaṇapati Ś ā s t r ī to situate him with precision[4]. Samudrabandha is the author of a commentary on the Alaṁkārasarvasva; in it he has alluded to Ravivarmadeva as

1. P r ā k ṛ t a r ū p ā v a t ā r a, a Prākrit grammar based on the Vālmīkisūtra, by Siṁharāja, son of Samudrabandhayajvan, edited by E. H u l t z s c h, London Royal Asiatic Society 1909 (Prize Publication Fund I).

2. Cf. H u l t z s c h, Preface to the edition 10. VII.

3. Ibid, p. VIII.

4. The Pradyumnābhyudaya of Ravivarmabhūpa, edited with notes by T. Gaṇapati Śāstrī, Trivendrum, 1910 (TSS, VII), preface, pp. I-VIII. The merit of Gaṇapati Śāstrī is so great that he does not know the prologue in which Siṁharāja says that his father had written a commentary on a treatise on alaṁkāra.

his contemporary. From the inscriptions we know that this ruler was born in 1265 A.D. in Kerala. So Siṁharāja should have been living towards the end of the 13th and 14th centuries[1].

In any event Siṁharāja would be posterior to Trivikrama and Trivikrama is to be placed in the beginning of the 13th century.

732. Let us revert back to the question of the sūtras of Trivikrama.

Appaya Dīkṣita and Lakṣmīdhara, who have utilized these sūtras, know and cite also the commentary of Trivikrama. Siṁharāja does not name Trivikrama and does not utilize his commentary, but probably he is posterior to him and he could have borrowed the sūtras from him. None of the three offers us any certainty that the sūtras are anterior to Trivikrama. And in a question so much discussed it is only the certainty that we need for discussing the problem of the sūtras of Vālmīki, because all the doubtful things have been interpreted differently according to the conviction of those who have made use of them.

I am not able to solve this problem in a definitive manner, so I am to be satisfied by placing the data here and leave the readers to take their own decision:—

1. The first of these data is provided by Trivikrama himself. Below will be found a reproduction and translation of the stanzas of the introduction and the conclusion of the Prākṛtavyākaraṇa:—

śrīvīraṁ prācyācalasamuditamakhilaprakāśakaṁ vande l
divyadhvanipaṭudīdhitimahamakṣarapaddhatiprāptyai ll 1 ll

śrutibharturarhananditraividyamuneḥ padāmbhujabhramaraḥ l
śrībāṇasukulakamaladyumaṇerādityaśarmaṇaḥ pautraḥ ll 2 ll

1. This affirmation is of Bhattanatha Svamin (p. 223)., that Samudrabandha flatters Ravivarmadeva is a fact; but flattery in India is limited to the living Why ? Ravivarmadeva could not be an ancestor of a patron of Samudrabandha, the ancestor whom he admires as a man of letters.

śrīmallināthaputro lakṣmīgarbhāmṛtāmbudhisudhāṁśuḥ I
bhāmasya vṛttavidyādhāmno bhrātā trivikramaḥ sukaviḥ II 3 II

śrīvīrasenajinasenāryādivacaḥpayodhipūrāt katicit I
prākṛtapadaratnāni prakṛtikṛtī sukṛtibhūṣaṇāya cinoti II 4 II

analapārthaḥ sukhoccāraḥ śabdaḥ sāhityajīvitam I
sa ca prākṛtameveti mataṁ sūtrānuvartinām[1] II 5 II

prākṛtaṁ tatsamaṁ deśyaṁ tadbhavaṁ cetyadastridhā
tatsamaṁ saṁskṛtasamaṁ neyaṁ saṁskṛtalakṣmaṇā II 6 II

deśyamārṣaṁ ca rūḍhatvāt svatantratvācca bhūyasā I
lakṣma nāpekṣate tasya saṁpradāyo hi bodhakaḥ II 7 II 13

prakṛteḥ saṁskṛtāt sādhyamānāt siddhācca yadbhavet I
prākṛtasyāsya lakṣyānurodhi lakṣma pracakṣmahe II 8 II

prākṛtapadārthasārthaprāptyai nijasūtramārgam anujigamiṣatāṁ I
vṛttiryathārthyasiddhyai trivikrameṇāgamakramāt kriyate II 9 II

tadbhavatatsamadeśyaprākṛtarūpāṇi paśyatāṁ viduṣām I
darpaṇatayeyamavanau vṛttis traivikramī jayati II 10 II

prākṛtarūpāṇi yathā prācyairā hemacandrāryāt[2] I
vivṛtāni tathā tāni pratibimbantīha sarvāṇi II 11 II

1. "To Śrī-Vīra, who has risen up from the eastern mountain, who illuminates all, the sun of the divine speech, I do offer my homage with the intention of obtaining an imperishable voice (and for finding the path of the syllables.)

2-3. "A bee on the lotus of the feet of Arhanandi Traividyamuni, who retained all that he had heard (or:

1. Some MSS have *sūktānuvartinām.*

2. This is the reading in all the MSS utilized by Pischel and also by T. Laddu. However, the MS No. 571 of Paris has *prācyairā hemacandramācāryaiḥ*, metrically possible (it should have been the first hemistich of a verse in the āryā metre and what appears clearer to me like an expression. Basically the meaning does not differ.

master of revelation)[1], grandson of Ādityaśarman—this sun for the water-lily, that is the noble family of Bāṇa—son of Mallinātha; born like a moon from the ocean of ambrosia that had given birth to Lakṣmī, brother of Bhāma, the temple of prosody, such is the great poet Trivikrama.

4. "From the waves of this ocean—the speech of Śrī-Vīrasena, Jinasena and other saints—he has collected some pearls—the Prākrit-words—with the intention of decorating his fine work, himself an expert in etymology.

5. "A word rich in meaning and convenient in pronunciation, is the life of poetry; this word is (also) of the (pure) Prākrit in the opinion of those who conform to the sūtras[2].

6. "Prākrit is divided into three parts: the Tatsama, the Tadbhava and Deśya. Tatsama are the words that have the same form as that in Sanskrit; they are to be deduced according to the rules of Sanskrit.

7. Local words (Deśya) like Ārṣa words, are not regulated according to the rules, because in most of the cases they do not have an etymology and they behave arbitrarily; their sole teacher is tradition.

8. "Tadbhavas are those that have their origin in Sanskrit, that are derived from themes and roots or from already formed words : this is this Prākrit of which we expose the rules according to the examples.

9. "For those who aspire to follow the path of his (or their) sūtras for acquiring a rich vocabulary of Prākrit and meanings, Trivikrama has composed according to tradition a commentary that will serve them in attaining this goal.

10. "May the commentary of Trivikrama succeed, because as a mirror it serves the scholars who see the Prākrit forms, Tadbhava, Tatsama and Deśya.

11. "The forms of Prākrit as explained by the ancient (teachers), including Hemacandra, are all reflected in it."

1. For Mr. U p a d h y e (An. *Bhandarkar*, XIII, p. 172) *Śrutabhartā* in the name of the teacher who teaches the Jaina scripture.

2. Or to nice speech (of Śrivīrasena, etc.) in case one prefers the reading *sūktānu°* of certain MSS.

733. The MSS consulted by T. Laddu have three concluding stanzas that are wanting in the MS of the Fonds Sanskrit 571 of the Bibliothèque Nationale of Paris that I have examined. The last MS on the whole is correct and is evidently incomplete. It stops in the middle of a stanza given as an example of nipāta of Apabhraṁśa :

kahiṁ sasaharu kahiṁ mayaraharu kahiṁ barihiṇu kahiṁ mehu

The whole stanza will be found in Hemacandra (IV, 422,7). After the nipātas of Apabhraṁśa (III, 3, 56) Trivikrama adds two more sūtras before closing the third pāda of the third and last adhyāya. So the Paris MS is wanting in the whole of the fourth (pāda devoted to declension and conjugation of Apabhraṁśa) and in addition the end of the third pāda.

734. The concluding stanzas of the grammar of Trivikrama are the following:—

sapratyayaprakṛtisiddhamadīrghasūtram I
satkārakaṁ bahuvidhakriyamāptadeśyam II

śabdānuśāsanamidaṁ praguṇaprayogaṁ I
traivikramaṁ japata mantramivārthasiddhyai II

viśantaḥ śrotraṁ padamadhurimā medurayati I
praṇetā nūtnorthaḥ pratipadamaho sādhuvacanam II

rasaḥ pātrīkuryād bhuvanam anubhavādiva kṛter I
yadi kāvyaṁ śravyaṁ mama rasikanāiyāyikajanaiḥ II

vaktāraḥ santu sarvepi svābhiprāyāprakaśane I
svapadāśayasaṁvādikathāsvekastrivikramaḥ II

"Count it like a magical formula, for the purpose of understanding the meanings (of words), this grammar of Trivikrama, excellent in the usage, which realises the themes

1. It has been so described by Cabaton in his catalogue Prākṛtavyākaraṇavṛtti par Trivikramadeva, 18th, Century? Grantha-writing 104 380 x 35 m.m., 31, 60 to 65 aks. (Sanskrit Grantha 32). In fact there are 8 lines per folio.

with their suffixes, of which the sūtras are short, which teaches the relations of cases, which explains the different verbs (allusions to the dhātvādeśa?), which understands (also) the correct local words.

"While penetrating into the ear, the sweetness of words fills it up; our new guide is the sense of each word; Oh! the beautiful language! what does the sentimental poetry make its receptacle the entire world, whilst my poem on account of the importance of my work, will be heard by men endowed with poetical sentiments and a philosophical spirit.

"Everybody is capable of explaining his own doctrine; but when there is a question of reconciling the meaning of the words used by him there stands Trivikrama alone[1]".

735. Bhattanatha Svamin and T. Laddu, who are convinced that the author of these *sūtras* is Trivikrama, find that this thing was pronounced by Trivikrama himself: but these very words, on the contrary, indicate to Hultzsch and K. Prāṇaśaṅkara Trivedi, the editor of Lakṣmīdhara, that Trivikrama is exclusively the author of the commentary. As regards Pischel, who has changed his opinion between the period of the publication of his dissertation on the grammarians and of his grammar, he is always dependent upon the words of Trivikrama. We are, therefore, obliged to accept that they admit of two different interpretations.

(a) *Trivikrama is the author of the sūtras* : In fact in stanza 3, he calls himself "a good poet" (*sukavi*) and calls his grammar a *kāvya* (verse 2 of the conclusion). Since his sūtras are in verses, he is their author.

(b) *Trivikrama is not the author of these sūtras* : In these two reprises, he himself calls his work a commentary (stanzas 9 to 10 of the introduction); he would not have done so had he composed these sūtras.

As to the stanza 9 and to the meaning of the word *nija*, it has been the field of an epic-battle : *nija* has the sense of *sva* and refers to Trivikrama (Bhattanatha Svamin, T. Laddu, Pischel, Gramm.); it has the sense of *sva*, but it

1. Trivikrama has compared his grammar with a *mantra* and has used in these verses a number of words from the language of magic. The allusions are obvious to an Indian, but I omit to translate them here.

has a reference to *anujigamiṣatām*, those (of the Jainas) who would like to follow the path of their sūtras (=religious precepts written in Prākrit)" (Pischel, de gramm. pr., K. Prāṇaśaṅkara T r i v e d i); should be taken in the sense of "proper, real" and finally "just" as in certain Dravidian languages (Hultzsch)[1].

(2) *The tradition attributes these sūtras to Vālmīki.* This tradition is not well established. Lakṣmīdhara (cf. § 723) is correct when he expressly calls Vālmīki *mūlasūtrakṛt*. Moreover, K. Prāṇaśaṅkara T r i v e d i reproduces a passage from a mythological work, the Ś a m b h u r a h a s y a[2] that praises Vālmīki as the founder of the Prākrit grammar:

ko vininded imāṁ bhāṣāṁ bhāratīmukhabhāṣitām I
yasyāḥ pracetasaḥ putro vyākartā bhagavān ṛṣiḥ II267II 13

gārgya-gālava-śākalya-pāṇinyādyā yatharṣayaḥ I
śabdarāśeḥ saṁskṛtasya vyākartāro mahattamāḥ II14II

tathaiva prākṛtādīnāṁ ṣaḍbhāṣāṇāṁ mahāmuniḥ I
ādikāvyakṛd ācāryo vyākartā lokaviśrutaḥ II15II

yathaiva rāmacaritaṁ saṁskṛtaṁ tena nirmitam I
tathaiva prākṛtenāpi nirmitaṁ hi satāṁ mude II16II

pāṇinyādyaiḥ śikṣitatvāt saṁskṛtā syād yathottamā I
prācetasavyākṛtatvāt prakṛtyāpi tathottamā II19II

prākṛtaṁ cārṣmevedaṁ yaddhi vālmīkiśikṣitam I
tadānārṣaṁ bhaved yo vai prākṛtaḥ syāt sa eva hi II24II

Śambhurahasya, pp. 17-18.

1. Interpretation refuted with excellent arguments by Bhaṭṭanātha Svāmin (p. 219).

2. Intr. to *Ṣaḍbhāṣācandrikā*, p. 13, note: "A portion of this voluminous work Śambhurahasya, comprising of four chapters devoted to the praise of poet and poetry, treatment of Prākṛita words (Prākṛtaśabdapradīpikā) and a poetical work called Rāghavayādavīya with a commentary is printed in Telugu characters in the year 1890." I have not been able to consult this work.

"Who dares despise this language, gracious speech of Goddess Eloquence, of which the grammarian is the son of Pracetas, this divine sage? As the sages G ā r g y a, G ā la v a, Ś ā k a l y a, P ā ṇ i n i, etc., have been the greatest grammarians of the mass of Sanskrit words, so the same great ascetic, so the author of the first poem, has been the celebrated grammarian of languages in the world, of six languages, the Prākrit, etc."

"And the same person, who has composed the history of Rāma in Sanskrit, has also composed it in Prākrit[1] for the pleasure of the respectable persons. As Sanskrit has attained its perfection through the teachings of Pāṇini, etc; so thanks to the analysis of the son of Pracetas, Prākrit too has become perfect. Prākrit is the language of Ṛṣis; it is taught by Vālmīki; if there is a man who may say that it is not worthy of Ṛṣis, this is he who will be called *Prākṛta* (uncultured)."

736. Moreover, in the Madras library[2] there is preserved a manuscript of a grammar that is attributed to Vālmīki, which exclusively comprises the sūtras of the first two adhyāyas of Trivikrama. The work is complete as the colophon indicates : *iti vālmīkīyeṣu sūtreṣu dvītīyādhāyasya pādaścaturthaḥ* ll *adhyāyaś ca samāptaḥ* l *prākṛtavyākaraṇaśāstram api samāptam* ll "Here ends the fourth chapter of the second lesson in the sūtras of Vālmīki. The lesson too ends : the grammar of Prākrit too comes to its end."

Unfortunately this undated manuscript is written on paper and its appearance is wholly modern.

737. Bhattanatha S v a m i n explains the tradition which attributes to Vālmīki the paternity of the sūtras commented upon by Trivikrama in an entirely ingenuous[3] manner. It might have its origin in a careless reading of the verse 11 of the introduction to P r ā k ṛ t a v y ā k a r a ṇ a. It would

1. Reference to S e t u b a n d h a.

2. A Descriptive Catalogue of the Sanskrit MSS in the Government Oriental Manuscripts Library, Madras, by M. R a n g a n a c h a r y a, Madras 1906, vol. III, No. 1548 (p. 1083).

3. IA. 1911, p. 220.

have been read as *prācetasa-hemacandrādyāt* in place of *prācyair ā hemacandrādyāt* (which is substituted in other MSS for the reading *prācyair-ā-hemacandraṁ ācāryaiḥ* (cf. § 732).

738. If the Śambhurahasya is posterior to Trivikrama, the hypothesis of Bhattanatha Svamin may by accepted: Vālmīki, the grammarian of Prākrit, had rather been embarrassing, and one will like to be relieved of him by a philological stratagem.

Is it, therefore, necessary to consider Trivikrama as the author of these sūtras?

I affirm that the alternative thus posited will be without an issue. I, however, believe that we may abandon Vālmīki without being constrained for this to attribute all the sūtras to Trivikrama.

739. In the chapter on Hemcandra (cf. § 619ff.) I have pointed out a case in which Hemcandra shows that he knew a sūtra of Trivikrama written in the technical terms that are characteristic of the Prākṛtavyākaraṇa. And since Hemacandra has been plagiarized by Trivikrama, for me there is no shadow of doubt that at least a certain number of sūtras are anterior to Trivikrama.

Moreover, I would be inclined to attribute some importance to the manuscript of the sūtras of Vālmīki preserved in Madras (cf. § 736).

740. It is admittedly very modern, but it rejects the third adhyāya, and the grammar of Trivikrama presents a curious peculiarity that I am astonished not to find to have been noted by the advocates of the theory of Trivikrama, being the commentator. The beginning of the third adhyāya does not coincide with a subdivision of the material to be treated. The following table will help us in understanding better this remark :—

Adhyāya I, Pāda I :-	Introduction, Technical terms, General Rules, Sandhi, etc.
Pādas II-IV :-	Phonetics.
Adhyāya II, Pāda I :-	Suffixes
Pādas II-IV :-	Declension and Conjugation, List of *Dhātvādeśas.*
Adhyāya III, Pāda I :-	Continuation of *Dhātvādeśas*; Irregular Words.

Pāda II :- Śauraseni, Māgadhī, Paiśāci and Cūlikā Paiśācī.

Pāda III-IV:- Apabhraṁśa and Deśī.

741. We cannot resist thinking that the whole of the third adhyāya might have been a later-day addition of which Trivikrama might have been the author[1]. Possibly there was a Prākrit grammar written in short sūtras of the Pāṇinian model before the time of Hemacandra. It appears that after the Siddhahemacandra was completed, Trivikrama summarised the different grammatical treatises known in his age and wanted to rewrite the whole thing in the style of this ancient grammar. And since he calls himself a poet (*sukavi* § 735), it appears that he had the idea of putting his ideas into verses.

742. In any case this primitive grammar of the principal Prākrit was current in the age of Trivikrama, and on this account, Trivikrama could not dare make any alteration in its essential plan. Hence in the third adhyāya he adds a portion of his own contributions, so far as they relate to the dialects and a certain number of Dhātvādeśas that probably the original grammar did not contain[2]. It is also probable that after Trivikrama, this ancient grammar went out of use but its souvenir continued to remain, and it was easy to give life to the personality of Vālmīki as a Prākrit grammarian, on the basis of a false reading. In addition the manuscript preserved in Madras attests that the ancient subdivision of the two adhyāyas and four pādas of the primitive work was still referred to.

743. Moreover, the third adhyāya of Trivikrama is of further interest: it is here that we find a rich collection of Apabhraṁśa-stanzas and a part of the lists of Deśīs and Nipātas. An edition of Trivikrama will not be superfluous if the editor be willing to treat Trivikrama as a

1. In the first concluding stanza, one may probably find some complaisance of the author: he would insist on the *Dhātvādeśas* and the *Deśīs* and the *Nipātas*, because it is in this domain that he had made his personal contributions.

2. At the end of the edition of the Ṣaḍbhāṣācandrikā (p. 19 of the pagination in Arabic figures) will be found the list of sūtras of Trivikrama in the original order.

lexicographer and literary man, rather than as a grammarian.

743. In fact the Prākṛtavyākaraṇa merits to be edited on account of lists of words and examples, but not for the grammatical principles of Prākrit, to which he has made no new additions.

744. On account of the technical terms, I have been simply wondering, solely on account of the sūtras, on which Trivikrama wrote his commentary, if the grammar that is the basis of the Prākṛtavyākaraṇa has not been the famous Prākrit grammar attributed to Pāṇini[1] by Jaina authors and of which we do not find the trace elsewhere.

745. The glory of Hemacandra has been so great among the Jainas that some grammarians wholly following Trivikrama have attempted to approach Hemacandra more and more closely.

746. One of them, Śubhacandra, is the author of Śabdacintāmaṇi of which Hoernle had found a manuscript[2] in 1873.

This m nuscript contained only the subject-matter of the first two adhāyas of Trivikrama, exactly like the Vālmīkisūtra of the Madras library. But the complete work has been found : Dr. A.N. Upadhye[3] has examined it and given some extracts.

747. Śubhacandra was a Jaina teacher, whose literary activities extended over a period of at least about forty years, since in the Pāṇḍavapurāṇa, written in 1608 of the Vikrama era (1551 A.D.), he cites a list of 27 works composed by him, of which one, the Adhyātmataraṅgiṇīṭīkā is of 1516 A.D.[4] Among them he cites also the Prākṛtacintāmaṇi, however, without indicating the date of its composition.

1. Cf. Hoernle, Introduction to the edition of Prākṛtalakṣaṇa of Caṇḍa, pp. I-II. The two citations are not found exactly as in Trivikrama, but this would not be a proof, because this ancient grammar would be submerged in the abundant materials of the Śiddhahemacandra, of which the Prākṛtavyākaraṇa is a plagiarist.

2. IA. II (1873), p. 29.

3. Śubhacandra and Prākrit Grammar : Annals of the Bhandarkar Oriental Research Institute XIII, p. 37-58.

4. *Ann. Bhaṇdarkar* XIII, pp. 43-44.

748. Śubhacandra was a *bhaṭṭāraka* (professor) at Sakavāṭa (actually at Sāgavāḍā) in Rajputana. But we do not know if he was a native of this country.

749. His Prākrit grammar is written in a servile manner exactly as that of Trivikrama. Even the absurd separation of the two groups of dhātvādeśas (cf. § 740) is faithfully respected[1]. But viewed from the external aspect Śubhacandra represents also a back-coming to Hemacandra. The conclusion of Upādhye wholly appears acceptable to me: Śubhacandra has mechanically followed H. (Hemacandra) and T. (Trivikrama) and as such he has made little contribution to the advancement of Prākritic studies. The independence of Śubhacandra's grammar, if it can be called so, consists mainly in changing the wordings of the sūtras, sometimes in changing the order, combining two sūtras into one, and in composing sūtras based on the matter that was included in the commentary by H. and T. Additional illustrations as such there are none"[2].

750. More dependent on Hemacandra than on Trivikrama there appears another Prākrit grammar : the Audāryacintāratna (°maṇi) for remarking the nominal analogy with the preceding work of Śrutasāgara. I know about this grammar only from its short extract published by the editor of the Saḍbhāṣācandrikā of Lakṣmīdhara[3]. This work is dated towards the close of the 15th century.

1. Ibid, p. 48
2. Ibid, p. 51
3. Cf. Introduction to the edition, p. 7-8. See also *Ann. Bhandarkar* XIII, 52-53.

Chapter VII

CAṆḌA

81. In case Hoernle, the editor of the Prākṛtalakṣaṇa[1] of Caṇḍa had been a less unsophisticated enthusiast, he would have been struck by the singular circumstance that all the manuscripts on the basis of which he established the text of his venerable sūtras as going back to an epoch hardly more recent than the 3rd century B.C.[2] were copies written in the second half of the 19th century. After the publication of the Prākṛtalakṣaṇa, the interest of the searchers of manuscripts should have been sufficiently aroused that none of the ancient treasures in any of the remote provinces has delivered a much more ancient MS of Caṇḍa. The history of the manuscripts consulted by Hoernle will be found at p. III of his introduction : the faith and the deep faith of the editor are admirable.

82. R. G. Bhandarkar[3] points to a MS dated 1857-58 A.D. (Śaka 1779) belonging to Govind Sastri Nirantar of Nasik. According to the its colophon one concludes that it gives the texts of the "revisionists", C and D of Hoernle.

83. Peterson[4] mentions the existence of another manuscript of the work belonging to Kalyana Chandra of Cambay; it is not dated, but since it is written on paper, it cannot be very old. We may go back to a century or two, but there always remains an age of almost two thousand years for rejoining with the supposed original. And during this

1. The Prākṛita-lakṣaṇam or Chaṇḍa's grammar of the ancient (Ārṣa) Prākrit, edited by A. F. Rudolph Hoernle, Part I, Text with a critical introduction and indexes; Calcutta 1880; published by the Asiatic Society.

2. Introduction, p. XX-XXI.

3. Lists of Sanskrit Manuscripts in private libraries in the Bombay Presidency, compiled under the superintendence of R. G. Bhandarkar, Part I, Bombay 1893, p. 58.

4. P. Peterson : Three Reports on a Search for Sanskrit Manuscripts...Bombay 1887, p. 265. The colophon indicates that this manuscript reproduces a version analogous to that of the manuscripts A and B of Hoernle. It adds a title of the work that we do not know elsewhere: *iti śrīcandakṛte prākṛtalakṣaṇe vyaṁjanāvidhānaṁ tṛtīyaṁ samāptam* ll *samāptā caiṣā prākṛtasāroddhāravṛttiḥ.*

long lapse of time the name of Caṇḍa had never been cited by any grammarian or commentator and it has never been included in the list and biographies of eminent Jainas.

It is also permissible even to doubt about the grammar of Caṇḍa being complete. There is not a single word on conjugation.

84. Naturally for Hoernle this fact is not disquieting: during this remote epoch Prākrit had not undergone any important modification on this point and did not "differ much from the prototype Sanskrit"[1]. In any case the form *vāhijjaī* replacing the Sanskrit *vādhyate* (III, 25), for example, merits some words of explanation. But Hoernle,[2] profoundly convinced of the antiquity of Caṇḍa interpreted every fact as an argument standing in support of his doctrine. In case any fact could not be brought to support his doctrine he modified it without remorse. His probability is always beyond discussion: in the critical apparatus all the readings are preserved, but the text of the Prākṛtalakṣaṇa in a great measure is a construction of his own intelligence.

85. In respect of the verb, for example, he states without any hesitation that "ancient Prākrit, like Pāli and Sanskrit, preserved the ātmanepada by the side of the parasmaipada (p. LII of the Introduction)". Now in reality he has nothing to justify this affirmation—except a few examples from the commentary—commentary that is not necessarily contemporaneous with the sūtras. Moreover, these examples are found mostly in the MSS C and D in unintelligible "revisionists". Examples A B C *dīsaï*, D *dīsae* (text of Hoernle *dīsae*) = Skt. *dṛśyate* (II, 5). AB *najjaï*, CD *najjae* (text : *najjate*) = Skt. *jñāyate* (III, 25).

86. It is probable that the grammar of Caṇḍa is not complete. In the MSS A and B it is made up of three sections: *vibhaktividhāna*, *svaravidhāna* and *vyañjanavidhāna*.

The "revisionists" have grouped four meagre sūtras on the dialects in a fourth section : the *bhāṣāntarvidhāna*. Have they not done this with the intention of giving to the *Prākṛtalakṣaṇa* the outlook of a complete work consisting of 4

1. Int. p. LII.
2. Hoernle reads *vāhijjate* on account of his reliance on the "revisionists" who say *vāhijjae*.

subdivisions, a thing that in the grammatical text is sacramental?"

Another proof of the fragmentary condition of the grammar of Caṇḍa, lies, in my opinion, in the fact that the sūtras are not enchained among themselves. The commentary often completes the sūtras by words that are not authorised to be understood from the preceding ones. And whether the commentary explains and sometimes betrays the sūtras, it never bothers about the force of *adhikāra*. Now Caṇḍa, in case, was so ancient as Hoernle wants him, the necessity of respecting the *adhikāra* should have weighed with him in the same manner in which it had weighed with Pāṇini.

87. Let us take for example the sūtras I, 12 *ṇo ṅaseśca* and 13 *ssaśca ṅasaḥ* : it is evident that these sūtras were related only to the themes in *-i* or in *-u*, which alone have the ablative and genitive singular in *ṇo*. But the limitation is not indicated by what precedes it.

88. I believe also that the declension of pronouns, other than the personal pronouns, cannot be comprehended within the single remark in respect of the form replacing the ablative and genitive singular and plural of the three genders of the pronouns *tad* and *idam* (Caṇḍa I, 17).

89. The arrangement of the subject-matter is little coherent: in the second section, the svaravidhāna, the section on vowels, we find the suffixes and the particles. And still more curious is the fact that two sūtras on the personal pronouns (Caṇḍa II, 26, 27) have come to interrupt the teaching on the particles.

810. When one reads in the introduction of Hoernle the grammatical exposition of the dialect taught by Caṇḍa and compares it with inaccurate and a small number of sūtras of the Prākṛtalakṣaṇa, one comes to know that a large number of rules and forms enumerated by Hoernle have been introduced by him on the basis of the "rule of three". Now this rule of three holds good in mathematics alone. His mode of reasoning is revealed in respect of the form of the abl. sing. *devato*[1].

1. Introduction, p. XXXII: "To these forms may be added the

811. The exposition of the verb (p. LII –LIV of the introduction) is based only on the forms found in the commentary.

812. However, in spite of the effort made by Hoernle for filling all the lacunae of Caṇḍa, he does not successfully either from the reading of the introduction or still less from that of the sūtras eliminate the impression that the Prākṛtalakṣaṇa teaches a unique language that is more ancient than the Māhārāṣṭrī of the gāthās.

813. None of the arguments advanced by Hoernle for demonstrating the higher antiquity of the Prākrit of Caṇḍa resists a careful examination. R.G. Bhandarkar[1] has already refuted a number of them :—

1. P. XXV : "The final vowel of the former part of a compound word is dropped, if the initial vowel of the latter part is followed by a conjunct consonant (Caṇḍa II, 2) ; e.g. *deva+indra* would in Sanskrit be *devendra*, but in Ārṣa the final *a* of *deva* is elided, hence the compound is *devinda*."

8131. Bhandarkar remarks that this rule is taught by Hc. I, 84, who gives in fact the examples *narendraḥ=narindo*; *adharoṣṭhaḥ=aharuṭṭhaṁ*[2].

As regards Vararuci, I am surprised to see that the commentary of Bhāmaha teaches exactly the same thing as Caṇḍa. All that we have to do it is to search for it under the sūtra IV, 1 devoted to the sandhi of vowels.

8132. Hoernle has translated a large number of words of the sūtras of Caṇḍa.

saṁyoge pare lopaḥ :

Commentary:—*saṁyoge pare svare parataḥ pūrvasvarasya nityaṁ lopo bhavati* ll *dhanāḍhyaḥ=dhaṇaḍḍho* l *deva indraḥ=deviṁdo* l

ablative made with the suffix *-to* (=Sanskrit—*taḥ*). It is not technically a declensional form. For the same reason it is separately noticed by Kachchāyana (II, 5, 1, p. 116). But its existence in Ārṣa is guaranteed by its occurrence in Pāli, and by its presence in the modified form *-tto* in later Prākrit (Hc. III, 8) and also by the existence in Ārṣa itself of the pronominal forms *maītto* and *taītto* (I, 24, 28)",

1. JBORAS XVII, 1887, p. 5 ss.
2. Cf. also Hc. I, 10.

kṛta udyogaḥ=katujjoo[1] ll 8133. In Bhāmaha we read (IV, 1): *saṁyoge pare sarvatra pūrvasyāco lopaḥ.* It is translated by Cowell as—"when a conjunct consonant follows, it is always the *first* of the two meeting vowels which is elided (when there is any elision at all, which is not always required)". Unfortunately Bhāmaha does not add examples, but there is no doubt that the subject relates to the same fact as taught by Caṇḍa.

8134. In other respects the treatment is normal in Māhārāṣṭrī, as indicated by Pischel (Gramm. §158).

8135. 2°p. XXV: "The preservation of the dental *n*, in every case, whether single or double, whether initial or medial in a word". Bhandarkar noted that demonstration of this affirmation was not rigorous and that the examples given in the edition, almost without exception, follow the rule propounded by Hemacandra, and I believe, that is common to all the grammarians, cf. § 4111 (i): intervocalic *n* always becomes *ṇ*; *n* that is initial or is in a group may become *ṇ*[2].

8136 3° p. XXVI: "The preservation of the medial single surd unaspirate consonant, with the exception of *k* which may be elided." Hoernle wants to justify his theory by the sūtra III, 34 *katṛtīyayoḥ svare* (understood *lopaḥ*) Commentary : *kakārasya vargatṛtīyasya ca svare pare lopo bhavati* ll *kokilaḥ=koilo* l *bhaugikaḥ=bhoio* l *rājī=rāī* (B *vanarājī=vaṇarāī*) *pratikulaḥ=paikulo* (in B only) l *nadī=naī* l *nupuram=neuraṁ* l *kūpaḥ=kūo* (the two last ones in A only). B adds a very long list of examples of the non-aspirate surds.

8137. Now in fact, as noted by Bhandarkar, non-aspirate surds undergo at least vocalisation :

Cd III, 12 does not leave any doubt on this subject:—

1. As throughout, I respect here the reading of Hoernle that is not always far from that of MS.

2. The starting point of cerebralisation of the initial dental was provided by the enclitics. Cf. for example under I, 3 CD *ṇo* for *naḥ* (p. 53) (cf. also § 2512).

prathamasya tṛtīyaḥ

Comm. : *prathamasya sthāne tṛtīyo bhavati* l *ekam=egaṁ* l *tīrthakaraḥ=titthagaro* l *piśācī=pisājī* l *jaṭā=jaḍā* l *kṛtam=kadaṁ* l *pratiṣiddhaṁ=paḍisiddhaṁ*...... (cf. the variants.)

A. the best manuscript, has a further reduced and more clear commentary: *spaṣṭam* l *piśācī=pisājī.*

8138. So it results that in the language taught by Caṇḍa, the intervocalic surds are normally vocalised; the sūtra III, 34 should probably indicate the case of dropping of surds and voiced consonants. The "revisionists" of the MSS C and D have, therefore, believed in effecting improvement through substitution of this sūtra in the unhappy edition by an analogous sūtra Vr. II, 2; Hc. I, 177: *kagacajatadapayavāṁ prāyo luk.*

8139. Moreover, the examples enumerated by R. G. Bhandarkar present in a large number of cases the dropping of intervocalic surds. But neither this constant usage of all the manuscripts nor the teaching of Caṇḍa III, 12 dissuaded Hoernle from believing that in this venerable dialect all the intervocalic surds were preserved. So he has restored it all through and this is a thing that gives to the language an appearance of its being hybrid: it is not of Prākrit and it is neither a different language. It is true that Hoernle always took pains to give at the bottom of the page the accurate reading, but in case one is not careful, he will every time imagine the presence of an exceptional error of the copyist.

This is a single isolated word that has brought in and invoked the passion for restitution.

81310. The MSS A and B (II, 26) give *bhe kṛtam=tvayā kṛtam* as an example of substitution of *bhe* for the pronoun of the second person. At p. XIII of introduction Hoernle "thinks" that the copyist had before him the form **kataṁ* with the intervocalic consonant *-t-* preserved and that he replaced it by the pure Sanskrit *kṛtam.* The suspicion soon after was transformed into certainty, because Hoernle did not hesitate to restore all the intervocalic surds. The weakness of this argument is evident. Of the two things, the one, for Hoernle, the commentary of the best manuscripts

A and B is contemporaneous with the sūtras, and in this case one is authorised to attach some importance to the form *kṛtam*, or the commentary is posterior and that it is not permissible to use it for rectification of the sūtras, unless one is able to prove that the sūtra has been subjected to an accident.

In case the commentary is contemporaneous, there remains to be explained the presence of the normal form *kayaṁ* (I, 23, 27; II, 18) *or kadaṁ* (III. 12) elsewhere in the same commentary in the MSS A and B, and why it did not retain the intervocalic surd in any other word.

81311. So the commentary is posterior, and in this case we are less authorised to make too much of a single isolated form.

And we do not insist on the circumstance that in reality this isolated form too is partly an invention of Hoernle, because the MS has *kṛtaṁ* and not *kataṁ* (when at the bottom one would rather restore *kaṭam* with a cerebral.[1]

81312. 4° p. XXVII: "The preservation of the medial single surd aspirate consonants with the only exception of *kh*, which may be reduced to *h*".

It should be noted that for Vararuci (II, 27) as well the ḍropping of the occlusive element among the aspirates is restricted to *kha* and *tha*, so the language of Caṇḍa would preserve only the *tha* at the most. But in this way we come to the dilemma set forth above just now—the commentary (of the manuscripts A and B) finds this exclusion of the *tha* so weakly justified, that it brings in the examples *mathurā mahurā*, *nāthaḥ nāho* in the sūtra III, 11

81314. 5° p. XXXVII: "The preservation of the single medial semi-consonants *y* and *v*."

It is exclusively deduced from the silence of Caṇḍa. In all events when Hoernle affirms that for Vararuci the *ya* is always elided, he makes a statement that is not accurate, since this elision is optional like that of *va*. Some examples of the dropping of *ya* and of *va* are given in

1. Cf. also Bhandarkar l. l., p. 7.

the commentary of the MS B under the sūtra III, 34 (cf. p. 35).

81315. 6° p. XXVII : "The insertion of the semi-vowel to fill up the hiatus whenever the second vowel is *a*".

Cḍ III, 35 *yatvamavarṇe.*

Now this corresponds exactly to Hc. I, 180 *avarṇo yaśrutiḥ.* So there is nothing that may indicate an archaic language in Caṇḍa. According to H o e r n l e, however, there should have been a difference in the comprehension of the sūtra. (But let us not forget that this would belong in all the cases exclusively to the commentary of Caṇḍa). For Hemacandra the *yaśruti* should take place exclusively between two *as*. Now it is true that Hemacandra explains the sūtra as *kagacajetyādinā luki sati śeṣovarṇovarṇāt paro laghuprayatnatarayakāraśrutirbhavati—titthayaro* l *sayadhaṁ.....* ll *avarṇādityeva* l *loassa* ll *dearo* ll *kvacid bhavati* l *piyaī.*

81316. For the same Hemacandra, so there are exceptions to his rule, that in addition, as noted by P i s c h e l in his note, is not respected by the Jaina-texts. But Hemacandra further contradicts it more explicitly in the commentary on I, 15: *bahulādhikārādiṣatspṛṣṭatarayaśrutirapi* ll *sariyā* ll *pāḍivayā* l *saṁpayā* ll "On account of the force of the adhikāra *bahulam* (Hc. 1, 2) one also hears lightly pronounced *ya* replacing the final consonants of the feminine themes.

Ex. *sariyā* (Skt. *sarit*), *pāḍivayā* (Skt. *pratipad*), *saṁpayā* (Skt. *saṁpad*).

So the accord between Caṇḍa and Hemacandra on this point is incapable of being discussed.

814. These divergences, that we believe to have eliminated, are the only ones that exist according to the same Hoernle, between the old Prākrit of the later-day grammarians, so for as phonetics is concerned[1].

815. In the declension of nouns another characteristic of the venerable dialect of Caṇḍa would be *-haṁ*, the termina-

1. P. XXVII "In all other respects there is no difference between the older Prākrit and that of the older grammarians."

tion of the genitive sing. that it possesses in common with the non-literary Apabhraṁśa.

816. This termination is unknown to Ārṣa and to classical Māhārāṣṭrī. Hemacandra attributes it to Māgadhī, but the texts do not attest his statement. As already noted by us, it is on the contrary the normal termination of Apabhraṁśa[1].

817. Let us first of all examine the sūtra of Hemacandra. Hc.IV. 300 *āmo ḍāha̐ vā* ll *māgadhyām avarṇāt parasyāmonunāsikānto ḍit āhādeśo vā bhavati* l *saayaṇāha̐ muhaṃ* l *pakṣe* ll *nalimdāṇaṁ* l *vyatyayāt prākṛtepi* ll *tāha̐* l *tumhāha̐* l *sariāha̐* l *kammāha̐* ll In Māgadhī one may substitute *ḍit āha* with the final *anunāsika* for the termination *-ām* of the genitive plural "when it is preceded by a short or long *a*. Examples—*śayaṇāha̐ muhaṁ*". (cf. the remark of Pischel).

"While applying the second alternative one says *nalimdāṇaṁ* as well. "On account of confusion (of the dialects) (Hc. IV, 447) (this termination *-āha̐* occurs) in Prākrit too:

Examples :—*tātha̐*, *tumhāha̐*, *amhāha̐*, *sariāha̐*, *kammāha̐* ll

818. So Hemacandra, like Caṇḍa, admits the termination *-haṁ* for the principal Prakrit too. It is even astonishing that this thing escaped the notice of Hoernle, Pischel and Th. Bloch. It is one of the rare cases in which the manner in which Hemacandra introduces this extension in his vṛtti may create the impression of a borrowing by Hc. from Caṇḍa: no grammarian, other than Caṇḍa teaches the genitive plural in *-haṁ*; moreover, some of the examples are common to Hc and Caṇḍa.

Caṇḍa I, 5 *sāgamasyāpyāmo ṇo ho vā* l

sāgamasyāmonāgamasyāpi ṇakāro bhavati ho vā l *tāṇaṁ tāhaṁ* ll *devāṇaṁ* l *devāhaṁ* l *kammāṇaṁ kammāhaṁ* l *saritāṇaṁ saritāhaṁ* l *tumhāṇaṁ*, *tumhāhāṁ*.

I do not even try to translate the sūtra *sāgamasya*, as I am unable to make anything out of it, and the explanation of the commentary is of no help.

Moreover, incited by Hemacandra, I would read in place

2. Cf. Pischel, Gramm. § 370.

of *māgadhyām* : "in Māgadhī" the termination of the genitive plural may have the consonant *ṇa* or *ha* optionally". I would like to believe that on account of this false reading, that paleographically is not impossible, this sūtra of the Prākṛtalakṣaṇa has been displaced. As a result of this displacement a dialectical treatment has been accorded to the principal Prākrit.

Hemacandra knew from a different source this treatment in Māgadhī; but on account of the sūtra that we know as of Caṇḍa, he chose to indicate in the note that the termination *-haṁ* is at times employed in the principal Prākrit.

But we should not forget that the affix *-haṁ* is not attested either in the Māgadhī of the dramas or in some other grammarians on Māgadhī. So Caṇḍa would agree with Hemacandra against the unanimous textual evidence. It is imprudent to think that one or the other of them knew of this termination in Ṭākkī, grouped among the vibhāṣās by eastern grammarians, but what according to Hariścandra, is an Apabhraṁsa dialect ? (cf. § 4102).

819. Mārkaṇḍeya (XVI, 6) and Puruṣottama (XVI, 5) indeed teach the terminations *-haṁ* and *-huṁ* for the genitive plural of Ṭākkī. Somebody who was not very much conversant with the dialects spoken on the scene could easily consider a vibhāṣā as a kind of Māgadhī. Śākārī has many points of contact with Māgadhī[1]; like and more than Māgadhī the vibhāṣās are reserved for inferior characters, so the confusion is not impossible.

820. In case this long chain of argument has appeared convincing, it would result that the termination *-haṁ* should not be taken out of Apabhraṁśa.

821. On the other hand the dialect described by Caṇḍa does not point to the characteristics that are more particularly relevant to Ārṣa. There is not a single word on the survival of the dative singular, a thing that was current in Ardhamāgadhī (cf. Pischel, §361).

None of the rules taught by Hemacandra for Ārṣa (cf. § 660-663) is found in the language of Caṇḍa, ex-

1. Cf. Mk. XIII, 1 *māgadhyāḥ śākārī siddhyatīti śeṣaḥ.*

cepting the form *suhumaṁ*, Skt. *sūkṣma* (cf. Hc. I, 118, II 101; II, 113; Caṇḍa III, 30) which indeed is attested in Ardhamāgadhī only.

822. Moreover, it is difficult to resume the characteristics of Prākrit of Caṇḍa; there is at the moment question of understanding the sūtras; it is the value of the commentary that has to be defined first.

823. H o e r n l e was right in making a distinction between the manuscripts A and B on one side and those of the "revisionists" (C and D) on the other. These last ones at times go in search of their examples in pure Apabhraṁśa[1].

Moreover, many of the sūtras, found only in the MSS C and D. present certain affinities with the sūtras of Hemacandra that cannot be considered to be simply accidental.

On the whole the Prākṛtalakṣaṇa, that is the MSS A and B, often confirmed by the MSS C and D, does not make sure a lien betweeen Hemacandra and Caṇḍa.

824. Hoernle[2] was the first scholar to note that the commentary on Hc. III, 81 might have in view Caṇḍa I, 17. Th. B l o c h[3] is opposed to it, but, he is unable to bring forward arguments different from the assumed confusion of all the Indian grammarians between *kaścit* and *kecit*. According to him they make the variation in the singular and the plural exclusively due to their love for variety and least importance should be attached to these indications[4]. P i s c h e l takes up the question with less enthusiasm and arrives at the conclusion that probably H o e r n l e is correct.

825. It is sufficiently disappointing to be satisfied merely with a probability after so much of efforts. I have pointed

1. Cf. C. I, lla, p. 36=Hc. IV, 353; C. II, 27h, p. 47=Hc. IV, 330; CD 27 1, p. 47; cf. P i s c h e l, Gramm. § 34. Since the examples are of *dohās* in pure Apabhraṁśa, we are not permitted to accord some importance to the form *haũṁ* of the pronoun of the first person taught by CD (I, 26 a, p. 42) too and to renounce faith in the infiltration of "vulgarisms" in Māhārāṣṭrī according to the evidence of Caṇḍa alone, as done by Jacobi (*Bhavisattakaha, p.* 62.)

2. Introduction, p. XXII.

3. KZ. XXXIII, p. 325.

4. G r a m m a r § 34. The use of the singular, on the contrary, is exceptional and consequently more important. Hemacandra, almost always makes use of Pluralis Majestatis (cf. E. L e u m a n n, *Übersicht über das Āvaśyaka-Literatur*, Hamburg 1934, p. 52 note.

above (§ 818) to another case in which Hemacandra appears to have followed Caṇḍa.

Hc. I, 84 *hrasvaḥ saṁyoge* reproduces also Caṇḍa II, 3 *hrasvatvaṁ saṁyoge,* a rule that is wanting in Vararuci.

Hc. II, 184. *ṇaī cea cia cca avadhāraṇe* resembles more with Caṇḍa II, 17 *evārthe ṇaïceyaciyāḥ* than does Vr. IX, 3 *cia cea avadhāraṇe.*

Again Hc. III, 123 *saṁkhyāyā āmo ṇha ṇhaṁ* like Cd. I, 6 *saṁkhyāyāḥ ṇhaḥ,* extends the termination of the genitive plural -*ṇha* to all the nouns, of number whilst for Vr. VI, 59 *eṣām āmo ṇhaṁ* its use will be restricted to the numerals for two, three and four.

826. Lastly the form *bhe* that might be substituted for Caṇḍa for the pronouns of the first and second persons in all the cases and numbers and has been noted by Vararuci (VI, 37) for the genitive plural of *yuṣmad* and by only the commentary of Bhāmaha, since the Prākṛtasaṁjīvanī replaces *bhe* by *te* and and the Prākṛtamañjarī by a still more funny form *haū* (sic). It may be that they are not correct, but they reveal the point at which *bhe* in the language of Vararuci had been an aberrant form.

827. For Hemacandra, on the contrary (III, 91, 93-95, 100, 106) *bhe* may replace the nominative and the accusative plural, the instrumental singular, the genitive plural of *yuṣmad* and the nominative plural of *asmad.*

828. The extension made by Caṇḍa, indeed exaggerated and not justified by the texts, is apparently due to the less critical edition of the Prākṛtalakṣaṇa.

829. Following these data I would not dare affirm that Caṇḍa was one of the predecessors of Hemacandra, but this remains established that Hemacandra and Caṇḍa have in common certain rules and certain forms that are unknown to lyric Māhārāṣṭrī taught by Vararuci. Caṇḍa appears to be continuing a traditional school of Jaina Prākrit, or to be more precise his work appears to be the reflection of an outline of a grammatical treatise made for the Jainas and made by the Jainas. Hemacandra has incorporated in his grammar a portion of this material, probably the most ancient skeleton of the Prākṛtalakṣaṇa.

830. For the MSS C and D of the Prākṛtalakṣaṇa the lien, on the contrary, is absolutely certain : there is no doubt that there exists a current between the Prākṛtalakṣaṇa and the Siddhahemacandra : the thing, that is not certain, is the meaning of this current. The objections of Pischel (§ 34) are partly refutable, and in all events he has not pointed to all the points where the two works are accordant.

831. I do not believe, for example, like Pischel, that *uddhṛta-* and *udvṛtta-* should be considered as two different technical terms: both of them indicate likewise (Hc. I, 8), *svarasyodvṛtte*; Caṇḍa II, I D *svarasyoddhṛte*), the vowel that remains after dropping of a consonant. I believe that the good reading is that of Caṇḍa and I have found its confirmation in the fact that Trivikrama calls this vowel by the term equivalent to *śeṣa*. *Udvṛtta* does not have a satisfactory meaning, but since all the MSS of Hemacandra attest it, one may consider it as a case of mistake of reading in Hemacandra himself.

832. As against this the agreement is evident in these following cases :—

Hc. I, 5 *padayoḥ saṃdhirvā*.
Cd. II, la D *saṁskṛtavat saṁdhikāryaṁ padayoḥ*.
Hc. I. 6 *na yuvarṇasyāsve*.
Cd. II, lc D *na yuvarṇasyāsve*.
Hc. III, 137 comm. *prathamārthepi dvitīyā dṛśyate*.
Canda II, 13 a CD *prathamāyā dvitīyārṣe*.
Comm. Hc. III, 137 *ārṣe tṛtīyāpi dṛśyate* (*ṣ-e saptamyāḥ*)
Cḍ. II, 13b C D *saptamyās tṛtīyā ārṣe*.
Hc. II, 127 *ijerāḥ pādapūraṇe*.
Cḍ. II, 27a C D *ijerāḥ pādāpūraṇe*.
Hc. IV, 422. *yadeśchuḍuḥ*.
Cḍ. II, 27e C D *yadeśchuḍu*.
Hc. IV, 444 *ivārthe naṁnaūnāināvaījaṇijaṇāvaḥ*.
Cḍ. II, 27i C D *ṇaṁ ṇaū ṇāiṁ ṇāvaī jaṇi jaṇu maṇu ivārthe*.

833. None of the these sūtras has its correspondence in Vararuci : so the "current" exists. As regards the "meaning" I would be inclined to believe that the "revisionists" have taken this from Hemacandra. For example the last two sūtras are applicable to Apabhraṁśa, the examples given by C and

D are in pure Apabhraṁśa. The confusion can be explained only by supposing that C and D took them from Hemacandra. Lastly the rules of syntax that Hc. III, 137 gives for Ārṣa are found in Caṇḍa with the same examples and preceded by the indication *ārṣe.* Only once this word appears in the Prākṛtalakṣaṇa: hence it may be concluded that here C and D give peculiarities of Ārṣa in opposition to the dialects that they are in course of studying. This is partly perhaps the case, but since they are silent on all the other points, it is reasonable to conjecture that they have, without giving much pain to themselves, transported the sūtra of Hemacandra.

834. I would not dare affirm that the sūtras of the *Prākṛtalakṣaṇa* teach Ārṣa, but the examples of the commentary are often taken, from the language of the canonical texts of the Jainas.

835. Thus for example, when Hoernle announces in the paradigm of the declension (p. XXXII-XXXIII) that the nominative singular of the themes in-*a* may optionally become those in -*o* or in -*e* (*devo* or *deve*), he says a thing that does not clearly come out from the teaching of Caṇḍa. He solely rests on the example *katare gacchati* of the sūtra II, 10, and this is not a solid basis, although he rejoices at his discovery, the same example has been cited under reference to Ārṣa (IV, 287).

In fact the example in Hemacandra occurs in the form *kayare āgacchai* and moreover, the rule of Caṇḍa is rather obscure.

836. On the other hand, this is an incontestable fact that should have been indicated more clearly by Hoernle in the whole of the first book on the declension. Caṇḍa, does never teach the nominative in -*e*, neither in the list of terminations (II, 3, ex. *devo*) nor in the examples of the commentary (cf. I 1; 2). It is so permissible to doubt that the language taught by Caṇḍa knows the nominative singular in -*e*.

837. The sūtra in question in addition is Caṇḍa II, 10:- *edodralopā visarjanīyasya* ll

Commentary :- *et-ot-ralopā visarjanīyasya sthāne bhavanti* ll *katare gacchati*l *dittarūpe* / (*deo*) *devo*l *vaṁbhaṇo* l *puṇarapi* l *sa* l *esa* l etc.

"The visarga is replaced by *-a*, *-e*, *-ra* or elision. Example (of *e*) : *katare gacchati*, *dittarūpe*; (of *o*) : *devo*, *vaṁbhaṇo*: (of *ra*) *puṇarapi* : (of elision) *sa*, *esa*, etc."

The example *puṇarapi* is difficult to follow; it would allow us to suppose that in Sanskrit too one said *punaḥ api*.

Then how could *ra* replace the visarga in Prākrit. Could this be the Prākrit of the Ṛṣi? It should also be noted that *-e* or *-o* does not uniquely replace the visarga, but the thematic vowel *-a* plus the visarga. Cf. Var. V, 1 *ata ot sau*.

838. In the face of this sūtra I cannot check myself from referring to Bharata, Nāṭyaśāstra XVII, 6 the source of Caṇḍa II, 6. Could it be sūtra in pure Prākrit?

[a]. *eoparalopo visarjaṇiaṣsa**

"In Prākrit, there do not exist sounds that follow *-e* and *-o* (that is to say *-ai* and *-au*) or the visarga."

839. That this sūtra of Caṇḍa was originally written in Prākrit is not a new idea. Hoernle had thought about it (cf. p. I of the Introduction), on account of a citation from Malayagiri reproduced by Weber[1]. Even the name Caṇḍa is sometimes substituted by its false Sanskrit translation Candra[2]. Malayagiri has some other rules in Prākrit: a grammatical Prākrit stanza is also cited by Haribhadra in his commentary on the Daśavaikālikasūtra: they have all been reproduced by A.N. Upadhye[3], who has collected all the grammatical citations in Prākrit that he has been able to locate in the texts. The result is rather poor: three citations from Malayagiri, one from Haribhadra. To these should be added at least the Prākrit stanzas of the beginning of the adhyāya XVII of Bharata (cf. § 310), one of which, as noted by me, occurs in the metrical Prākrit treatise composed by Nanditāḍhya, and the citations from the commentaries of Caṇḍa that we are just going to examine.

840. The stanza that is repeated most often is that

1. *Indische Studien*, X, 273.

2. Cf. for example R.G. Bhandarkar, List of Sanskrit Manuscripts in private libraries in the Bombay Presidency, Bombay 1893, p. 58 and Bühler, ZDMG 42, 556.

3. Ann. Bhandarkar, XIII, 45 ff.

which summarizes the syntactical peculiarities of Prākrit: the duel in it is replaced by the plural and the dative by the genitive.

841. Malayagiri in his commentary on the Āvaśyakasūtra[1] says : *bahuvayaṇeṇa duvayaṇaṁ chaṭṭhī vibhattīe bhaṇṇaī caütthī* l *jaha hatthā taha pāyā namotthu devāhidevāṇaṁ* ll

"The duel is replaced in conversation by the plural and the fourth case (dative) by the sixth (genitive). Ex.

"As the hands (plural), so that feet (plural); salutation to the Jinas (gen)."

The choice of the second example reveals the Jaina.

The sentence *chaṭṭhī vibhattīe bhaṇṇaī caütthī* is cited also by the same Malayagiri in his commentary on the Nandīsūtra[2] and by Haribhadra in his commentary on the Daśavaikālikasūtra. Under a form slightly different the stanza occurs in full in the commentary of the MS C in Caṇḍa II, 13 :—

duvayaṇe bahuvayaṇam caütthīvibhattīe chaṭṭhī bhaṇṇae l
jaha hatthā taha pāyā vaṁdāmi devāhidevāṇaṁ ll

Malayagiri cites also a stanza on the suffixes that are substituted in Prākrit for *-mant*, *-vant* of Sanskrit. *matuvatthammi*† *munijjaha*† *ālaṁ illaṁ maṇaṁ taha ya.*

The MSS C and D have reproduced a śloka in Sanskrit retranslated in this context; cf. p. 45 on Caṇḍa II, 20·

842. Another well known stanza is the one that enumerates the sounds that have disappeared in Prākrit. Bharata (XVII, 6) and Nanditāḍhya have cited them. The MSS C and D know its Sanskrit version : under Caṇḍa II, 14, p. 44

eosvaraṅ tataḥ paścāt ṛ, ṝ ḷ, ḹ *catuḥsvarāḥ* l
aḥṅañanaśaṣaḥ saṁti prākṛte naiva kārhicit ll

C adds also a Prākrit gāthā that enumerates the sounds of the Sanskrit alphabet :

1. P. 26 of the edition of the Āgamodaya Samiti according to Mr. Upadhye.

2. P. 43 of the edition of the Āgamodaya Samiti.

tettīsa viṁjaṇāiṁ sattavīsā sarā tahā bhaṇiyā l
cattāri ya jogavāhā caūsaṭṭhī mūlavaṇṇā o ll

"In Sanskrit they pronounce 33 consonants, 27 vowels 4 accessory sounds (ansuvāra, visarjanīya, upadhmānīya and the jihvāmūlīya) in all 64 original sounds."

843. The fact that the commentary of Caṇḍa contains some grammatical citations in Prākrit confirms the hypothesis that the Prākṛtalakṣaṇa had been retranslated from Prākrit. It is an impression that one often has when he reads it, but I am not able to transform it into a veriety susceptible of demonstration ; it is as if one sunk in water casts his glance and finds nothing better.

844. This exception to the general rule that prescribes writing of Prākrit grammar in Sanskrit would find its justification among the Jainas in the honour that they accord to the dialect of the Ṛṣis, that they put face to face in a certain manner with Sanskrit :-

ārisavayaṇe siddhaṁ devāṇaṁ aḍḍhamāgahā vāṇī"[1]

But loyal to its misfortune[2], the Jaina community has never done an original creative work. The grammar of Ārṣa still remains to be written and in the Prākṛtalakṣaṇa of Caṇḍa, as in certain Prākrit rules, that have come down to us (wholly except in the beginning of the adhyāya XVII of the Nāṭyaśāstra, cited by the Jainas) technical terms, case order etc. have been taken from Sanskrit grammar.

845. The Jainas probably wanted to have a different grammatical school in opposition to the Brāhmaṇical tradition, but they did not make progress in realisation of this ambitious plan. Some *āryās* on grammatical generalities and some isolated sūtras should have been circulating among them; one day they put them together to make of them a grammar of the Jaina texts, independent of the grammars of the Māhārāṣṭrī lyrics and of their sisters, the grammars of Apabhraṁśa and of Paiśācī. But the material was neither

1. Namisādhu, commentary on the Kāvyālaṁkāra of Rudraṭa II, 12; cf. p. 159.

2. Sylvain Lévi, Preface to the *Album Au. Indes* d O. Brūhl, Paris, Hartmann.

abundant nor properly classified. And in vain they tried to arrange in imitation of the famous grammar of Pāṇini, that is particularly a morphology, whilst on the contrary the grammars of the Māhārāṣṭrī lyrics are above all phonetical treatises—the result does not merit being called by the name grammar.

486. To what epoch does this effort for assembling reach ? The Prākṛtalakṣaṇa appears to lie in its actual form to be a wholly recent work, but perhaps it contains ancient parts reproduced from Prākrit. Although this appears so probable, we cannot arrive at a certainty unless there are new discoveries in grammatical literature of Prākrit.

Appendix I

List of Abbreviations.

Generally the abbreviations used are easily intelligible. It is only the names of grammars that may present some difficulty. The following one is their list :

Pu. (=Puruṣottama=The Prākṛtānuśāsana of Puruṣottama, edited and translated into French with annotations by L. Nitti-Dolci, Paris 1838); Mk. (=Mārkaṇḍeya=Prākṛtasarvasva of Mārkaṇḍeya Kavīndra by Bhaṭṭanātha Svāmin : Vizagapatam Granthapradarśanī Series, 1912); Vr. (=Vararuci=Prākṛtaprakāśa, ed. E. B. Cowell, London 1868); Hc. (=Hemacandra — Grammatik der Prākritsprachen, ed. R. Pischel, Halle 1877-80); Kī. (=Kramadīśvara =Saṁkṣiptasāravyākaraṇa, Aṣṭamapāda, an Indian edition that in my copy does not contain either the name of the editor or its date : printed by Pitambar Bandyopadhyaya at the Anglo-Sanskrit Press. No. 2 Nababdi Ostagar's Lane) ; CD (=Caṇḍa=Prākṛtalakṣaṇa, ed. A.F.R. Hoernle, Calcutta. 1880; RT (=Rāmaśarman Tarkavāgīśa=Prākṛtalakṣaṇa, parts devoted to the dialects other than Māhārāṣṭrī, ed. by G. A. Grierson, Indian Antiquary, 1922, 1923, 1927, 1927 and Sir Asutosh Mookerjee Silver Jubilee Volume, pp. 121-141) : Pish. (=R. Pischel, Grammatik der Prākṛit Sprachen, Strassburg 1900—the references are to paragraphs); [Pc. (=Prākṛtacandrikā of Kṛṣṇadāsa, edited by Prabhākara Jhā, Varanasi 1968.)]

Appendix II

Index of Names

Appendix III

Index Locarum

CORRECTION SLIP

Page	*Line*	*Read*	*For*
Preface	13	aware of the	aware of
x	12	II	11
5	4 from the bottom	*dantyasaḥ*	*antyasaḥ*
6	9	colophons	Colophones
10	21	*Siddhānta-*	*Sidhānta*
15	4 from the bottom	offenbar	offerbar
18	11 from the bottom	121	12
21	15 ,,	2514 a	2514
21	8 ,,	V, 1-13	V-13
29	7	*gahijjaï*	*gahijjai*
,,	8	*gāhijjaī*	*gahijjai*
,,	10	*geṇhijjaī*	*geṇhijjai*
31	1	*Hc.*	*He.*
72	10	*ṛ, ṝ, ḷ, ḹ*	*ṛ, ṛ, ḷ, ḷ*
86	21	book of F. W. Genthe	book
96	2 from the bottom	42	43
98	14	38	48
99	3 from the bottom	II, 2, 25	II, 25
100	23	14	4
101	4	Haraśaṅkara	Haraiśaṅkara
101	10 from the bottom	*karmaṇyapi*	*karmanyopi*
101	3 from the bottom	*-bhāṣām*	*-bhāṣāṁ*
101	2	*vaṭṭaï*	*vattaï*
102	13	make	do
104	11 from the bottom	originality	originally
106	8 from the bottom	98	981
107	9 from the bottom	R. III, 4	R.
108	5	*Śakuntalā*	*Śakuntolā*
108	7 from the bottom	Insert	*Kāvyapradīpa-* (Kāvyamālā No 24, 1891
110	5 from the bottom	*ḷkāraḥ*	*lkāraḥ*
112	1 from the bottom	see	se

121	1 from the bottom	155	153
147	18	Vr. 1, 3	Vr. 3
150	1 from the bottom	53	50
154	11 from the bottom	carried	carrid
161	6 ,,	elsewhere	else werfe
181	2 ,,	on his	onhis
183	2 ,,	à l'histoire	àl' histoire
186	8 ,,	Ann	And